ELITE FIGHTING FORCES

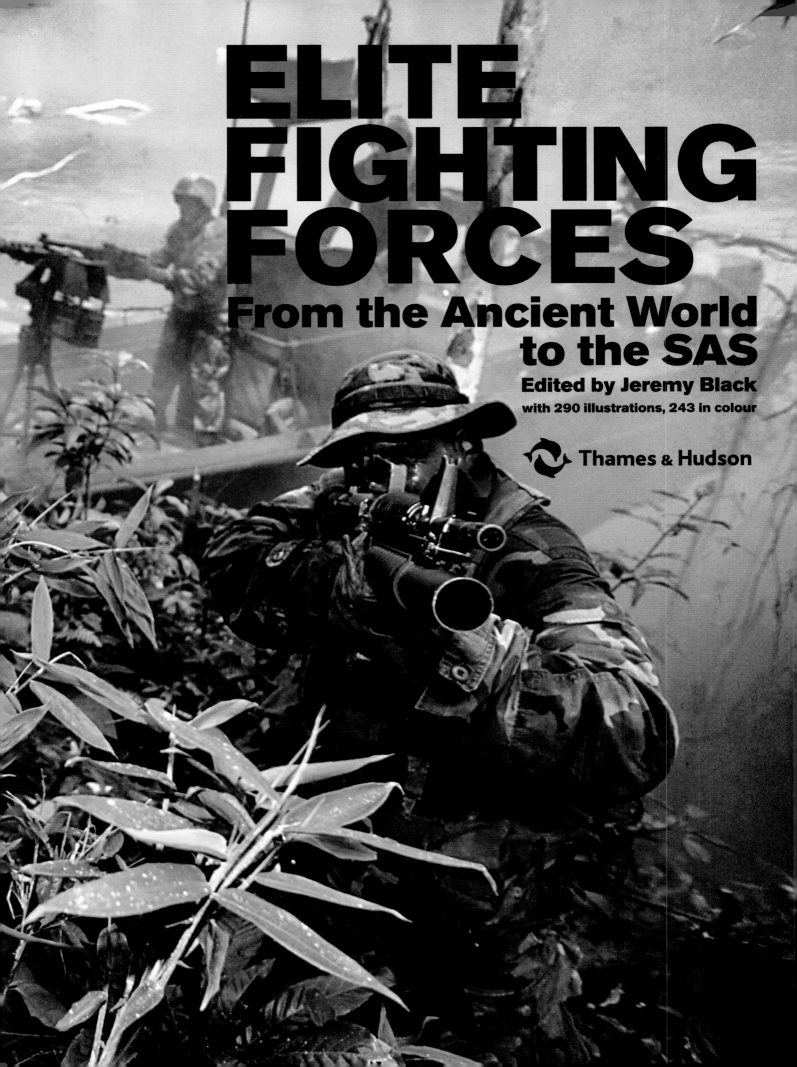

# ELITE FIGHTING FORCES

## From the Ancient World to the SAS

**Edited by Jeremy Black**

with 290 illustrations, 243 in colour

Thames & Hudson

Half title: Charge of the
Swiss pikemen at the battle
of Marignano, 1515.

Title page: US Navy SEALs on an
operation in Panama land on the
shore from a small gunboat.

Right: A 14th-century sword
with a Mamluk hilt and
a European blade.

pages 8–9
Ranks of the Terracotta Army.
pages 34–35
Mongol horsemen in battle.
pages 70–71
The Polish Hussars.
pages 134–35
Royal Marine Commandos,
Helmand Province,
Afghanistan, 2007.

First published in the United Kingdom in
2011 by
Thames & Hudson Ltd, 181A High Holborn,
London WC1V 7QX

British Library Cataloguing-in-Publication
Data
A catalogue record for this book is available
from the British Library

ISBN 978-0-500-25176-8

Printed and bound in China by 1010 Printing
International Ltd

To find out about all our publications, please visit
**www.thamesandhudson.com**.
There you can subscribe to our e-newsletter, browse
or download our current catalogue, and buy any
titles that are in print.

# Contents

*I*n warfare a unique dynamic is brought to the battlefield by elite fighting forces – those elements of a power's armed forces singled out in some way as special fighting groups for particular tasks. This history of such key forces provides an instructive way to look at war, its history and its process – even its future.

Across time and around the world, the composition, character and purpose of special forces have varied, but certain central factors can be identified. They include a willingness on the part of the men to take heavy casualties, and if necessary to fight to the death, a determination shown by the 300 Spartan hoplites who fought the Persians in the pass at Thermopylae, or the Knights of Malta who resisted the forces of Süleyman the Magnificent at St Elmo. Technical and professional skills are also important, as demonstrated by the longbowmen of Edward III of England, or the British light infantry defying Napoleon five hundred years later.

Linked to such fearlessness and high levels of expertise is a spearhead role. Elite forces have generally been the core of the army, the units that make crucial breakthroughs and are deployed against their opponents' leading troops. This is true of cavalry – the Companion Cavalry of Alexander the Great, the Mongol *keshik*, the core cavalry of the Mamluk army and the Polish Hussars

The longbow in the hands of Edward III's archers, depicted here at the battle of Poitiers (from Froissart's Chronicles), struck fear into the hearts of the enemy. But it was the qualities of the men themselves, their determination, courage, strength and skill, that made them such formidable soldiers.

– and also of infantry: the imperial Roman Praetorian Guard, the Viking
Varangian Guard, the Swiss pikemen, the Aztec Eagle and Jaguar Knights, the
Ottoman (Turkish) Janissaries and the Prussian Grenadiers all took on axial
roles in their respective armies.

Unwavering loyalty has always been a key factor, often expressed in terms no
just of military steadfastness, but also of political allegiance to a ruler, as with
the Zulu impis. Ideological and religious factors could play a role in this, as they
did in the case of the Sikh Khalsa, and so could ethnic identity, as with the
Manchu Bannermen of the Chinese Imperial Guard. Personal loyalty to a leader
and his cause was also crucial, as exemplified by Caesar's 'Larks' and Garibaldi's
Redshirts. Endurance was (and is) always a vital characteristic. Sometimes
tenacious resistance in gruelling hand-to-hand fighting is not enough: the
special forces face critical tests of resolve, particularly if the combatants are
fellow citizens, as they were in the American Civil War, in which the Iron Brigad
and Mosby's Rangers fought on opposite sides.

The increasingly complex demands of warfare require both the capacity to
master new skills and quick adaptability. These traits are well illustrated in the
annals of 20th-century air warfare – by the Red Baron's Flying Circus, the Few of
the Battle of Britain and the American 'Top Gun' pilots of the Korean War. And
elite forces have become more important in recent decades, as developments
in warfare, notably the end of conscription and an increased concentration
on distant power projection (the use of force in regions far from one's own
territory), coupled with the need for covert, behind-the-lines operations, have
very much focused attention on quality, not mass. Such factors are reflected in
some more recent elite forces, including the British SAS and SBS, the American
SEALs and Green Berets, and the French Foreign Legion. The fame of the last
serves as a reminder of the reputation and fascination often attached to such
units. Some, for example the Japanese samurai, have had a key role in national
identities; all have had an important part to play in the fates of nations.

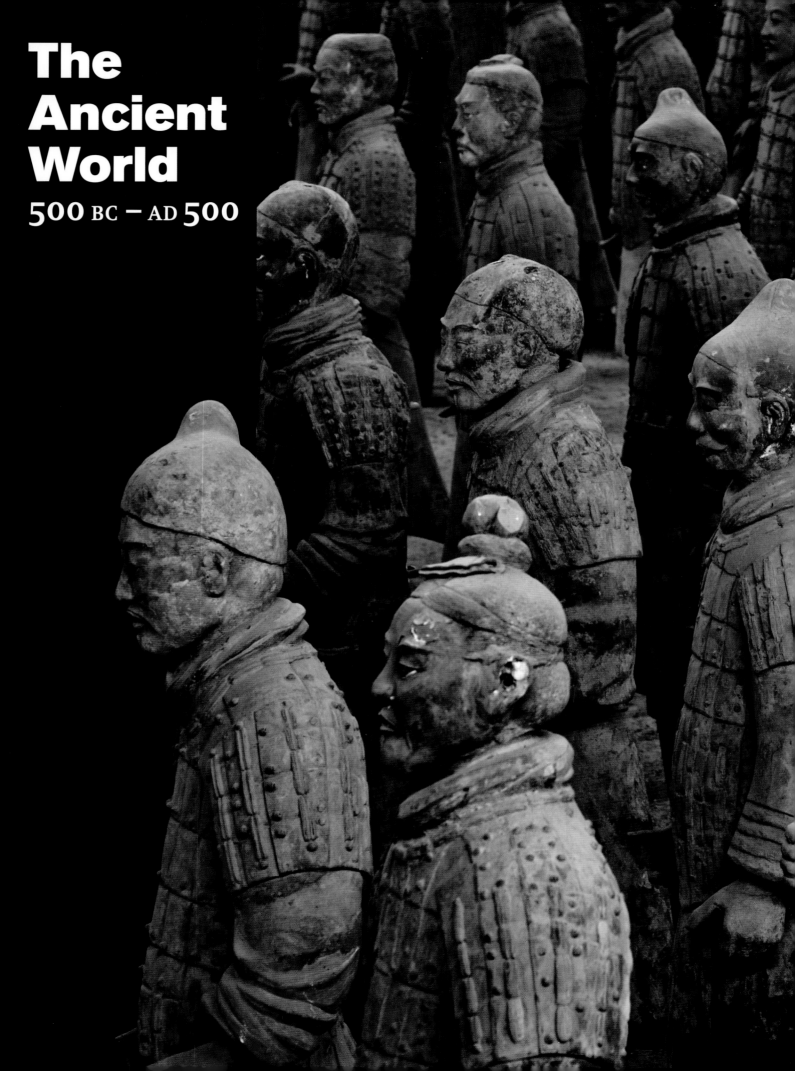

# The Ancient World

## 500 BC – AD 500

# The Persian Immortals
## The Deathless Ones

**T**he Immortals (Greek *athánatoi* – 'those without deaths') is the name of an elite corps of 10,000 Achaemenid Persian infantry soldiers. Much of our information about them comes from the *Histories* of the Greek writer Herodotus, who describes the Immortals' involvement in the invasion of Greece by the Persian king Xerxes in 480–479 BC. Calling them a 'body of picked Persian troops' under Hydarnes as their Commander-in-Chief, Herodotus accounts for the name 'Immortals' by explaining that the body of select troops 'was invariably kept up to strength: if a man was killed or fell sick, the vacancy he left was at once filled, so that the strength was never more or less than 10,000'.

The Immortals were regarded as standing apart from the common Persian soldiery. Herodotus describes them as wearing a tiara, or soft felt cap, an embroidered tunic, a coat of mail 'looking like the scales of a fish', and trousers. Their weapons consisted of light wicker shields, powerful bows and quivers of cane arrows, and short spears and swords. He also notes – probably referring to the Immortals – that 'every man glittered with gold', that they accompanied the carriages of the royal concubines, and that they were provided with special food, brought to them separately from the rest of the army on camels and mule wagons.

At the battle of Thermopylae the Immortals played a particularly important role. They were brought into the action on the fifth day of battle after a Median regiment had failed to secure the pass of Thermopylae or to overcome the small Spartan force defending it. 'Their place was taken', says Herodotus, 'by Hydarnes and his hand-picked Persian troops – the king's Immortals – who advanced in full confidence of bringing the business to a quick and easy end'. However, it was not until the Greek Ephialtes betrayed the Spartans by alerting the Persians to a mountain path leading to the narrow pass that the Immortals were able to help secure a victory for Xerxes.

When the king began his withdrawal from Greece, following the Persian defeat at Salamis (and possibly to put down a revolt in Babylonia), his general Mardonius was instructed to stay behind to continue the campaign in Greece the following spring. His impulse was to command the Immortals to remain with him, without Hydarnes,

Detail of a glazed brick panel depicting a procession of royal guards, possibly Immortals, from the palace of Darius I in Susa (western Iran). Each guard wears a spectacularly decorated court robe with ornamental borders, geometric patterns and inlaid floral designs. They carry a bow and finely worked quiver and a tall spear, the ball of which (in the shape of a silver pomegranate?) rests on their feet.

'When the Medes had been roughly handled, they retired, and the Persians whom the king called Immortals, led by Hydarnes, attacked in turn. It was thought that they would easily accomplish the task.' Herodotus, c. 450 BC

Fragment of a relief from the ceremonial city of Persepolis (southwest Iran) of a row of imperial guards. It is possible these are the Immortals, who were certainly the elite of the army and may also have formed the Great King's personal bodyguard.

who 'refused to be separated from the King'. However, given that the Immortals make no (obvious) appearance in Herodotus' description of the campaigns of 479 BC, it is probable that they returned to the Persian heartland with Hydarnes and the king, acting as his bodyguard.

Persian sources for the Immortals are surprisingly elusive. They are generally thought to be depicted in particular reliefs, but, importantly, there are no references to a corps of Immortals in the Persian written sources. Probably, Herodotus heard the Old Persian word *anûšiya* ('companions [of the King]'), which certainly is found in Persian texts, but confused it or associated it with the phonetically similar Persian word *anauša* ('Immortals'). All in all, there are more questions surrounding this special corps of the Persian army than there are answers: their exact tasks, and even their Persian name, remain unknown because authentic Achaemenid sources with this information do not exist.

## Battle of Issus 333 BC

In November 333 BC the armies of Alexander the Great of Macedon and Darius III, Great King of Persia, met on the plain of Issus in southern Turkey. The battle would help to determine who would rule Asia; consequently Darius placed himself at the centre of the battle, surrounded by his nobles and his fighting elite, the Immortals. The decisive moment of the battle came when Alexander broke through the right of the Persian ranks and headed for the centre of the Persian army. The Macedonians swiftly slaughtered Darius' Immortals and many of his key generals, causing widespread panic in the Persian forces. Darius fled the scene of battle, pursued by Alexander, who followed the royal chariot for 25 km (15 miles) before finally giving up the chase.

Darius III turns round to face Alexander while fleeing from him at the battle of Issus, depicted in a Roman mosaic from Pompeii.

# The Spartan Hoplites
## Disciplined Citizen Soldiers

**T**he true Spartan hoplite was a Spartiate – a full citizen of Sparta. What distinguished him from the others who served in the Lacedaemonian army –

the *perioikoi* and helots – was that he was born and raised a soldier. The *perioikoi* were from allied states who fought alongside the Spartiates. Some of these also were hoplites, which means that they had a spear, armoured cuirass, helmet and the distinctive round shield (*hoplon*) after which this type of warrior was named. Helots were a people enslaved by the Spartans early in that state's history; those helots who were trusted to bear arms fought as light infantry or skirmishers.

### Training and tactics

In some ways Sparta was the world's first totalitarian state. Spartan land was controlled by the state, which ensured that farms worked by helots were allocated to support each Spartiate. The only profession allowed to Spartiates was soldiery, and training began from birth. Young children generally went naked until the age of 12 when they were allowed a tunic which sufficed for summer and winter. Education

'Our arrows will darken the sky.'

**Persian envoy to the Spartans at Thermopylae**

'So we will fight in the shade.'

**Spartan response.**
**Herodotus, c. 450 BC**

Above: A hoplite helmet from around the 6th century BC. Spartans originally used Corinthian-style helmets, but there was a tendency in later years to adopt the Chalcidian helmet, which had a slightly more open face and openings for the ears, which allowed the hoplites to hear shouted commands better.

Opposite: The Leonidas Monument, depicting the Spartan king in battle. The base carries the inscription 'Come and get them!' – the Spartan response to a Persian demand that they give up their weapons. This modern monument is now accompanied by an even later memorial to the soldiers from the little town of Thespis who also fought at Thermopylae.

was minimal, apart from physical education, which was intense. The boys were encouraged to fight among themselves and were slightly underfed as this would make them steal food and so become better foragers. Discipline was harsh, and even before they reached their 20th year and formally joined the army, young men lived together in a barracks – something they continued to do even after marriage. Military service lasted for 40 years. Other Greek nations feared and respected the Spartans in equal measure. Among other city-states practice for warfare was a much less organized affair, and was to a large degree left up to the individual at the gymnasium.

Spartiates were immediately recognizable by their long hair and distinctive red cloaks. In battle they were generally to be found at the right of the line (the place of honour), with their round shields bearing the distinctive Λ, capital *lambda* – the initial letter of Lacedaemon, their native state. The Greeks fought in a phalanx, a block of soldiers formed into a solid battle-line. In the phalanx each hoplite was partly protected by the overlapping shield of the soldier to his right. The hoplite's main weapon was his spear, which was used overhand to stab over

A Spartan phalanx at Thermopylae as depicted in the film 300, a vigorous if not completely accurate homage to the enduring legend of the Spartans who held back the invading Persian hordes.

the enemy shield. Most casualties came when one or the other phalanx broke, and the defeated soldiers fled from the field after first casting aside their heavy shields as an encumbrance in flight. For this reason, fleeing a battle-line was the most heinous crime a Spartiate could commit; loss of a shield came a close second. The large shield was often used to carry casualties from the battlefield, and this underlies the famous admonition of a Spartan mother to her son: 'come back with that shield, or on it'.

The Spartan state was generally under the control of five elected magistrates called ephors, but there were also two hereditary kings, one of whom led them in war. The king had 300 bodyguards (*hippeis*), and they and their commander fought as infantry. It is believed that the Spartan army fought in large blocks called *morae*, each of which was divided into smaller units known as *lochoi*. The Spartiates trained intensively until manoeuvring in their ranks was almost second nature, and this, together with their famed discipline, meant that every Spartiate was deemed worth three or four of the opposing side.

### Triumphs and decline

Spartan military history had as its high point the defence of the pass at Thermopylae by King Leonidas and his famed band of 300 men in 480 BC. With a large Persian army advancing on Greece, Leonidas and his small force held the pass of Thermopylae for several days, and with their lives purchased time for the rest of Greece to prepare for the coming invasion. The Spartans were able to withstand the overwhelming odds partly because of their superb discipline, and partly because at close quarters hoplite armour was vastly superior to Persian equipment.

Spartans continued to lead the Greek resistance to the Persian invasion thereafter and played a decisive part in the victory at Plataea in north central Greece in 479 BC. The next generation fought the Peloponnesian War against the expansionist Athenian empire, and one Spartiate weakness was revealed at the battle of Sphacteria in 425 BC. The Athenian general Demosthenes had trapped

Above: 'Leonidas' – a 5th-century BC marble statue of a hoplite discovered in Sparta, which may possibly depict the famous battle king. Ancient statues were painted, and the huge arc atop the helmet probably represented a feathered crest. Since most Spartan helmets were unadorned, this would have made the leader more distinctive on the battlefield.

Right: Long-haired warriors carry the body of a fallen comrade on his shield, on a Spartan vase of the 6th century BC. As can be seen (opposite) the hoplite shield was large and firm enough to double as an impromptu stretcher for wounded casualties or as bier for those killed in battle.

## Battle of Plataea 479 BC

Sparta fielded some 5,000 Spartiates among the city's contribution to the Greek army of about 100,000 men who fought around 250,000 Persians at Plataea. The battle saw Sparta at its best and worst, with individual commanders refusing to retreat even for tactical reasons, and the overall commander almost paralysed until the last moment by religious scruples. When they closed with the Persians, however, the Spartans were unstoppable. They spearheaded the drive that broke the Persian army and killed the enemy commander, effectively bringing to an end the Persian invasion of Greece.

A hoplite shown on a Greek krater (wine-mixing bowl) of c. 530–520 BC. This huge krater was found at Vix in modern France and testifies to the range of Greek influence.

some 500 Spartans on an island off the headland of Pylos, but his army was reluctant to face their formidable foe. The ingenious Athenian came up with a solution whereby a mix of light and heavy infantry harassed but refused to engage with the Spartans, while bombarding them with missiles from all sides. Whenever the Spartans rushed forward to attack, the Athenians gave way, and then fell on the Spartans as they withdrew. Finally, the exhausted Spartans surrendered – an event previously unheard of.

However, after 30 gruelling years of combat which saw few major land battles the Spartans managed to grind out a victory, making Sparta the supreme land power in Greece, but there were already signs that its hegemony was waning. It is believed that the number of Spartiates was in decline, and many other Greek states were now taking their own military training more seriously. In 371 BC the Greek world was rocked by the news that the Spartans had been defeated in the open field at Leuctra by the innovative tactics of the Theban general Epaminondas. The innate conservatism of the Spartiates left their version of the phalanx unequal to more modern equivalents, as was proven with yet another defeat in the battle of Mantinea in 362 BC. The Spartans were unable to replace their casualties, and with the loss of the territory of Messenia, the helot state they had struggled to hold on to for so long, Sparta became a second-rate Peloponnesian power, and the Spartiate hoplites a largely disregarded anachronism.

# The Theban Sacred Band
## Devoted Company of Warriors

A bronze statuette of an armoured Greek warrior carrying a so-called Boeotian scalloped shield, from Dodona, *c.* 500 BC. The raised right arm would once have held a spear.

**S**ecure attestation for an elite unit of 300 men at Thebes begins shortly after the liberation of that city from Spartan domination in 379/378 BC. Perhaps in imitation of similar units elsewhere, including the 300-strong *hippeis* at Sparta, the Theban politician Gorgidas created an elite force which would be maintained at public expense to uphold his city's independence. To enhance the unit's fighting spirit, the soldiers selected were 150 pairs of male lovers whose devotion to each other would ensure the highest standards of bravery and commitment. They appear to have been equipped as standard hoplites – heavy infantry armed with spear and sword and protected by a large circular shield and bronze armour. The original intention may have been for the men to be distributed through the standard brigades of citizen heavy infantry, quite possibly constituting the front line behind which less experienced soldiers would take their positions. However, after an early success when fighting as a single unit under the leadership of Pelopidas at Tegyra in 375 BC, this became their standard method of deployment.

At Leuctra in 371 BC the Sacred Band, again commanded by Pelopidas, contributed to the stunning victory of the Theban general Epaminondas over the apparently invincible Spartan army, to the extent that Pelopidas was honoured equally with Epaminondas, though the precise details are unclear. The Band may have spearheaded the mass assault on the left wing which killed the Spartan king Cleombrotus and broke down subsequent resistance; alternatively, they may have been deployed as a flank guard to hold off an attempt by the Spartans to extend their formation to the left of the 50-deep Theban block and disrupt its advance by flank attacks. The Sacred Band must also have been involved in Epaminondas' subsequent campaigns, including the encounter at Mantinea (362 BC), again against the Spartans and their allies, in which he died, but their contribution there is not recorded.

'When Philip was surveying the dead at Chaeronea and saw the place where the 300 were lying, and learned that this was the band of lovers and beloved, he burst into tears and said, "As for anyone who thinks that these men did or suffered anything disgraceful, may they perish miserably".' Plutarch, 1st century AD

### Key Dates

378 BC
  Creation of the Sacred Band
  by Gorgidas.

375 BC
  Victory at Tegyra under
  Pelopidas.

371 BC
  Participation in defeat
  of Sparta at Leuctra.

338 BC
  Annihilation at Chaeronea.

315/285 BC
  Erection of lion monument
  at Chaeronea.

Scenes of hand-to-hand combat between Greek warriors armed with spears and shields, on an Athenian vessel of *c.* 560 BC. In some of the details a defeated warrior has fallen to the ground, his spear broken, and is about to be killed by his opponent.

Their final engagement was in the defeat of Thebes and Athens by Philip of Macedon at Chaeronea in 338 BC, the one occasion on which the Sacred Band fought on the losing side. Their personal contribution to the battle secured unstinting praise from Philip after he observed that their corpses all lay where they had fallen while facing the enemy. In the battle they had probably occupied a place of danger on one flank of the Theban contingent, but their greatest service may have come as the Greeks started to flee from the victorious Macedonians. The members of the Sacred Band were buried in a precinct where the stone lion erected to commemorate the event still marks the battlefield – its location suggests that they had been deployed as a suicide force to cover the disorganized retreat of the rest of the army, saving them from massacre.

## Battle of Tegyra 375 BC

In 375 BC Pelopidas was returning from a raid with the Sacred Band against Spartan-held Orchomenos in northwestern Boeotia when he was confronted by two Spartan divisions blocking his route back to Thebes. Pelopidas decided on a frontal attack against the overconfident and numerically superior Spartans, and led the Sacred Band and some accompanying cavalry directly at the Spartan commanders, who were killed. The Spartans then decided to open their ranks, in the belief that the Thebans would take the opportunity to resume their march towards Thebes, but Pelopidas exploited this move to continue his onslaught right through the Spartan force until the survivors were forced to flee. Although the numbers engaged on either side were small, 300 infantry plus some cavalry for the Thebans and somewhere between double and treble that on the Spartan side, the psychological impact of the victory was considerable. This was the first occasion on which a Theban force had driven Spartans to flight.

Young warriors putting on their arms and armour, on a 5th-century BC cup.

# Elite Contingents of the Warring States Period

## Chosen Vanguard of Early Chinese Armies

In Warring States period (c. 480–221 BC) China, the primary military trend was the replacement of small forces organized around noble charioteers by huge, mass armies composed mainly of footsoldiers conscripted from the peasantry of the seven major kingdoms that made up the Chinese world at that time. Perhaps to compensate for the decline in quality that necessarily accompanied this new emphasis on quantity, the military treatises of the period, such as those attributed to the famous generals Wu Qi and Sun Bin, often recommend the formation of elite contingents within the army capable of acting as a 'picked vanguard' or spearhead in offensive actions. The *Xunzi*, a philosophical text of the mid-3rd century BC, describes the standards expected of the 'martial

## Key Dates

**341** BC
The battle of Maling sees the first recorded use of the crossbow in Chinese warfare.

**320** BC
King Wuling of Zhao is the first Chinese ruler to include cavalry forces in his army.

**259** BC
After victory at Changping, Qin besieges the capital of Zhao; the siege is eventually broken by relief forces sent by Wei and Chu.

**246** BC
Prince Ying Zheng, later to be the First Emperor (Qin Shihuangdi), becomes king of Qin.

**221** BC
Qin armies overcome the last of the rival kingdoms, creating the first unified empire in China's history.

**210** BC
The First Emperor dies while on an inspection tour; the collapse of his empire follows within three years.

Among the weapons and armour buried with the Terracotta Army were stone-tile helmets (above; surely never intended for battlefield use), bronze *ge* dagger-axes (above left), bronze spearheads (left) and bronze swords (below). *Ji* halberds (not shown here) combined spearhead and dagger-axe on a single shaft.

Opposite: The life-sized terracotta warriors found near the tomb of the First Emperor of Qin include chariot-drivers (second from left) and senior commanders (on the right), as well as cavalrymen and many different types of footsoldiers.

Right and overleaf, below: A kneeling crossbowman of the Qin Terracotta Army, viewed from front and back.

soldiers', the elite force of the kingdom of Wei: once a man demonstrated his ability to march 100 *li* (about 48 km/30 miles) in a single morning while wearing a helmet and full body armour and carrying a sword, halberd, crossbow, 50 arrows and three days' rations, he and his family were rewarded with exemptions from taxes and corvée labour. Elite contingents such as the 'martial soldiers' must have been present on many battlefields of the Warring States period, but the limitations of the literary sources surviving from that period make it impossible to describe their exploits in any particular engagement.

### The Terracotta Army

Archaeology provides at least a partial corrective to the deficiencies of the written record. The 'Terracotta Army' of life-sized warrior replicas, discovered near the tomb of the first emperor of the Qin dynasty, Qin Shihuangdi, in 1974 and subsequently excavated and partly reconstructed, dates from the end of the Warring States period. It is reasonable to suppose that its appearance does not differ greatly from that of an elite contingent in the army of the Qin state. The force consists of upwards of 7,000 soldiers, mostly infantrymen but also including chariot-borne warriors mixed in with the infantry formations and a smaller cavalry group of 108 men (and their horses).

The weapons found with the warriors include swords, spears, halberds (*ji*), dagger-axes (*ge*), bows and crossbows, with the archers and crossbowmen mostly

Right: The unique faces of the Qin terracotta warriors once led researchers to suppose that they were portraits of actual soldiers of the 3rd century BC. Further study has made it clear that they were assembled in modular fashion using a limited range of standardized components to create the appearance of great diversity.

Opposite: The largest of the Qin warrior-and-horse pits contains a formation of nine parallel columns with additional lines of troops covering the front, flanks and rear; each of the columns consists of infantry interspersed with four-horse chariots.

'Within the army you must have soldiers with the courage of tigers, the strength to lift tripods easily, and the fleetness of barbarian horses ... If you have men such as these, select and segregate them into special units; favour and honour them. They are referred to as the "army's fate".'

*Wu Zi*, a military treatise, c. 300 BC

positioned around the outer face of the main formation of infantry and chariots. The blades and arrowheads are bronze, not iron, and the soldiers lack shields and helmets (though there is reason to believe that their real-life counterparts would have been provided with both). Most of the soldiers are represented with armour of the lamellar type, which would have been made from numerous small plaques of leather or metal intricately laced together. Since the cavalrymen are only lightly armoured and their mounts are entirely without armour, it would seem that they were used for scouting, pursuit and archery attack rather than shock combat. It was with such forces of infantry, chariots and light cavalry that the kingdom of Qin overcame the other six states to create a unified Chinese empire in 221 BC.

### Battle of Changping 260 BC

In 260 BC the kingdoms of Qin and Zhao clashed over control of the Shangdang region (in today's Shanxi province). After initial skirmishes, the two armies eyed each other from entrenched camps in the vicinity of Changping. The removal of the experienced Zhao commander Lian Po made it possible for the Qin general Bai Qi to lure Lian's reckless replacement out of his earthworks with a feigned retreat; Qin columns striking from ambush then cut off the pursuers from

their camp, and the camp itself from its supply lines to the interior of Zhao. To maintain the encirclement of the Zhao army, the king of Qin mobilized all males over the age of 15 in one part of his kingdom and sent them to the front at Changping. An attempt by the Zhao commander to break out with his best troops failed, and after 46 days the starving Zhao army surrendered. Almost the entire force, reportedly 400,000 men, was then put to death by the victors.

# Alexander the Great's Companion Cavalry
## Charging into Battle with the King

In the 4th century BC Macedonian monarchs had different categories of companion. There was a select group of royal companions – friends, advisers and dining and hunting companions of the king, who included some non-Macedonian Greeks, as well as his closest Macedonian entourage. At some point the Macedonian cavalry was dignified with the title of Companions and included one elite Royal Squadron. Under Philip II (359–336 BC) this honorific appellation appears to have been extended also to the main infantry units of the phalanx, who became known as Foot Companions.

### Growing numbers and success

During Philip's reign the numbers of Companion Cavalry significantly increased, in large part thanks to the progressive annexation of the fertile territories of Greek cities such as Amphipolis, Olynthus and Methone, whose confiscated farmlands were reassigned by the king as grants to support his new cavalrymen. As a result, Macedon developed the most powerful cavalry force in the Greek world, over 3,000 strong by Philip's death, and one which was closely attached to the royal house. The horsemen were equipped with lances (made from cornel wood, which was more resilient than

## Key Dates

**359–345 BC**
Philip II expands the Macedonian cavalry and honours them as Companions.

**338 BC**
Cavalry contributes to the Macedonian victory at Chaeronea.

**331 BC**
Cavalry spearheads Alexander's victory charge at Gaugamela.

**330 BC**
Command structure of the Companion Cavalry is reorganized.

**324 BC**
Alexander proposes to include a large Persian element in the Cavalry.

**323 BC**
Death of Alexander.

Opposite: A bronze statuette of Alexander on horseback, a Roman copy of a Greek original. Alexander developed the army he inherited from his father, Philip, and was a brilliant cavalry general.

Below: The frieze on one side of the so-called Alexander Sarcophagus from the tomb of King Abdalonymus of Tyre (c. 320 BC) shows Alexander (at left) and Macedonian horsemen in battle against the Persians, reflecting Alexander's use of his Companion Cavalry to strike a decisive blow.

other timber), swords and some body armour for the riders. Not much is known about its operation under Philip, but at the crucial battle of Chaeronea in 338 BC, when Philip defeated the coalition of his main Greek enemies, Athens and Thebes, it was the Companion Cavalry under the command of the 18-year-old Alexander, that delivered the charge that broke the Theban formation.

When Alexander crossed to Asia in 334 BC, he took with him 1,800 Companion Cavalry under the command of Philotas, son of one of his generals, Parmenio. Shortly afterwards, at the Granicus, Alexander led the Companions across the river into a confused skirmish on the east bank, where they routed the Persian nobility, enabling the annihilation of the opposition. In November 333 at the Issus, Alexander again led his Companions in the crucial charge that opened up the left of the Persian formation and prompted Darius III to take to flight.

## Reorganization

After the battle of Gaugamela in 331 BC, where the Companions, who now numbered 2,000, once more made a vital contribution, Alexander faced the issues of both how to assimilate his former Persian enemies into his new hybrid kingdom and how to develop his force of soldiers originating in the Greco-Macedonian League of Corinth into a more personal army. Philotas was executed in 330 BC for conspiring against Alexander, and a single overall commander of the Companion Cavalry was replaced by a dual leadership of Clitus the Black, the former commander of the Royal Squadron, and Hephaestion, Alexander's closest friend and supporter.

Unit organization also evolved, from squadrons whose geographical basis may have become a disadvantage in the new supra-national army to eight hipparchies under the commander of some of Alexander's leading courtiers. The Royal Squadron, now renamed the *agema* in line with practice in the infantry brigades, remained a separate, ninth unit. Squadrons survived as sub-units of the hipparchies, and at this time there was a significant but unquantifiable increase in numbers. Alexander was joined by 500 more Macedonian Companions, but the main growth resulted from the progressive incorporation of Persian horsemen, a development that aroused considerable opposition among traditionalists. Initially, the Persians and other orientals probably served in specialist units – for example as mounted javelinmen or horse-archers – and may not have held the title of Companions. However, in 324 BC Alexander proposed to create four Companion hipparchies from

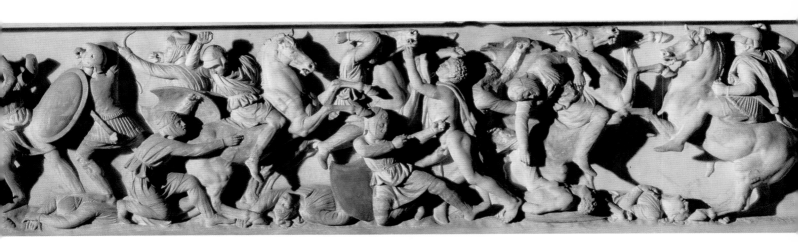

> **'When the cavalry on the right wing had, to some extent, broken the front of the Persian formation, Alexander wheeled towards the gap, and making a wedge of the Companion Cavalry and the part of the infantry phalanx stationed there, led them at the double with a loud battle cry straight at Darius.'** Arrian, 1st century AD

Above: A Macedonian coin showing a cavalryman riding down a fallen enemy. It was often a well-timed cavalry charge that gained Alexander victory in battle.

Opposite: Alexander charging on his horse in pursuit of the fleeing Persian King Darius III at the battle of Issus, 333 BC (see also p. 11), a detail from a Roman mosaic from the House of the Faun, Pompeii, but probably modelled on a painting from Alexander's lifetime. Alexander frequently put himself at the very front of the fighting.

oriental troops, with a mixed fifth hipparchy under the command of a Persian. Complaints about the incorporation of orientals into the royal *agema* and the use of Macedonian equipment by non-Macedonians point to the full extent of the amalgamation being attempted. During the Opis Mutiny, when Alexander was facing down the discontent of his veterans, his suggestion that he would reform the Companion Cavalry from among his Persian subjects was one of the proposals that particularly stunned the mutineers.

### Decline

After Alexander's death, the Companions initially sided with the regent, Perdiccas, and other supporters of the claims of Alexander and Roxane's unborn child, the future Alexander IV, but the decline in their importance is reflected by the choice of the relatively junior Seleucus to be their commander: their status and relationship with the Macedonian leadership inevitably changed in the absence of a king who participated actively in their campaigns. The competing generals naturally developed their own personal cavalry forces, with honorific titles to reward loyalty and denote special status, and as the successor dynasties emerged they continued to find benefit in the notion of Companions of the king. But even the cavalry of the most dynamic leaders, such as Demetrius Poliorcetes or Antiochus III, did not establish the reputation or track record of Alexander's Companion Cavalry.

### Battle of Gaugamela 331 BC

In 331 BC Alexander faced Darius at Gaugamela on the east bank of the Tigris near modern Erbil (Arbela). Alexander's army of 47,000 was substantially outnumbered, and Darius had also prepared his battlefield in order to deploy scythed chariots. Alexander countered this by adopting a square formation against the inevitable outflanking, and then by advancing diagonally towards the right to remove his troops from the prepared chariot ground and outflank the Persian left. As the Persians struggled to respond, a gap opened up in their formation into which Alexander charged at the head of the Royal Squadron and the rest of the Companion Cavalry, with the elite infantry hypaspists and the other phalanx brigades following in support. This charge progressively rolled up the Persian left and centre, forcing Darius into flight with Alexander in close pursuit. The Macedonian left sustained a stubborn defensive battle against overwhelming Persian cavalry, until Alexander broke off his chase to return to the rescue.

# The Persian Cataphracts
## A Heavily Armed Cavalry Assault Force

**A**fter their experiences fighting against the Greek hoplites and their phalanx formation during the Greco-Persian Wars, and of the campaigns of Alexander, the Persians of the following generations realized that they needed to create a new type of military force. The result was the creation of a heavily armed and highly professional cavalry. This was capable of causing great disorder in the massed ranks of an opposing army by attacking them at vulnerable points with bowshots that could pierce armour and with lances effective against shields.

The Parthians first used this tactic in repelling the Greek Seleucids from their lands in central Iran from around 130 BC, and it was still being deployed effectively at the end of the succeeding Sasanian dynasty in AD 650. The Persians have been the source of major advances in equestrian skills throughout history and the Parthian and Sasanian cataphracts – horsemen clad in coats of scale-mail (from the Greek *kataphraktos*, 'armoured' or 'enclosed') – with their arched saddle-bows, prefigured the heavy cavalry of the later medieval world. Cataphracts performed as elite cavalry or assault forces in successive eastern and western empires up until the Middle Ages, being used primarily to charge through, and break up, infantry formations.

Cataphracts wore a kind of scale armour made from linked pieces of bronze flexible enough to allow both horse and rider a high degree of mobility yet strong enough to take heavy blows as the cavalry charged at full speed into an opposing army. To withstand a head-on collision of this sort, it has been estimated that the scale armour must have been made from overlapping, rounded plates of 4 to 6 mm (⅕ in) in thickness. These were threaded with a

Above: This remarkable graffito dating to the early 3rd century AD was scratched on to the wall of a residence in Dura Europus, Syria. It shows a fully armed cavalryman on his armoured war horse – it is clear that the image of the Persian cataphract was well known enough in parts of the Sasanian empire to enter into popular imagery.

Below: A photograph taken in the 1930s of a suit of horse armour made up of overlapping scales found at Dura Europus, which was preserved in the destruction of the site in the AD 250s.

## Battle of Callinicum AD 531

On 19 April AD 531, during the Iberian War, the Persian forces under the skilled leadership of the general Azarethes met the army of the Eastern Roman Empire under the command of General Belisarius at Callinicum, on the banks of the River Euphrates in Iraq. The cataphracts played a key role in the battle, placed in the front line together with the infantry. The Persians broke through the Roman front line and drove Belisarius' army back to the river, where many men drowned. Although the Persians celebrated a victory, they chose not to press further into Roman territory. The battle was the first of Belisarius' series of unsuccessful wars against the Sasanians, which cost the Eastern Roman empire heavily.

**Key Dates**

**250 BC**
Arsaces elected leader of the Parni tribe; the beginnings of the Parthian Dynasty.

**130 BC**
Parthia suffers numerous incursions by nomadic tribes.

**AD 224**
Parthian dynasty overwhelmed by the Sasanians; accession of Ardashir.

**AD 309**
Accession of Shapur II; the golden age of Sasanian history begins.

**AD 531**
Battle of Callinicum.

**AD 637**
The sack of Ctesiphon and the fall of the Sasanian empire.

At Taq-i Bustan, in western Iran, a series of grottos is decorated with Sasanian-period reliefs. Inside the arch here is a relief showing, in the top register, the investiture of Shah Khusro II (AD 591–628), while below is a depiction of a fully armed cavalryman, probably also Khusro II. The military power of the Sasanian empire is nowhere better displayed than in this wonderful sculpture.

bronze wire that was then sewn on to an undergarment of leather, animal skin or toughened linen. A full set of cataphract armour of around 1,300 scales would have weighed about 40 kg (88 lb). The rider usually wore a close-fitting helmet, leaving only eye-slits and a nose gap for visibility and breathing. In addition to the horse mail, the scale-armour corselet, breastplate, leg armour, sword and lance, the cavalryman carried a mace and, fastened at his waist with a girdle, a battle axe and a bow case containing two bows and 30 arrows.

Cataphracts were deployed as the heavy assault force, acting as 'shock troops' to deliver the impact of an offensive manoeuvre. Clearly the most important part of the army, their weapons were costly and their status high; only the wealthiest men of high-ranking noble birth could afford the full panoply of weaponry and armour of the cataphract, not to mention the cost of supporting several war horses, grooms and armourers. By the 6th century AD, the Sasanian royal Chancery of Warriors set a stable stipend for cavalrymen. It was from among this group of warriors that an elite corps known as the Immortals (in commemoration of the Achaemenid practice; see p. 10) was chosen.

The charge of the super-heavy cataphract was very effective thanks to the discipline of the cavalryman and the huge numbers of horses used. Roman authors lay much emphasis on the terror of merely facing cataphracts, let alone receiving their charge. Parthian and Sasanian armies therefore repeatedly repelled Roman incursions across the River Euphrates, due in no small measure to the Romans' fear of, and ineptness in dealing with, the Persian cataphracts.

'... all parts of their bodies were covered with thick plates ... the forms of human faces were so skilfully fitted to their heads, that since their entire body was covered with metal, arrows that fell upon them could lodge only where they could see a little through tiny openings opposite the pupil of the eye, or where through the tip of their nose they were able to get a little breath.'
Ammianus Marcellinus, 4th century AD

# Caesar's 'Larks': Legio V Alaudae
## One of Rome's Bravest Legions

Above: The eagle of the Fifth, here commemorated on a coin of Mark Antony. This is one of a series of coins depicting the legions that were loyal to Antony in his struggles in Rome's civil wars.

Below: The Roman legionary dagger, *pugio*, was both a utility knife and a back-up weapon for a soldier who had lost his sword. As these richly decorated examples show, the *pugio* sheath could be used for displays of ostentation.

**W**hen formed in the late 50s BC, the 'Larks' were a completely unofficial legion. Raised in Gallia Transalpina, the first unit raised from provincials, the soldiers were originally paid out of Julius Caesar's own pocket and not recognized by the Roman senate. It was possibly originally called V *Gallica*, but the plumes on the men's helmets resembled those of a species of lark, and Pliny the Elder in his *Natural History* (11.121) explicitly says this gave the legion the name by which it later became known. Perhaps because the Latin for 'lark' (*galerita*) also means 'with a wig', the unit adopted the Gallic equivalent, *alauda* (the modern form of this word for lark, *alouette*, is also the name of a French military helicopter).

Though V *Alaudae* served with distinction in Gaul, *legio X* was Caesar's favourite until that unit disgraced itself by its mutinous behaviour. Only the Thirteenth legion was with Caesar when he crossed the Rubicon and initiated the civil wars that brought the Roman republic to an end. It is possible that the Larks were disbanded by this time. They were remobilized by Caesar for his African campaign of 47 BC, when V *Alaudae* was one of the precious few veteran units in his army. So high was morale in the Larks at this time that its men requested to face the enemy elephants of Metellus Scipio at the battle of Thapsus on 6 April 46 BC. The unit withstood the charge and performed so well that thereafter the elephant became its emblem (most Caesarian legions had a bull).

The early 40s BC had marked the prime of the *Alaudae* as an elite unit, and after Caesar's assassination in 44 BC, the legion was never really the same. They transferred their loyalty to Mark Antony, and in 44 BC Cicero wrote that Antony was marching on Rome 'with the Alaudae'. Later the unit probably went east with Antony in his failed Parthian campaign. Antony was defeated in the naval battle of Actium in 31 BC by Augustus, who subsequently reorganized the army. The Larks seem to have been moved to Spain (where contemporary coinage featuring a distinctive crested helmet has been found). The historian Velleius Paterculus (*History* 2.97.1) says a 'fifth legion' – probably the *Alaudae* – lost its eagle (standard) in 'a disaster' which required imperial intervention. By this time the unit was on the Rhine frontier, where its members briefly joined in the mass mutiny of AD 14. However, the legion fought well against Frisian rebels in AD 28, and a vexillation (detachment) might have crossed to Britain with the invading army of Claudius in AD 43.

Snubbed for supporting Nero against the rebel Vindex in 68, the Larks strongly backed Vitellius, another imperial claimant, in the following year. At least part of the legion was in Italy at the first battle of Bedriacum (Cremona) that same year, but much of it remained at Castra Vetera (Xanten) on the Rhine. Outnumbered and without support, these men surrendered to Batavian rebels and were massacred as they left camp. Thereafter the legion's history becomes hazy. Probably the remnants were replenished by Gallic levies and sent to the Danube frontier to block barbarian incursions. Some believe that the last of *V Alaudae* perished in the late AD 80s, when two legions under Cornelius Fuscus were wiped out in battle with the Dacians. Certainly there is no trace of the once-proud legion after this.

Caesar's *Alaudae* in action in Gaul, with siege towers in the background. At this time the Romans had adopted the superior Gallic helmet.

## Battle of Munda 45 BC

The battle of Munda in southern Spain was the final battle of Caesar's civil wars. The Larks fought on the left alongside *legio III* against the army of the son of Pompey. The enemy had the higher ground, leading to hard fighting – Caesar afterwards said that in his other battles he fought for victory, but at Munda he was fighting for his life. Victory came when the Tenth broke the enemy left wing, and the Larks and cavalry broke the right.

'He could not rely much on the light-armed foot, and so dispatched the Fifth to sustain them.'
Julius Caesar, 1st century BC

# Rome's Praetorian Guard
## Makers and Breakers of Emperors

A gold coin (*aureus*) of Claudius: the reverse shows the Castra Praetoria, the Praetorians' camp, with a figure holding a spear and standing in front of a standard. The coin type was first minted in AD 41–42 and was reissued on each anniversary of Claudius' succession for the next five years.

Opposite: Roman soldiers, possibly Praetorians, from the Arch of Claudius (now in the Louvre and much restored). The identification of these soldiers as Praetorians rests on the oval shields and the standard in the background. They wear the Attic helmet, which is an artistic convention.

**T**he Praetorian Guard of the Roman imperial period served primarily as the emperor's bodyguard, though they were also engaged in many other tasks, such as maintaining public order in Rome and keeping watch on those deemed a threat to the principate. But the Praetorians were perhaps best known for their involvement in transitions of power, whether providing support for the new candidate – who often paid a bribe called a donative – or occasionally assassinating the incumbent, as they did Caligula.

Instituted by Augustus in 27 BC on the model of earlier republican Praetorian Guards, the unit initially consisted of nine cohorts, though the figure was fixed at 10 by the early 2nd century AD. The number of men per cohort continues to be a controversial issue, however, and it is not clear whether there were 500 or 1,000 men in each. The Praetorians were paid at a higher rate than regular legionaries and they served for a shorter period of time; as a result, the unit attracted the best recruits, who were restricted to Roman citizens of free birth, generally from Italy. While the overall commander of the guard was the emperor himself, the Praetorian prefects supervised the unit, with the day-to-day management of the soldiers handled by tribunes (one per cohort), assisted by centurions. The task was made easier when, in AD 23, at the instigation of Sejanus, all cohorts were moved into a specially constructed camp, the Castra Praetoria, on the outskirts of Rome.

### Distinguishing the Guard

The uniform and equipment of the Praetorians were virtually identical to those of the typical legionary soldier of the imperial period – their basic garment was a short white tunic, sometimes augmented by a cloak called a *paenula*. In battle, the Guard used segmental armour, and was armed with a javelin and sword. It is only in their shields that the Praetorians may have stood out: in the 1st century, it is likely that the Guard had oval shields (as opposed to the legionary's usual rectangular shield), though by early in the 2nd century they too adopted the rectangular style.

The blazon on these shields, however, sometimes distinguished soldiers of the Guard, for they often carried devices distinct from the legionaries: winged thunderbolts with moons and stars, or vine tendrils, or scorpions – the last was seen as the unique emblem of the unit. The standards of the Praetorian cohorts were also unusual in that they had the image of the emperor affixed directly to them, unlike their legionary counterparts (where the image was borne separately). The Praetorian soldiers who carried the standards also wore distinctive lion pelts over their helmets.

## Evolution of the Guard

The history of the Praetorian Guard can be divided into three phases. During the first, from its inception to the late 1st century AD, the unit was primarily involved in administrative tasks in the capital. At this time the Praetorians rarely left Rome, apart from occasions when a contingent of soldiers accompanied the emperor if he travelled outside the city. The exception was during the civil wars of AD 69, when the Praetorians were involved in the various battles between rival candidates, both in and outside Rome.

The second phase, starting in the late 1st century AD under the emperor Domitian, saw the Praetorians actively involved in fighting in the field. This was especially the case under emperors such as Trajan, who undertook a series of wars against Dacia, and Marcus Aurelius, who was forced to defend the northern frontiers of the empire against the Germans. By the early 2nd century, then, administrative tasks had become secondary, since the Praetorians were spending most of their time away from the capital.

The third and final phase falls after AD 193, the year in which the entire guard was dismissed with dishonour by Septimius Severus upon his accession. The purge came after several Praetorians had been involved in the assassination of the emperor Pertinax in March of that year and the resultant auctioning of the empire to the highest bidder, in this case Didius Julianus, who survived as emperor for a mere three months. From this point, the Praetorians are virtually a different unit, since their members were no longer selected only from the oldest areas of the empire, and recruitment was thrown open to any legionary. The Guard thus became more integrated within the Roman army, and its 'elite' nature diminished.

Throughout the 3rd century AD, when the empire was often in great turmoil, the Praetorians were involved in the struggles for power among the many candidates and became closely associated with these individuals, a situation reminiscent of the Praetorian Guard in the late republican period. But, at the same time, the unit was also becoming more of an irritation, and, in particular, the cost of maintaining it was problematic. The number of men per cohort was reduced by Diocletian in the late 3rd century AD, and then, after they had fought on the losing side against Constantine in AD 312, the unit was disbanded.

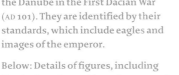

Opposite: Scene from Trajan's Column – this image shows Praetorians crossing the Danube in the First Dacian War (AD 101). They are identified by their standards, which include eagles and images of the emperor.

Below: Details of figures, including Praetorians dressed in scale armour, from the base of the column of the emperor Antoninus Pius.

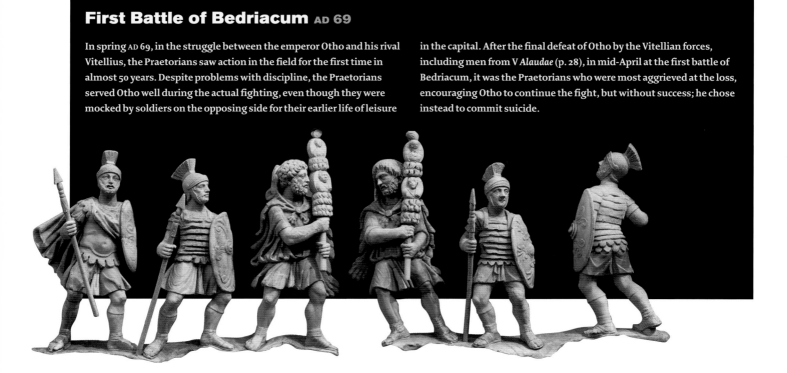

## First Battle of Bedriacum AD 69

In spring AD 69, in the struggle between the emperor Otho and his rival Vitellius, the Praetorians saw action in the field for the first time in almost 50 years. Despite problems with discipline, the Praetorians served Otho well during the actual fighting, even though they were mocked by soldiers on the opposing side for their earlier life of leisure in the capital. After the final defeat of Otho by the Vitellian forces, including men from V *Alaudae* (p. 28), in mid-April at the first battle of Bedriacum, it was the Praetorians who were most aggrieved at the loss, encouraging Otho to continue the fight, but without success; he chose instead to commit suicide.

'[Sejanus] increased the influence (previously limited) of the prefecture by gathering into a single camp the cohorts scattered across the City, so that they would receive commands simultaneously and, given both the number of the resulting hard core and their sight of one another, there would be a rise in their own confidence and in the dread of everyone else.'

Tacitus, early 2nd century AD

# The Medieval World

500 – 1500

# The Viking Varangian Guard
## Scandinavian Axemen in Byzantine Service

Below: A rare contemporary illustration of axe-wielding members of the Varangian Guard, from the 11th-century chronicle compiled by John Scylitzes.

**'The Varangians fight like madmen, as if ablaze with wrath ... They do not spare themselves, they do not care about wounds, and they despise their bodies.'** Michael Psellus, 11th century

**T**he Varangian Guard was an elite unit of Scandinavian mercenaries who served as part of the Byzantine emperor's imperial guard. The term 'Varangian' (Old Norse *Væringjar*, Greek *Varaggoi*) was used in eastern Europe from the mid-10th century onwards to describe itinerant Scandinavian mercenaries and merchants. It is probably derived from Old Norse *vár* ('pledge'), and *gengi*, ('companion'), possibly because bands of Scandinavian merchants and warriors travelled in sworn fellowships. Scandinavians serving with the Byzantine army are recorded as early as the reign of Michael III in the mid-9th century, but there was no specifically Scandinavian unit before the Guard itself was founded in 988 by Basil II

## Battle of Beroia (Stara Zagora) 1122

Highly effective shock troops, the Varangians were usually held in reserve until the battle reached a critical point. At Beroia an invading army of Pecheneg nomads had set up a wagon laager. While pretending to negotiate, the Byzantine emperor John II launched a surprise attack on the laager. All Byzantine assaults failed, however, with heavy losses, and the emperor himself was wounded. At this crisis point John sent the Varangians into the attack. Using their axes, the Varangians hacked their way through the circle of wagons, causing the Pecheneg position to collapse.

Above: Runic graffito carved by a bored Varangian guardsman called Halfdan on a marble balustrade in Hagia Sophia, Constantinople.

Below: The emperor Theophilus flanked by his bodyguard, almost certainly modelled on the Varangian Guard.

after his Greek bodyguards proved disloyal. The Guard fought in battle for the first time at Chrysopolis the same year, impressing observers with their merciless aggression. Subsequently they fought in every major Byzantine campaign until the late 12th century, and accompanied the emperor wherever he went.

In battle the Varangians were used as shock troops, fighting on foot using traditional Scandinavian weapons and tactics. The two-handed axe was their favoured weapon and they were often described as 'the emperor's axe-wielding barbarians' (or, on account of their heavy drinking, 'the emperor's wine-swilling barbarians'). They were usually heavily armoured. The Varangians' reputation for ferocity suggests that many practised *berserksgangr* ('going berserk'), working themselves up into a trance-like battle frenzy that left them immune to the pain of wounds. Strict discipline was imposed by a regimental tribunal. When based in the capital, Constantinople, the Varangians performed police duties, suppressing civil unrest and arresting suspected traitors – killing, torturing or blinding them as required by the emperor.

Early recruits to the Varangian Guard were mainly Swedes or the descendants of Swedes who had settled in Russia. The first 6,000 recruits were sent by Prince Vladimir of Kiev in return for the hand of a Byzantine princess. Glad to be rid of them, Vladimir advised Basil to disperse the Varangians, lest they cause the emperor as much trouble as they had caused him. In the early 11th century, Norwegians, Icelanders and Danes began to join the Guard, attracted by the generous pay. Regarded as outstandingly loyal, Varangian guardsmen were the highest paid mercenaries in Byzantine service, receiving the equivalent of one-and-a-third to two-and-a-half pounds of gold a year. They also received a larger share of war booty than other mercenaries.

The most famous member of the Guard was Harald Hardrada, who served as an officer from 1034 to 1043 on campaigns in Sicily, Bulgaria and the Holy Land. He made enough money to finance a successful bid for the Norwegian crown in 1046. Few did quite so well, but *Laxdæla saga* describes Bolli Bollasson on his return to Iceland (c. 1026–30) after serving in the guard as being dressed in fine silks, a scarlet cloak and a gilded helmet and carrying a richly decorated shield and a gold-hilted sword.

After 1066 many English exiles joined the Guard and it is likely that by the 12th century they outnumbered Scandinavians. The Guard survived until 1204, when Constantinople was captured by the Fourth Crusade. The Guard's last hour was certainly not its finest: the Varangians refused to fight the crusaders unless given an exorbitant pay rise.

# The Knights Templar and Hospitaller
## Martial Monks in the Holy Land

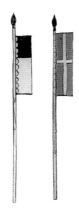

Above: The banners of the Temple (left) and the Hospital (right). Knights would have aligned their formations on these, and rallied around them in the confusion of battle.

Below: This metal water jug provides a fine picture of the armour of a well-equipped knight of the 13th century. Members of the Orders would have needed such protection because of their constant involvement in warfare.

*T*he idea of monks devoting their lives to war – which lies at the heart of the Templar and Hospitaller orders – is strange to modern eyes. Yet to the people of the 12th century the Knights Templar and Hospitaller represented a double elite – men devoted like other monks to the spiritual life, but also to fighting the infidel in defence of Christian possession of the holiest shrine and greatest relic in Christendom, the Church of the Holy Sepulchre in the Latin Kingdom of Jerusalem. At the root of their existence lay the crusading ideal, by which men and women undertook a religious exercise subject to strict regulation and fought against the enemies of Christ and His Holy Shrine. The religious orders were an institutionalization of this ideal, and just as laymen and -women paid monks to pray for them, so the devout of Christendom, stirred by events in the East, could purchase the prayers of the orders and pay them to fight on their behalf.

### The Order of the Temple

The first military order was the Temple, which appears to have grown out of a small confraternity of pious knights led by Hugh of Payns from Champagne. They probably took vows to the Patriarch of Jerusalem and were granted residence in the captured al-Aqsa mosque, which they named the 'Temple of Solomon'. At first they guarded the roads pilgrims travelled along from the Levantine coast to Jerusalem, but they were soon caught up in the wider defence of the kingdom. A tiny group, they were initially unknown in the West, until Hugh arrived at the Council of Troyes in France in 1129, where the order was given a Rule and wide publicity. It was enormously strengthened by the support of St Bernard, whose admiring tract, *In Praise of the New Knighthood*, calmed many doubts that had arisen about the very concept of combining war and monasticism.

The wave of publicity following this council triggered an extraordinary spate of gifts to the order, revealing the very real popularity of its role in Europe. Remarkably, in 1131 Alfonso I of Aragon made the Temple, the Hospital and the Canons of the Holy Sepulchre his heirs. While this settlement was never implemented, it profited

**1099**
First Crusade captures Jerusalem.

**1113**
Papacy recognizes the Hospitaller Order as autonomous under their Master, and subject only to the Pope.

**1120**
Knights Templar are given their first headquarters at the al-Aqsa mosque, which they believe to be the Temple of Solomon. They are called the *Poor Knights of Christ and the Temple of Solomon.*

**1187, 5/6 July**
Saladin captures Jerusalem at the battle of Hattin and commands that all the Templar and Hospitaller prisoners be executed.

**1307**
Philip IV of France accuses the Templars of heresy and suppresses the Order in France. By 1312 the Order has been dissolved, and in 1314 its master, Jacques de Molay, is burned for heresy.

**1310**
The papacy inspires a Holy League which enables the Hospitallers to capture Rhodes, where they establish their headquarters.

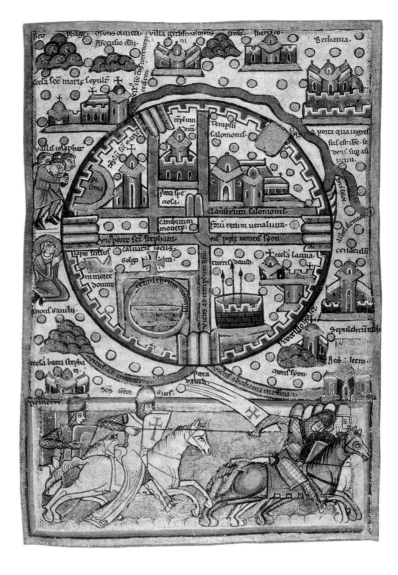

A stylized map of Jerusalem of *c.* 1170; below the circle representing the city Knights Templar charge and put Muslims to flight.

the order enormously because the barons of Aragon effectively bought off the claims of the orders, leaving the knights richly compensated. Their reputation was then firmly cemented when, during the Second Crusade (1145–49), Louis VII of France, after a defeat, placed the divisions of his army under the command of Templars.

### The Hospital of St John of Jerusalem

By this time another order had militarized. Founded before the First Crusade to care for pilgrims, the Hospital of St John of Jerusalem emerged as an independent order in 1113, and always maintained the charitable function that made it so popular in the West. But under Raymond du Puy, Grand Master 1120–58/60, it began to militarize. In 1136 the King of Jerusalem gave Bethgibelin Castle to the Hospital, and in 1144 the Count of Tripoli made over to them his most exposed frontier, including the imposing fortress of Crac des Chevaliers. It is unlikely that the Hospital merely imitated the Temple – more probably its military role grew out of its earlier role in aiding pilgrims. With their enormous resources in the West the orders became major and often rival forces in the Latin East. The Hospital, for example, strongly backed attempts by the kings of Jerusalem to conquer Egypt, to the point where the order was almost bankrupted, while the Templars held aloof.

## Military power

By the 1170s both orders seem to have been able to put into the field 300 knights, each fully armoured and equipped like the best of their lay counterparts with chainmail, sword, shield and lance. The entire Latin Kingdom of Jerusalem could raise only some 600 knights, so their importance is self-evident. Moreover, the knights of the orders were supported by strong forces of infantry and Turcopoles, native light horsemen who were useful in harassing the enemy and reconnaissance. The great strength of the orders lay in their organization and discipline which, in the case of the Templars, was embodied in their Rule. Their bravery was hardly in doubt, though they could be reckless. On 1 May 1187 a force of Templars and Hospitallers and a few secular knights, about 140 in all, disastrously attacked 7,000 Muslims near Nazareth. Roger of Les Moulins, Master of the Hospital, was unwilling to fight, but was taunted by Gerard of Ridefort, Master of the Temple: 'You love your blond head too well to want to lose it!' Almost all the men of the orders, except Gerard and a few Templars, were killed, though the secular knights surrendered.

Their Muslim enemies had a very high respect for the military power of the orders, which is why Saladin, after he had crushed the army of Jerusalem at Hattin on 4 July 1187, paid his men to bring in all Templar and Hospitaller

A detail from the 13th-century chronicler Matthew Paris of two Templars mounted on a single horse – a symbol of their poverty as monks. By the mid-12th century the Order was so rich that its enemies were accusing it of greed.

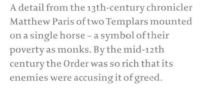

### Battle of Arsuf 1191

After the capture of Acre, Richard I of England marched the army of the Third Crusade down the coast of Palestine towards Jaffa. His knights were grouped into three squadrons and encircled by infantry whose crossbows and spears protected them from Turkish harassment. Most enemy attacks fell upon the vanguard and rear of this moving fortress, and because of this Richard placed the Temple at the front and the Hospital at the rear. At Arsuf Saladin forced a battle, attacking the Hospitallers with special ferocity, so that they launched a counter-charge compelling Richard, who would have preferred to wait until Saladin was fully committed, to join them. Even so, the result was a great victory for the crusaders.

'Go forward in safety, knights, and with undaunted souls drive off the enemies of the cross of Christ, certain that neither death nor life can separate you from the love of God which is in Christ Jesus, repeating to yourselves in every peril: "Whether we live or die we are the Lord's." How glorious are the victors who return from battle! How blessed are the martyrs who die in battle!'

**St Bernard of Clairvaux, c. 1136**

Right: The hauberk was a shirt of chainmail usually worn over a padded *aketon*. Although not proof against a heavy blow falling squarely, it provided real protection against glancing strikes in the mêlée of battle.

Above: A Hospitaller knight of the early 14th century. He is entirely covered in mail, while his knees are protected by *poleyns* and his elbows by *cowters*, both of steel plate.

Above right: The Knights Hospitaller on Rhodes under the Grand Master Pierre d'Aubusson, an illustration from Guillaume de Caoursin, c.1482/83. The rich setting of this picture indicates the wealth of the island, arising from its agriculture and its strategic position, which enabled it to levy tolls on passing ships. When the knights moved to Malta in the 16th century (see p. 80), they compared it very unfavourably to Rhodes.

prisoners and had them executed. The orders recovered, and on the Third Crusade (1189–92), Richard I of England gave them the task of holding the most difficult position, the rearguard, at the battle of Arsuf on 7 September 1191. They played a major role in the Fifth Crusade (1217–21), and in 1244 were so prominent at the battle of La Forbie that virtually all of their 600 knights were lost. In 1250 King Louis IX entrusted the Templars with the delicate business of crossing a hidden ford as part of his assault on Mansurah. Unfortunately, with them he sent his brother Robert of Artois, who impetuously rushed into the town, drawing the Templars into a massacre in its narrow streets.

The orders were the elite fighting force of the Latin Middle East. In all its battles they stood in the most exposed positions. They were great holders of castles, which became increasingly vital to the Latin States. The Hospital built Belvoir in 1068–70, a highly developed concentric castle in which the inner defences could support the outer wall. At the very turn of the 13th century they rebuilt Crac des Chevaliers. The Temple held Baghras in the principality of Antioch, while in the 13th century they built mighty Athlit.

It is a mark of how highly the orders were regarded that they were widely imitated. In Spain they were richly endowed in the hope that they would join in the Reconquista (the reconquest of Spain from the Moors), and when their part proved disappointing due to their preoccupation with the East, new orders, notably Calatrava, were founded. In Livonia the 'Sword Brothers' and in Prussia the 'Knights of Dobyrzyn' assisted in the advance of Catholicism there, but were later replaced by the Teutonic Order (see p. 56).

## Dissolution and reinvention

After the fall of Acre in 1291 the orders had to find a new role and they first fled to Cyprus. The Templars tried to re-establish themselves in the Holy Land by seizing the isle of Ruad off Tortosa, but were driven from there by the Mamluks in 1302. Their order seemed to have no real function as a result of such failure, and its spiritual life was uninspiring. However, its riches attracted the attention of Philip IV of France who in 1307 accused its knights of heresy and sexual malpractice in a series of show-trials. Despite lack of evidence, the Templars were convicted, though most of their wealth was directed by the papacy to the Hospital.

The Hospitallers enjoyed much respect because of their charitable work, but the order also found a new military role. In 1310, in alliance with Genoa and Cyprus, the Hospital seized Rhodes, establishing it as a bone in the throat of the Ottoman Turks. The island was massively fortified and strengthened by the very latest in heavy cannon, acting as a base for a small but effective navy. In 1480 they gained enormous prestige by repelling a serious Ottoman attack. But in 1522 Sultan Süleyman I led an overwhelming assault with 100,000 men, and the Hospitallers surrendered on terms after a highly creditable resistance. They were then given Malta, successfully defending the island against the Ottomans in 1565 (see p. 80).

Despite the failure of the crusades in the Middle East, the valour of the Templars and Hospitallers earned them much respect and emulation. Even the British Order of the Garter is ultimately an imitation. Despite the destruction of the Temple, the Hospital persisted as the very embodiment of the fighting spirit of the crusade down to modern times.

On 13 October 1307, Philip IV of France ordered the arrest of all Templars in his kingdom on charges of heresy. Over time it became clear these charges were trumped up, but the French monarchy persisted and in 1314 Jacques de Molay, the Grand Master, and some of his associates were burned at the stake. Philip had probably hoped to acquire the wealth of the Order, but although the popes agreed to its dissolution, they transferred its worldly possessions to the Hospital.

# The Japanese Samurai
## From Ruthless Warriors to Ruling Class

**A**n array of enduring myths and misconceptions continues to inform popular understandings of the history of the early samurai today. A heavily romanticized and seemingly timeless image of the samurai as honour-bound swordsmen of unsurpassed skill, bravery and devotion remains prevalent both inside and outside Japan. Yet such a portrayal is problematic, for despite the apparent consistency invoked by the term 'samurai', this group of warriors was subject to repeated and marked changes over the course of their lengthy history.

The precise origins of the samurai are obscure. The word 'samurai', which stems from the verb *saburau*, initially meant 'to serve', though not only, or even primarily, in a military sense. The earliest recorded armies in ancient Japan in fact comprised not self-identified samurai, but rather contingents of commoners conscripted for military service by local elites. By the latter half of the 7th century early Yamato kings – the leaders of the lineage that would eventually become recognized as the imperial family – centralized this process even further through the creation of a conscript army. This force, with an overall

A scene from *The Picture Scrolls of the Tale of Heiji*, depicting the burning of the Sanjō Palace. Sources describe the carnage as 'beyond description', and countless warriors and courtiers were killed by a combination of arrows and the all-consuming flames.

structure based closely on established Chinese precedents, consisted primarily of infantry. Officials came to regard this organizational model as cumbersome and ineffective, however, and, after a series of partial reforms, the system was abolished throughout most of the country from 792 onwards. Thereafter, in order to secure needed military support, the court frequently called upon a much smaller cadre of highly trained and well-armed cavalry drawn from units of the capital guard and from members of powerful provincial families. It was from a combination of these two sources, then, that the group of warriors known as samurai probably first emerged.

## Amassing power and influence

Some samurai continued to serve the court in later centuries, but most were essentially free agents whose loyalties were far from fixed. As the central government entered into a period of waning authority, these skilled warriors discovered that there were a number of other potential employers eager to recompense them for their expertise. Provincial governors wished to recruit armed followers who could offer protection while they journeyed to and from the capital. In addition, these fearsome men might also be called upon forcibly to intimidate reluctant taxpayers in these same regions if and when the need arose. And, having been granted lands exempt from such dues and levies, high-ranking noble families and major temple establishments turned to warriors as a means to keep their scattered holdings secure. Entrusted with preventing unwanted intrusions by rapacious neighbours and overzealous officials, warrior defenders were in turn rewarded with a portion of the income derived from the revenues collected on these private estates. Samurai thus operated in a number of different, and at times conflicting, capacities, with the result that they both contributed to as well as benefited from the steady militarization of

# 'Whether called a dog or a beast, a warrior's purpose is to win.'

Article 10 of the *Asakura Sōteki waki* [A Record of Asakura Sōteki's Words], first compiled in the mid-16th century

the countryside. Yet at no point during this early period were they able to seize power exclusively for themselves.

Still, it was not long before the leaders of certain extended lineages of samurai began to amass ever-greater amounts of both personal wealth and official prestige. As a result, from the middle of the 12th century onwards these individuals came to wield an increasingly large degree of control over political as well as military affairs. Chief among the leading contenders for influence at this time were the heads of the Taira and the Minamoto, two warrior families distinguished by their extensive networks of provincial followers and close ties to prominent figures at court.

For the Taira, their pre-eminence was short-lived, lasting for only a few decades following the conclusion of the Hōgen and Heiji Disturbances of 1156 and 1160. Although they were initially successful in their efforts to obtain a variety of key posts in both the capital and the provinces on account of their military support for the winning side in these conflicts, their rapid advancement at court sparked unease and resistance that culminated in the Genpei War. Fought from 1180 to 1185, this struggle was marked by a string of crushing defeats for the Taira at the hands of the Minamoto family. In its wake,

## Battle of Okehazama 1560

The battle of Okehazama was brief, beginning on the morning of the 19th day of the fifth month of 1560 and over by early afternoon. The conflict was the latest in a series of border skirmishes between two families that stretched back decades and was not, despite what later war tales claimed, part of any larger plans by the Imagawa leader to march on Kyoto.

An advancing army of roughly 20,000 warriors under the command of Imagawa Yoshimoto confronted the defending side, led by Oda Nobunaga, which numbered only 5,000–6,000 men at most. Yoshimoto had attacked two outlying forts the day before; this was a provocative move that threatened Nobunaga's territory, and he was determined to meet it head on. Rejecting advice to prepare for a siege and likewise refusing to wait for the arrival of additional troops, Nobunaga set out with his small force and managed to locate Yoshimoto's the supreme commander of the victorious forces, Minamoto no Yoritomo, received the title of *shogun* from a grateful court. This was neither the first instance in which this post of 'barbarian-subduing general' had been granted to a samurai commander, nor was it the highest rank held by Yoritomo during his lifetime. Nonetheless, Yoritomo's receipt of this title and its transfer to his descendants, together with their decision to establish a separate administrative headquarters at the city of Kamakura, signalled the beginning of a semi-independent samurai bureaucracy and provided a model framework for the successive warrior governments of later years.

## Weapons and methods

Thus, from the end of the 12th century onwards the status of samurai rose substantially, even though, at least initially, their overall number remained quite small. The vast majority of battles fought during the Genpei War involved no more than 200 to 300 samurai on each side. In the case of the very largest engagements, numbers perhaps rose to as many as a few thousand. These warriors fought primarily from horseback and their weapon of choice was the bow, rather than the sword. Though swords of superior craftsmanship were produced throughout this period and most samurai did generally carry either a curved, single-edged blade called a *tachi* or the slightly shorter, straighter

vanguard, who were resting unawares as they waited for the rest of the army to catch up to their position.

Seizing the opportunity, Nobunaga attacked. If subsequent accounts are to be believed, a violent rainstorm may have also added to the general confusion of the mêlée and helped to distract Yoshimoto's men. At the end of the engagement Yoshimoto was dead and Nobunaga victorious.

The battle of Okehazama demonstrated that, with the proper initiative, a smaller, highly disciplined group of samurai were capable of defeating a much larger adversary. It also marked the rapid decline of the Imagawa family's fortunes while simultaneously catapulting Nobunaga from his origins as an obscure regional warlord to a position of ever-greater military and political prominence on the national stage.

Kuniyoshi prints of Imagawa Yoshimoto (left) and Oda Nobunaga (right); 19th century.

Right: Detail of part of a folding screen which depicts the siege of Osaka Castle (1615). One of Tokugawa Ieyasu's captains, Honda Tadatomo (wearing the horned helmet), leads an attack on the defenders of the castle.

Below: An *ebira*, or quiver for arrows. These devices could carry up to a few dozen arrows of different sizes and shapes, and were generally worn over a samurai's right hip.

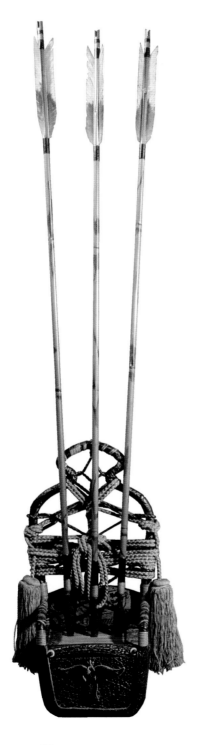

*katana*, they only rarely chose close combat as their method of attack. Rather, mounted archery remained heavily favoured, leading contemporaries to refer to these men as practitioners of 'the way of the horse and bow'. Their armour, made of small, overlapping plates of either leather or iron linked together with silk or leather cords, was designed both to blunt the impact of projectiles and to allow the wearer mobility in aiming and firing a bow while on horseback. The effectiveness of this armour notwithstanding, available evidence suggests that even as late as the 14th century arrows, not swords, still accounted for the majority of all battlefield wounds.

Significant alterations were made to the methods and tools of samurai warfare, however, especially from around the time of the Ōnin War. This widespread and intensely destructive conflict, from 1467 to 1477, signalled a transition in fighting styles and tactics that was to continue into the 16th century and beyond. Hereafter, commanders relied primarily on footsoldiers to secure victory, carefully deploying whole units as part of massed formations in a manner at odds with the highly individualistic style of combat practised in earlier centuries.

Warriors were now equipped with spears for fighting at close quarters and, after the arrival of European traders in the mid-16th century, firearms for use at a distance. Previous battles had been brief and only loosely co-ordinated, with most samurai focusing on securing proof of their own prowess while devoting little attention to the pursuit of larger strategic goals. But given the immense size of the armies now mobilized, it was essential for the successful leader to maintain order and discipline at all times. Gone were attempts by warriors to spend their energies on seeking out a worthy opponent or rushing headlong into battle in order to claim rewards as the first to enter the fray. Such actions, now deemed both futile and reckless, were subject to severe restrictions as outlined in a growing body of comprehensive military codes. By 1600 the 'way of the samurai' therefore required discipline and sacrifice – not simply on account of individual honour but rather because such ideals were necessary both to ensure victory on the battlefield and to reinforce the moral legitimacy of the samurai as a new and distinctive ruling class.

# 'Because the realm is comprised of warring states, it is of the utmost importance to keep one's military equipment at the ready.'

**Article 20 of the *Kōshū hatto no shidai* [The Fundamental Laws of Kai Province] issued by the local warrior leader Takeda Shingen in 1547**

Right: The helmets worn by high-ranking military commanders in the late 16th century were often distinguishable by elaborate, eye-catching designs. This one was supposedly owned and worn by Naoe Kanetsugu (1560–1619).

Below: Typical armour worn by low-ranking warriors towards the latter half of the 16th century, including body armour and a conical helmet known as a *jingasa*.

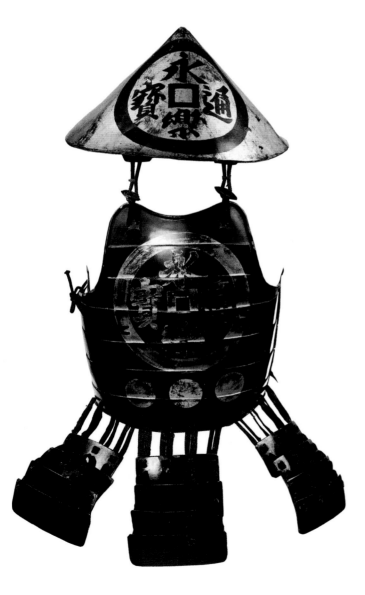

# The Mongol Keshik
## Bodyguard of the Khans

**T**he *keshik* was the bodyguard of the Mongol khans from the rise of Chinggis Khan to the end of the empire. From its earliest inception, however, the *keshik* always did more than guard the khan. In addition to their security duties, they were commanded by the Khan in battle, served as his household staff, and also functioned as a military training academy for the future generals and governors of the Mongol empire.

Dressed in black lacquered lamellar armour and mounted on similarly accoutred black mounts, members of the *keshik* were an intimidating prospect. During the rise of Chinggis Khan the *keshik* began as a force of a few hundred men but was then expanded. Originally it consisted of 80 *kebte'ül*, or nightguards, 70 *turqa'ud*, or dayguards, and 400 *qorchi* or quiverbearers. In addition, there was a regiment of 1,000 men who escorted the khan into battle. But in 1206, when Chinggis Khan re-organized his empire, numbers grew to 10,000 men, the increase coming from recruiting the sons of the commanders. Furthermore, as Chinggis Khan always welcomed talented individuals regardless of rank or social status, he also included sons of commoners who were deemed suitable in appearance and ability. These recruits were to be fully equipped, and their mounts were supplied by their original units. After 1206, the *keshik* comprised 1,000 nightguards, 8,000 dayguards and 1,000 *qorchi* or quiverbearers. It is believed that only the *qorchi* could carry bows within two bowshots (500–600 m/1,640–1,970 ft) of the khan's tent.

When not on guard duty members of the *keshik* served in a variety of positions, including as cooks, shepherds, camel herders, horse milkers and so forth. Simple tasks helped keep the *keshik* humble, but it also allowed the Khan to form personal bonds with the men and judge their talents. Virtually all the generals and

> 'Jamuqa said "My sworn friend [Chinggis Khan] has been feeding four 'hounds' on human flesh, leashing them with iron chains. They are the ones approaching in pursuit of our patrol"'.
>
> *Secret History of the Mongols*, mid-13th century

## Battle of Chakirma'ut or Naqu Cliffs 1204

In the final battle for the unification of the Mongolian plateau, the Mongols marched approximately 1,290 km (800 miles) to launch a surprise attack on the Naiman of western Mongolia. Chinggis Khan and his *keshik* formed the vanguard. One brigade from the *keshik* (the 'hounds') advanced quickly to hem in the more numerous Naiman as they came out of a mountain pass to surround the Mongols. With the *keshik's* furious attack, the Naiman found themselves outflanked and forced back to the mountains, while the Mongols held the steppe and thus had more mobility and were able to prevent the Naiman from bringing their full force to bear. This ultimately gave Chinggis Khan his most important victory, thus unifying Mongolia.

Opposite above: The *keshik* tended to be better armoured than the average Mongol warrior, reflecting both their different role and higher status. Lamellar armour, as seen here, could be made of plates of either metal or laquered leather. It provided excellent protection and was also easy to manufacture and repair.

Opposite below: A Mongol convoy, depicted in a 14th-century scroll. The *keshik* accompanied the Khan everywhere, not only into battle but also as his bodyguard; in addition they also performed more menial chores.

Below: Today the Mongolian army contains a unit of 500 men who play the role of Chinggis Khan's army on ceremonial occasions. Their equipment and horsemanship provide a glimpse of how the Mongols conducted warfare.

military governors of the Mongol empire emerged from the *keshik*. This model of performing menial chores also has roots in the rise of Chinggis Khan himself, as some of his early generals, such as Sübedei, started off not as warriors but as a servant or slave.

One of the main benefits of the ideology of the *keshik* was that the generals who emerged from it gained consistent and systematic training in the tactics and strategies used by the Mongols. Thus they were better able to co-ordinate actions on the battlefield, rather than acting as individual commanders directing personal armies as was the case in European and Middle Eastern armies. Indeed, one key difference between the Mongols and their opponents was the consistency of command among the Mongols. It is rare that one power produced several generals of such high quality in such a short period: Sübedei, Jebe, Muqali, Bayan, to name just a few.

The *keshik* appears to have lasted as long as the Mongol empire – well into the 14th century. As the various khanates declined, so did the size and function of the *keshik*. By the end of the Great Khanate (the Yuan dynasty in East Asia) in 1368, the *keshik* was still a bodyguard, but their role and effectiveness had diminished.

# The Mamluk Core Cavalry
## Swift-Moving Horse Archers and Shock Troops

**W**hile they had been used since the 9th century, the Mamluks were primarily the Muslim answer to their most formidable foes: the crusading military orders (see p. 38) and the Mongols. Capable of withstanding the shock attacks of the European knights, and delivering them themselves, the Mamluks could also function as swift-moving horse archers able to counter the forays of more nimble opponents such as Turkic nomads and Arab Bedouin.

The Mamluks entered Islamic civilization in the 9th century, as the caliphs sought to form a military from slaves who held loyalty only to the caliph and were without regional, tribal or other personal ties. Most Mamluks were of Turkic origin, primarily because they were viewed as better, or at least more natural, warriors than Persians and Arabs – Turks of nomadic origins possessed riding and archery skills from an early age. After purchasing Turks as slaves, they could be transformed into soldiers simply by refining their skills.

A Mamluk horseman depicted in a print of 1853. The Mamluks only grudgingly adopted firearms as they initially viewed them as a weapon requiring little skill or talent. This belief contributed to their defeat by Janissaries of the Ottoman empire (see p. 72), who were equipped with firearms.

### The army of the Mamluks

Over the centuries, Mamluks became a common feature in Muslim armies throughout the Islamic world, though they were always limited in numbers due to the expense of purchasing and training the slaves. The high point of the Mamluk institution came in 1250, when the Mamluks seized power in Egypt during Louis IX's (Saint Louis) ill-fated crusade there, saving the country not only from the crusaders, but also from the Mongols. They thus established the Mamluk Sultanate of Egypt and Syria, which lasted until 1517.

The army of the sultanate consisted of three parts. The first, and typically the centre of their army, comprised the Royal Mamluks.

Two warriors practising their swordsmanship from a Mamluk manual of cavalry tactics. Training was a crucial part of the identity of the Mamluks and was what made them an elite force.

Royal Mamluks were those directly purchased and trained by the sultan. The sultan also possessed Mamluks who had belonged to other masters (including the previous sultan and deceased or dismissed amirs or commanders). Those obtained from amirs comprised the second part of the Mamluk forces. *Halqa* or non-Mamluk cavalry formed the third part, and were typically forces of non-Mamluk amirs. Generally these last were regarded as inferior, if not in ability then in terms of social status, at least in the eyes of the Mamluks. Bedouin forces often served as ancillary forces and as scouts.

At their peak in the late 13th century the Royal Mamluks numbered around 10,000 men. These were the elite of the Mamluk forces and carried out most of the fighting; virtually all were stationed in Cairo. Compared to most of the enemies of the Mongols, the Mamluk Sultanate was relatively weak in numbers,

Sabres were the preferred weapon of the Mamluk. Before learning to fence, the Mamluks built up their endurance and strength for sword-fighting by cutting layers of felt and then clay repeatedly.

and could muster 29,000 Mamluk fighters in the late 13th century. Because of the need to garrison the numerous fortresses of Syria, the non-Mamluk forces were almost double the number of Mamluks.

## Military tactics

As medium or heavy cavalry the Mamluks wore chainmail armour as well as helmets, and carried shields, lances and other mêlée weapons such as sword and mace. They all of course carried bows and were extremely proficient in their use. Their primary opponents were the Mongols and the Franks of the crusader states, and they became adept at fighting both. Tactically, against the Mongols

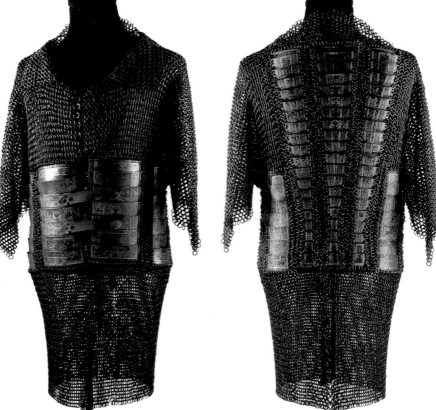

‘Islam seemed mortally wounded, and the Franj were about to reap the fruit of their victory when the Mamluk Turks arrived.’

Ibn Wasil, in relation to the defeat of King Louis IX at Mansurah, 1250

Above: While not innovative, the steel helmet of the Mamluks provided adequate protection for the head. An aventail, or skirt of chainmail, that protected the neck and often the face, was usually attached. A simple nasal guard protected the nose. This example dates to the 15th century.

Right: Chainmail was the preferred armour of the Mamluks throughout their existence. Forged from Damascus steel, it provided superior protection to other forms, while also being relatively light. In the 14th and 15th centuries the armour was augmented with overlapping steel plates.

the Mamluks typically remained on the defensive until an opportune moment came since they had insufficient horses to match the constant movement of the Mongols. However, as they were all archers, they could keep up a steady rate of fire to deter the Mongols. In addition, the Mamluks maintained the utmost discipline and rarely succumbed to feigned retreats. With their armour and lances they also served as a shock force and could deliver devastating charges like the European knights, as well as fighting them blow for blow.

Strategically, the Mamluks focused on defensive measures against the Mongols, who outnumbered them. They tried to minimize the Mongol numerical advantage by using scorched earth policies on the frontier to eliminate pasture lands. Without pasture lands, the Mongols could either bring more men and fewer spare mounts, or fewer men with more spare mounts. In either case, Mamluk strategy was effective – denying the Mongols the mobility that allowed them to dominate the battlefield, and preventing them having a sufficient number of men to compensate for the Mamluks' superior skill.

## Battle of Ayn Jalut 1260

Ayn Jalut was the battle that legitimized the Mamluks as rulers after their rise to power through regicide. In 1260, rather than await an expected Mongol invasion, 10,000 Mamluks led by Sultan Qutuz marched across the Sinai and forced the scattered Mongol enemy of 10,000 to face them in present-day Israel at Ayn Jalut (the Well of Goliath). The Mamluks rallied and defeated the Mongols, driving them from Syria.

The *furusiyya* – training in horsemanship – that the Mamluks received included group tactics and playing polo, as well as individual skills such as mounting a horse by vaulting on to it while wearing full armour. This illustration is from a 14th-century Mamluk manual, *Treatise on the Art of War*.

Recognizing the limitations of their military and having fewer men, the Mamluks rarely invaded Mongol territory. Instead, they struck at Mongol allies such as the Crusader lord, Bohemund, Prince of Antioch and Count of Tripoli, or at Cilicia (Lesser Armenia). The Mamluks usually timed these operations when Mongol troops were either not in the vicinity or were occupied in the civil wars that wracked the Mongol empire after 1260.

### A fading power

With the collapse of the Mongol Ilkhanate in the Middle East in 1335 and the threat it posed, the martial prowess of the Mamluks faded. Rather than focusing on training, the Mamluks occupied themselves with political squabbles between different factions, usually ending in bloodshed in the streets of Cairo. While they remained a potent military power, they were found wanting when faced with threats from Tamerlane in 1400/01 or the Ottomans in 1516/17. Unit discipline increasingly diminished and the Mamluks adapted to new weapons slowly. They only grudgingly accepted gunpower weapons and belittled those Mamluk units (mainly Africans rather than Turks or Circassians) who used them. In 1517 the armies of the Ottoman Selim the Grim conquered Syria and Egypt – the Mamluks continued to exist, but their era was over. Although their bravery impressed Napoleon, his troops had little difficulty in sweeping them off the battlefield in 1798. The Mamluk institution in Egypt ended once and for all with the rise of the Albanian Muhammad Ali who in 1811 killed their leaders and replaced them with an army conscripted from the Egyptian peasantry.

# The Teutonic Knights
## A Crusading Power in the Baltic

**T**he Order of the Hospital of St Mary of the Germans of Jerusalem, or Teutonic Order, was a military religious order whose members embraced warfare as a meritorious and devotional exercise and engaged actively in crusading, most famously in the Baltic. Founded by German crusaders as a field hospital in *c*. 1190, the Order received papal recognition in 1191 and was militarized by 1198. Its head was the Grand Master, to whom all other officers, regional masters, local commanders and individual brothers were bound by chain of command.

The Order's fighting convent consisted of two types of member: the brother knight and the brother sergeant. Brother knights were distinguished by their white habit with black cross. In the 13th and 14th centuries their battle armour consisted of a long-sleeved mail hauberk, a coat-of-plates covered with white cloth with a black fabric cross sewn to the front and a long white tunic, mail chausses for the legs, a wooden shield and great helmet. Brother sergeants were also heavily armoured, but wore a grey-covered coat-of-arms with a black T-shaped symbol to indicate their lower rank. Swords and lances were standard weapons of Teutonic knights, but they were also familiar with recent innovations in military technology, including the crossbow (which the Order produced on a large scale). The Order used ships in military operations and, most importantly, it had developed an expertise in breeding and training warhorses, making the heavy cavalry its most effective instrument in open battle.

Established in the Holy Land, the Teutonic Order was from the 1220s also involved in crusading activities in the Baltic, owing to the visionary leadership of Grand Master Herman of Salza. In 1226 their presence was made permanent when Emperor Frederick granted Prussia as a marcher lordship to the Order and the title of imperial

Above: The Teutonic Order produced crossbows on an industrial scale. In battle 'whistling bolts' were often used to weaken the enemy's spirits. During sieges crossbows allowed castle garrisons to keep larger forces at bay until relief forces could arrive.

Below: Depiction of the Teutonic 'Tree Castle' of Thorn in 1231. In Prussia the Teutonic Knights were the first to build castles using stones, bricks and mortar, rather than timber and mud. These fortifications allowed the Knights to sustain long sieges in deeply hostile territory and gave them a decisive advantage over their enemies, who often found these strongholds impenetrable.

> **'As so often as they showed their faces to the enemy, so often did the enemy flee, but as they gradually returned, these men had to sustain the blows and weapons of the enemy.'**
> Oliver of Paderborn, *The Capture of Damietta*, 1217–22

prince to Herman of Salza. Using forced labour to build river-forts and stone castles, the Knights rapidly expanded their power throughout Prussia and into Livonia. By the end of the 13th century, despite major setbacks in the form of large-scale uprisings, the conquest of Prussia and its consolidation as an Order state was complete. After the Fall of Acre in 1291 the Order shifted headquarters to Venice, and from there, in 1309, to Marienburg (Malbork) in western Prussia.

The 14th century witnessed the Teutonic Knights' ruthless involvement in local politics in the Baltic, which gained them additional territory and brought them into opposition with Poland. A new wave of crusader campaigns was also waged under the Order's command against the pagan Lithuanians – fought with great brutality on both sides. But ambitions to conquer Lithuania had to be abandoned after a combined Polish-Lithuanian army destroyed the Order's army in the battle of Tannenberg (Grunwald) in 1410. The battle marked the beginning of the end of the Order's predominance in Prussia. Invading armies ravaged Prussia on three occasions in the first half of the 15th century, and a 13-year-long war with Poland followed. In 1466 the Second Treaty of Thorn divided the Order state, allowing pocket-lordships to survive in Prussia until 1525 and in Livonia until 1562.

## Battle of Tannenberg 1410

On 15 July 1410, the combined army of Poland and Lithuania engaged with a numerically weaker Teutonic army (including a large number of crusaders, foreign knights and mercenaries) at Tannenberg. Involving about 60,000 people, among them 50,000 cavalry, it was the biggest battle in the history of Poland, Lithuania and the Order up to that point. Although better equipped and more skilled than the enemy, the Knights failed to prevent the Polish cavalry from successfully encircling their flanks, causing the banner of Chełmno to capitulate and driving the rest of the army into the marches. Grand Master Ulrich of Jungingen, most Order officials and about 400 knights of the Order were left dead on the field.

A re-enactment of the battle of Tannenberg.

# Edward III's Longbowmen
## Formidable Archers for the English King

The longbow was a simple, but deadly, weapon – 1.8 m (6 ft) or more in length and carved from a single piece of yew. Great strength and experience were required to pull it and to shoot up to a dozen arrows in a minute. The effective range was up to 180 m (200 yards); even at that distance, with a high trajectory the arrows came down with great force in a terrifying volley. It was the bow that made the English king Edward III's archers so feared on the battlefield, but they no doubt also possessed qualities of determination and courage, as well as strength and skill, which made them the formidable soldiers they were.

The archers who served Edward III were different from those who had mustered in large numbers to fight for Edward I in Wales and in Scotland in the late 13th century. One major development came in Edward III's campaigns in Scotland in the 1330s, when some of the archers were, for the first time, mounted. They did not fight on horseback, but rode with the cavalry, so enabling armies to move far faster. A second development was that the government took it upon itself to provide vast quantities of bows and arrows; in the past, archers had provided their own equipment, coming on campaign with no more than a quiver of two dozen arrows.

Little is known about the way in which men trained as archers. Many will have been familiar with the bow from childhood, and the government encouraged regular practice in villages. There was regional expertise: the men of Cheshire in particular were notable archers, and they formed a royal bodyguard as early as the 1330s. An archer took to war his bow, a bag for his arrows, a dagger and perhaps a sword, a simple helmet and a padded jerkin.

'The English archers then advanced one step forward, and shot their arrows with such force and quickness that it seemed as if it snowed.'

Jean Froissart's *Chronicles*, on the battle of Crécy

Both pages: Illustrations from the 14th-century Luttrell Psalter. The archers are not equipped for war – they have no quivers or bags for their arrows, and only one of them has a dagger. They also wear plain tunics, rather than any form of uniform. The man on the page opposite is shown stringing his bow. The archer on the right holds a bulbous-headed arrow intended for shooting at a target. Below are men at archery practice. Much training was needed if men were to acquire the strength required to use a longbow. In 1363 Edward III ordered all able-bodied men to practice shooting on feast days, forbidding them to play worthless games such as football.

Men from a particular county, or those attached to a particular retinue, might have had uniform jackets (such as the green and white of Cheshire), but there was no single uniform for an entire army. In the field, the archers were normally organized in groups of 20, each headed by a *vintenar*, and of 100, with a mounted constable or *centenar* in charge. In the case of Welsh troops, records reveal standard-bearers, criers, chaplains and doctors for each group of 100 men. Numbers were considerable – at the battle of Crécy in 1346 Edward III probably had about 10,000 archers, of whom roughly a third were mounted.

In battle, the longbowmen were normally drawn up in wedge formations, placed on the flanks of units of dismounted knights and men-at-arms. They transformed the balance of power on the battlefield; the archers provided the foundations for the great English victories at Crécy in 1346 and Poitiers ten years later. Although in the 1370s the French began to develop tactics to deal with the English archers, these bowmen were still a decisive battle-winning force at Agincourt in 1415.

Because the archers were men plucked from village society, we do not have much information about them as individuals. They rose in status during Edward's reign; the mounted archers, who were paid double the footsoldier's rate, were often drawn from the elite of local yeomanry. A few men, of whom Sir Robert Knollys was the most notable, rose from the ranks of the archers to become renowned commanders in the French war.

## Battle of Crécy 1346

In July 1346 Edward III led a campaign in France. The English army faced a numerically superior French force at Crécy in August, where the English archers, drawn up on high ground, forced the enemy crossbowmen to flee. They then devastated the initial French cavalry charge, maddening the horses with their volleys of arrows. In the later stages of the battle, they joined in the hand-to-hand fighting. The battle had begun in late afternoon, but by the time it was over and the English were victorious it was dark; French casualties were exceptionally heavy.

In this 15th-century illustration of the battle of Crécy the English archers are in the foreground on the right, with the Genoese crossbowmen employed by the French on the left. The man in a blue jerkin shows the way that the archers used a two-fingered draw to the ear. The longbowmen could shoot at least three times as fast as the crossbowmen.

# The Catalan Company of the East
Battle-Hardened Mercenaries in the Byzantine Empire

Detail of a mural, dating to the late 13th century, showing *Almogàvers* setting out; from a former royal palace in Barcelona.

**T**he Catalan Company of the East, often known as the *Almogàvers*, was an independent mercenary force that came to play a leading role in the military struggles of the Eastern Mediterranean during the 14th century. Its deeds were recorded and celebrated by one of the Company's members, Ramon Muntaner. The Company was established in the aftermath of the dynastic struggle known as the 'War of the Sicilian Vespers' between the kings of Aragon and the Angevins. In 1303, at the request of the Byzantine emperor Andronicus II Palaeologus, Roger de Flor (a former Knight Templar of German extraction) recruited a company of mercenaries who had fought in the Sicilian wars and transported them to Constantinople to help the emperor and his son, Michael, in their war against the Turks. According to Muntaner, the force that left Sicily comprised 36 ships, 1,500 knights, 4,000 *Almogàvers* (foot) and 1,000 sailors, all of Catalan or Aragonese extraction, together with their families. On arrival, Flor married the emperor's niece and was appointed Grand Duke.

The Company soon demonstrated its worth by defeating the Turks and driving them out of Anatolia. However, friction arose between the Catalans and their Byzantine paymasters, the latter fearing that the Company was out of control. In 1305 Flor was ambushed and murdered at the instigation of Prince Michael and the Company suffered severe losses. Thereafter, in what came to be known as the Catalan Revenge or Vengeance, the Company declared war on the

**1303**
Formation of the Catalan Company by Roger de Flor, recruited by the Byzantine emperor.

**1305**
The murder of Roger de Flor unleashes the 'Catalan Vengeance' against the Byzantines.

**1308**
The Company transfers its main base of operations from Thrace to Thessaly.

**1311**
Victory at the battle of Halmyros on 15 March 1311 allows the Company to seize control of the duchies of Athens and Neopatria.

**1388**
The Company is defeated by the Florentines, loses control of its duchies and is disbanded.

The Company and its leader, Roger de Flor, arriving in Constantinople, as imagined in a painting by José Moreno Carbonero (1888).

## Battle of Halmyros 1311

The battle of Halmyros (also known as Kephissos), which took place on 15 March 1311, was the most decisive battle fought by the Company. The Company had taken up position behind the River Kephissos in Boeotia. When a heavy cavalry charge by the knights of the Duke of Athens became bogged down in some flooded ground, the outnumbered but more manoeuvrable Catalans and their Turkish allies were able to overwhelm them.

Byzantines and raided far and wide throughout Thrace and Macedonia, causing widespread devastation and loss of life.

In 1306 the Catalans were joined by a large force of Turkish mercenaries, who had previously served the emperor. In 1310, the Duke of Athens, Walter of Brienne, recruited the Company to help him campaign against his neighbours, but when he refused to pay the Catalans' wages he was defeated and killed by them at the battle of Halmyros in 1311. As a result, the Company was able to take possession of the Duchy of Athens, as well as that of Neopatria soon after. However, the Catalans were to lose control of both duchies after their defeat by the Florentines in 1388 and the Company disappeared as an independent military force thereafter.

The Catalan Company was made up of highly mobile mixed forces of armoured horsemen and footsoldiers, supported by ships. The chronicler Ramon Desclot described the *Almogàvers* who fought in the Catalan-Aragonese campaigns in the Iberian Peninsula as 'men who live only by war'. They wore no armour and carried lances and short swords. Questions of strategy and leadership were debated by the Company Council, while Muntaner relates that written tallies were kept of the shares of spoils to be divided up and paid to each man. The success of the Company may be explained partly by its skilled and battle-hardened troops, and partly by the military weakness of the Byzantine empire, which lacked sufficient forces to impose its will on the Catalans.

# The Swiss Pikemen
## Highly Organized Peasant Armies

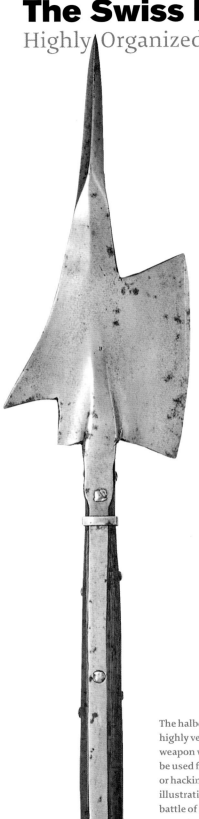

The halberd was a highly versatile weapon which could be used for thrusting or hacking, as in the illustration of the battle of Sempach, opposite. It was retained by the elite squad guarding the flags when the rest of the infantry adopted pikes around 1490.

*T*he Swiss were unusual among the elite forces of late medieval and early modern Europe in being poor peasants and townsmen without the wealth needed to equip and maintain the armoured horsemen associated with military success at the time. They developed their unique organization and methods in the course of a protracted struggle to free themselves from the feudal overlordship of the Austrian Habsburgs. An initial alliance of three mountain cantons in 1291 seemed doomed in the face of the far superior Habsburg forces, until the surprise victory at Morgarten in 1315 when the peasants destroyed a much larger Austrian force by rolling tree trunks and rocks down a hillside and then using halberds and swords to finish off the disabled horsemen. A more impressive victory followed at Laupen in 1339, when the Swiss managed to defeat both horse and foot on an open plain by remaining in a tightly packed square. This became their hallmark tactic and was honed over further conflicts, each one persuading more cantons to join the confederation until it totalled 13 cantons plus allied regions by 1513.

## 'Where are my Switzers? Let them guard the door.'

Shakespeare, *Hamlet*, Act IV, Scene 5

The Swiss system was based on universal service, but in practice only the fittest men were actually mobilized as usually there were enough volunteers to avoid the need for conscription. Each urban guild or rural parish provided a contingent, and these were combined in the field as the confederate army. Initially, most Swiss carried halberds, two-handed swords or crossbows, and only two in five were armed with long pikes even in the mid-15th century. But pikemen performed a key role in the Swiss offensive and defensive capacity.

### Successful tactics

Most late medieval infantry fought from behind barricades and other defences to protect them from cavalry. By forming themselves into a large solid square of up to 10,000 men, with the pikemen on the front and flanks, the Swiss were able to move into the open. If cavalry appeared, the square would halt, with the pikemen facing outwards to protect against a charge. The Swiss became adept at combining different infantry weapons, mixing several ranks of pikemen with others armed with crossbows, handguns or halberds. The square would

Above: Detail of one of a series of 16th-century tapestries depicting the battle of Pavia (1525). Charles V inflicted a severe defeat on the French army of Francis I, and his Swiss allies.

Below: At the battle of Sempach, 1386, 1,400 Swiss (seen on the left) defeated around 6,000 Austrians who had dismounted to attack them over broken ground, as depicted in this 16th-century woodcut by Niklaus Manuel Deutsch.

advance at a brisk pace, relying on its sheer size and momentum to terrify its opponents. If the latter chose to stand, the halberdiers would sally forth in attack, always ready to fall behind the protective pikes should cavalry appear. Such tactics were only effective because the Swiss imposed strict discipline. Men were forbidden to take prisoners to prevent the unit losing cohesion as individuals left the ranks. The system worked because the soldiers knew there would be enough booty if the enemy forces could be routed and their baggage captured. They also had confidence in their officers, most of whom they elected rather than having to serve under lords like most other Europeans.

The Swiss narrowly avoided destruction at Arbedo (1422) at the hands of the much larger army of the Duke of Milan, seen here in a 15th-century German manuscript. The outcome accelerated the replacement of the halberd by the pike as the principal weapon.

These tactics proved successful against the Habsburgs, who were eventually forced to renounce their overlordship in 1499. What really brought the Swiss to prominence, however, was their spectacular success against Duke Charles the Bold of Burgundy. Burgundy was one of Europe's best-organized and richest states, encompassing modern Belgium, the Netherlands and much of France. It had a large, well-organized and well-equipped army with a good train of artillery and a powerful force of armoured cavalry. Charles began conquering the Rhineland after 1467, soon threatening the Swiss cantons. Though France and Austria also opposed Burgundy, the Swiss were left largely to fight on their own.

Charles crossed the Jura mountains into western Switzerland in 1476, massacring the garrison of Grandson. Now over-confident, he raced to meet the Swiss who approached on 2 March and was unexpectedly routed. A key factor in the Swiss victory was their modification of the conventional medieval tactic of deploying an army in three 'battles' or divisions. Whereas the Burgundians lined their battles one behind the other, the Swiss deployed *en echelon*. They grouped their shot as a relatively small advance guard to harass the enemy and tempt him to leave any favourable position he may have occupied. The main body formed a massive square staggered some distance behind, with another smaller battle in support to the left or right rear. These tactics proved decisive in further conflicts at Murten (1476) and Nancy (1477). Charles' death in the latter cemented the Swiss victory and their international reputation.

## A lucrative mercenary trade

France and other powers soon paid good money to hire Swiss to stiffen their own infantry. This mercenary trade initially made the confederation a major factor in European politics, enabling it to seize more territory. However, serious problems arose when Swiss contingents faced each other on the same battlefield and refused to fight, giving rise to a reputation for unreliability. Other powers also began training their own soldiers in Swiss tactics, notably Emperor Maximilian I, who organized a German equivalent known as the *Landsknechte*. The *Landsknechte* employed a far higher proportion of pikemen, and largely replaced crossbows with handguns. Serious defeats by the *Landsknechte* at Marignano (1515) and Pavia (1525) forced the Swiss confederation to disengage from international politics. However, the Swiss remained sought after as mercenaries, and individual cantons were allowed to recruit regiments for foreign powers, notably the papacy and France.

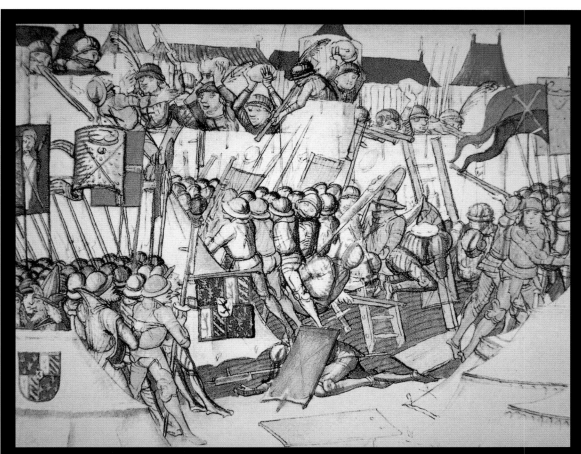

Duke Charles besieging the Swiss force at Grandson. The Swiss later charged, forcing the Burgundians to flee.

## Battle of Grandson 1476

Grandson was the first Swiss victory to have a serious international impact. The 20,000 strong Burgundian army left its entrenchments to confront the Swiss infantry numbering 18,000. Having seen two attacks fail, Duke Charles tried to switch his reserves to replace his battered first line. The Swiss charged, turning what was intended as a tactical withdrawal into a full rout which left 1,000 Burgundians dead. Having lost only 70 men, the Swiss captured the duke's entire baggage.

# Aztec Military Orders
## Fearless Knights of Ancient Mexico

**A**mong the Aztecs' knightly military orders, the Eagle and Jaguar warriors are undoubtedly the most famous. They were not an officer corps as such but an elite group, membership of which was the result of military achievement rather than special training, requiring an aspirant to take at least four captives in battle. Since military achievement was crucial for holding many higher political offices, members of the nobility dominated these orders, and they acted as a group to advise the king.

A life-size terracotta statue of an Eagle Knight dressed in battle costume, one of two nearly identical figures that once flanked the entrance to the House of the Eagles, close to the Templo Mayor in the Aztec captial Tenochtitlan (modern Mexico City).

> '**Each [of the Shorn Ones] had sworn not to flee if faced by twenty enemies, nor to retreat one step even if this meant death.**'
> Diego Durán, 1581

Distinguished only by insignia and ornament, the knightly orders used the same arms as other veteran warriors: atlatls (spearthrowers) and darts when first closing, and oak broadswords or thrusting spears edged with razor-sharp obsidian blades for hand-to-hand combat. They also carried shields and wore jerkin-like quilted cotton armour under full body suits of feather-covered fabric or hides. However, their arms were supplied from the royal armouries, rather than from the city or ward armouries, and so were presumably of the best quality. In battle, the Eagles and Jaguars fought as a group in the centre near the king or commanding general, but were readily identifiable in suits resembling the animals whose names they bore.

Despite being the most famous, Eagle and Jaguar knights were not regarded among the Aztecs as the highest of the elites – these were the Otomies and, especially, the Shorn Ones. To be named an Otomí, a warrior had to take five or six captives; to become one of the more elevated Shorn Ones, more than 20 brave deeds were required. Otomies wore their hair in a tassel bound with a red ribbon and both they and the Shorn Ones had distinctive suits and shields. The Shorn Ones shaved their heads to leave only a shock of hair braided with a red ribbon over the left ear, and painted one half of their head blue and the other half red or yellow. Although becoming an Otomí or Shorn One could bring political benefits, they were primarily warriors of great status and did not constitute an organized political group like the Eagle and Jaguar knights. Instead, they were superior individual fighters, and were used where their skills would have maximum effect.

The Otomies and Shorn Ones preceded the rest of the army into battle. Sworn not to retreat even in the face of 20 warriors, the Shorn Ones advanced

## Key Dates

**1428**
The Aztecs become an empire and are able independently to establish warrior elites.

**1428–40**
During the reign of Itzcoatl, the number of four captives is established as the standard for an elite warrior.

**c. 1450**
King Moteuczoma Ilhuicamina conceals the Shorn Ones and Otomies, who then ambush the Huaxtecs as they pursue the fleeing Aztec army.

**1481–86**
During the reign of Tizoc the requirement for an elite warrior is increased from taking four captives to taking four captives in a flower war – that is four enemy veteran warriors.

**1521**
The year of the Spanish conquest, after which Aztec warriors fight as Spanish auxiliaries.

first, followed by the Otomies, who were sworn not to retreat in the face of 10 or 12 warriors. Thereafter came the other knightly orders and veteran warriors leading organized units. Occasionally, individual knights and veterans led small groups of novice warriors into their first battles. Similarly, when the army withdrew from the battlefield, the Shorn Ones formed the rear guard to protect the rest; they did not turn their backs but instead performed a fighting withdrawal. Two or three Shorn Ones could reputedly rout an army, and once a Shorn One planted his foot, he could not be moved.

Unlike the bulk of the Aztec army, which was composed of commoners employed seasonally, the military orders were available year-round in case the need to fight arose. Nevertheless, as they formed a minority of the army, they did not have the manpower to launch major offensive actions themselves.

## Defeat of the Huaxtecs c. 1450

During an attack on the Gulf Coast in the 1450s, rather than employing the Otomies and Shorn Ones to initiate the battle, King Moteuczoma Ilhuicamina (now popularly known as Moctezuma or Montezuma) concealed a force of these elite fighters behind the battlefield, then engaged a large Huaxtec army. During the battle, the Aztecs feigned panic and fled, pursued by the Huaxtecs. Once their opponents were drawn past their place of concealment, the Otomies and Shorn Ones attacked from the flanks and rear, devastating the enemy.

Left and above: Details from the Codex Mendoza (c. 1541–42) showing Aztec warriors seizing defeated enemies by the hair. In the upper row above are warriors wearing the garb for taking two, three and four captives; the last of these is wearing a Jaguar suit. In the lower row are an Otomí and a Shorn One, as well as a general.

# The
# Early
# Modern
# World

## 1500 – 1900

# The Ottoman Janissaries
## Household Infantry of the Sultan

**E**stablished in the 1370s under the Ottoman ruler Murad I, the Janissaries initially served as the sultan's bodyguard and comprised a few hundred men. However, the corps soon became the elite household infantry of the Ottoman sultans and one of the first standing troops in Europe. The name Janissaries derives from the Turkish *yeni çeri*, or 'new soldiers', and they gradually replaced the Turkish warrior lords of the frontiers and their tribal levies, upon whom earlier Ottoman rulers had relied.

At first, the sultan used prisoners of war to create his own independent military guard. Later, in the 1380s, the child levy system was introduced to recruit new soldiers. Under this system, Christian boys, preferably between 12 and 14 years of age, were periodically taken at varying rates – usually one child from 40 households. A group of 100–200 boys, called 'the flock', was collected and a detailed register was compiled, with each boy's name and physical description. The 'flock' then travelled on foot to the capital. On arrival, the survivors who had not escaped or perished during the long journey were inspected, circumcised and converted to Islam. The brightest were singled out for education in the empire's elite Palace School; the rest were hired out to Turkish farmers for seven to eight years, learning the rudiments of the Turkish language and Islamic customs. After this the boys were recalled to the capital, where they joined the ranks of Janissary novices and lived in their own barracks under strict military discipline.

The levies occurred haphazardly in the 15th century, but more regularly in the 16th century, when the frequent and prolonged wars often decimated the Janissaries. By the end of that century, however, the ranks of the Janissaries were filled from within the corps, and thus the system became redundant. Practised sporadically in the 17th century, the levy was 'wholly forgotten by the 1660s', according to English author and diplomat Sir Paul Rycaut, though in 1705 Ottoman authorities attempted to levy 1,000 boys in Greece.

*c.* 1370s
  Founding of the corps by Murad I.

*c.* 1380s
  Introduction of the 'collection' or child levy system.

1444
  Janissaries are instrumental in the Ottoman victory at the battle of Varna against a European crusading army led by Vladislas of Hungary and Poland.

1453
  Janissaries play a crucial role in the conquest of Constantinople.

1514
  Janissary firepower and cannons annihilate the Safavids at the battle of Chaldiran.

1516/17
  Janissary volleys crucial in the Ottoman victories in battles against the Mamluks, including Marj Dabiq (Syria).

1517
  Battle of Raydaniyya outside Cairo; Ottomans end Mamluk rule in Egypt.

1526
  Battle of Mohács.

1826
  Destruction and formal abolition of the Janissary corps.

Above: The siege of Rhodes in 1522, with Süleyman I on horseback surrounded by Janissaries; from the *Süleymanname* of 1558. The Ottomans were quick to adopt gunpowder weaponry, and as well as the traditional recurved bow, the troops now also possess firearms.

Opposite above: A late 18th-century Turkish *miquelet*-lock musket. The Janissaries used the matchlock musket well into the 17th century, though from the later 16th century on their muskets featured the flintlock firing mechanism.

Opposite below: 'Janissary off to war', after a drawing by Nicolas de Nicolay, who travelled with the French ambassador to the Ottoman empire in 1551. Europeans were fascinated by this well-organized standing army, gorgeously uniformed and armed with a range of weapons.

With the broadening of the pool of recruitment, the original bodyguard was soon transformed into the ruler's elite household infantry, so that by the battle of Kosovo against the Serbs in 1389 they numbered some 2,000 men. By the mid-15th century under Mehmed II their number increased to 5,000, and by the end of his reign in 1581 the sultan had doubled the size of the corps. By the middle of the 16th century there were some 12,000 Janissaries and 7,700 Janissary novices whose salaries were paid from the central treasury. The Janissaries received five *akçes* pay per day, that is, four times more than the Streltsy of Muscovy (see p. 78). In addition, they were allocated one gold piece per year for their bows, as well as a shirt, a large trouser and other garments annually.

## Firepower

The Janissaries were equipped with their formidable recurved bow, sabre, shield and light coat of mail, while other units used crossbows, javelins and war-axes. Under Sultan Murad II in the mid-15th century they started to use matchlock arquebuses, but it was not until around the mid-16th century that most of the Janissaries carried firearms. Murad III equipped his Janissaries with the more advanced matchlock musket, which they used well into the 17th century, although flintlock muskets with the Spanish *miquelet*-lock were also manufactured in the empire from the late 16th century.

> '... if the imperial Janissaries were once decisively defeated and remained on that field, the Turkish emperor could never recover ...'

Konstantin Mihailović, a Janissary 1456–63

The Janissaries' firepower, especially in the early 16th century, often proved fatal for their adversaries. They could fire their weapons in a kneeling or standing position without the need for additional support or rest. Unlike musketeers in western Europe, they did not use pikes to defend themselves. Contemporary Ottoman chronicles and minature paintings show that as early as the battle of Mohács in 1526 the Janissaries formed several consecutive rows (from two to nine) and discharged their weapons row by row, firing volleys.

Until the early 17th century they maintained their firing skills by practising regularly, usually twice a week. However, in 1606, the author of *The Laws of the Janissaries* was already complaining about the decline of this exercise, noting that the members of the corps were no longer given powder for the drills and that the soldiers used their allotted wick for their candles and not for their shooting practice. By the time of the Long War (1593–1606) in Hungary, the Janissaries had lost their firepower ascendancy over their Hungarian and Habsburg opponents.

### Increasing numbers, decreasing discipline

To counter superior Habsburg firepower, the Ottomans increased the size of the corps of arms-bearing Janissaries. Their number reached 37,600 by 1606 and fluctuated between 50,000 and 54,000 in the 1650s, attaining a peak of almost 79,000 men in 1694–95 during the war against the Holy League (1684–99). This

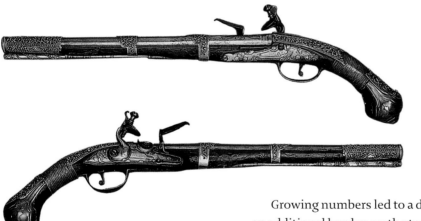

Below: A pair of ornate late 18th-century flintlock Ottoman pistols.

number decreased after the war, but was again raised in the Russo-Ottoman War of 1768–74. However, these paper figures are misleading as only a small proportion of the Janissaries participated in military campaigns. In 1660–61 the figure was only 33 per cent (18,013 men), and by 1710 only 17 per cent (7,255 men) of the total number of Janissaries listed in the account books fought. Many others were deployed in frontier garrisons, guarded the Janissary barracks in Istanbul or were pensioners.

Growing numbers led to a decline in the Janissaries' military skills and put an additional burden on the treasury. To ease the cost, the Janissaries were allowed to engage in trade and craftsmanship in the 17th century. By the 18th century Janissary service had been radically transformed and most Janissaries had become craftsmen and shop-owners, privileged with tax-exempt status as a reward for their supposed military service, for which they continued to draw pay. Far from the life of rigid military discipline that characterized the origins of the corps, the Janissaries married and settled in cities, established relationships with the civil population, and were more interested in providing for their families than fighting the enemy. Like the Streltsy, Ottoman Janissaries jealously guarded their privileges and fiercely opposed all military reforms aimed at undermining their status. Apart from a diminished military value, they were also unable to fulfil other vital functions as they had done in the 15th and early 16th centuries, when they served in Istanbul and in major provincial capitals as military police, guards, night-watchers and firefighters.

Opposite: A drawing of a Janissary by Gentile Bellini, c. 1480. Seated cross-legged on the ground, he wears a government-issued woollen cloak and cap. At his waist are visible his weapons, including the recurved composite bow, which had formidable armour-piercing capability.

# Battle of Mohács 1526

Janissary volleys decided the fate of several battles in the 15th and 16th centuries against the Aqqoyunlus (1473), Safavids (1514), Mamluks (1516/17) and Hungarians (1526). Of these, the battle of Mohács on 29 August 1526 led to the collapse of medieval Hungary. At an early stage of the battle, the Hungarian artillery opened fire at the Rumelian army, the first of Sultan Süleyman I's troops. It was followed by a successful Hungarian cavalry charge that broke the resistance of the Ottoman cavalry. But instead of chasing the fleeing enemy, the Hungarians set out to loot. At this point, the Janissaries inflicted major destruction on the Hungarians with their volleys.

Although the Hungarian infantry and the left wing fought bravely, they were unable to break the obstacles erected in front of the cannons and the Janissaries, and were slaughtered by Janissary volleys. Contrary to general belief, it was not Ottoman cannons (which shot beyond the Hungarians), but rather the insurmountable wall and firepower of the Janissaries that decided the fate of the Hungarians and their kingdom.

Two illustrations of the battle of Mohács, from the *Süleymanname*, 1558; the Janissaries' firearms volleys were crucial to the Ottoman victory.

By the latter part of the 16th century the corruption of the Janissaries was endemic and instead of protectors, they had become the terror of the cities. During the 1588 Istanbul fire, for instance, instead of fighting the flames, they engaged in looting. They also went on rampages when their taverns or coffee shops were closed down or their privileges threatened. The Janissaries had always occasionally mutinied, but in the 17th and 18th centuries these revolts became frequent. One revolt blocked the reforms of Selim III and their mutiny resulted in his murder in 1807. The Janissaries thus ultimately became Ottoman society's kingmakers, confirmed in the habits of privilege and corruption.

Learning from Selim III's mistakes, his successor Mahmud II carefully prepared his military reforms and made alliances within Ottoman religious

قلعه صالديدى عبر ويه يحرق عاده

Sultan Mehmed II had failed to capture Belgrade in 1456, but in 1521 Süleyman succeeded in taking the city, as seen in this illumination, opening the way for the conquest of Hungary.

and military establishments. When in 1826 the Janissaries revolted against his reforms, the sultan was ready for them. Obtaining a *fetva* or religious ruling that sanctioned the killing of the rebellious Janissaries, the sultan ordered his modern artillery corps against the Janissaries. The cannons destroyed and set aflame the Janissary barracks, killing some 6,000 men. The remaining Janissaries were slaughtered in the ensuing manhunt. Other Janissaries living in provincial cities were killed by the local population, which rose against their tyranny. Known in Ottoman history as the Auspicious Incident, the destruction of the Janissaries was regarded by the long-suffering Ottoman people as a form of liberation and it opened the way for substantive military reforms during the Ottoman reform era of 1839–76.

# Ivan the Terrible's Streltsy
## Elite Marksmen Armed with Muskets

*T*he Streltsy were Russia's response to the growing importance of firearms as infantry weapons from the mid-15th century. Unlike the infantry of western Europe, those of Russia, Poland and the Ottoman empire relied on massed firepower, preferably delivered from behind entrenchments or movable barricades. These tactics required considerable discipline and courage to be effective. Finding his existing infantry inadequate, Tsar Ivan IV, 'the Terrible', created the Streltsy (literally 'shooters') as a bodyguard in 1551. Each man carried a musket and a long-bladed axe known as a *berdysh*. The latter could be used as a rest to steady the musket while firing, as well as a vicious weapon for close combat.

Initially around 3,000 strong, the Streltsy were soon expanded with additional regiments, each distinguished by the colour of the men's long kaftan coat, which was decorated by contrasting braid; their uniform was completed with a fur hat and red, yellow or green boots. They soon proved their worth during Ivan's many wars, including the defeat of the khanates of Kazan (1552) and Astrakhan (1556), and the capture of Polotsk, which enabled Ivan to overrun Livonia (modern Latvia), in 1563.

By 1600 the Streltsy numbered around 25,000, including the 2,800-strong elite Moscow regiment. This was a significant force by contemporary standards, all the more impressive considering it was maintained permanently at a time when most European monarchs still raised and disbanded the majority of their forces as need and finances dictated. They guarded the tsar, garrisoned fortresses and enforced public order in peacetime. In wartime, the Streltsy were supplemented by less-reliable militia infantry, as well as by cavalry provided by the Russian boyars (nobles), Cossacks and other irregulars.

The Streltsy were most effective in siege warfare and in defending fixed positions, but were unable to match the offensive potential of western-style infantry units

'They are most insolent whenever an occasion presents itself and inspire the greatest fear in Moscow.' A Czech visitor to Moscow, 1680s

Opposite: Coloured engraving of 17th-century Streltsy, showing a commander (on the left) and a musketeer (on the right) carrying a *berdysh*.

Below: Streltsy shown using their favourite tactic of fighting from behind a wooden palisade, from a painting by Victor Vasnetsov (1918).

armed with both pike and shot. These units, introduced during the 1630s, were chiefly a response to the Polish adoption of such infantry. The Streltsy resisted change, partly because the new-style infantry achieved only mixed success, but largely because they had become a powerful, self-interested military caste similar to the Ottoman Janissaries (see p. 72). Recruited from free-born inhabitants at a time when most Russians were serfs, the Streltsy regarded themselves as a social as well as a military elite.

They increasingly intervened in Russia's turbulent domestic politics to safeguard their pay and privileges, especially after 1672 during the long regency of Sophia for the future Peter the Great. Peter was confined under internal exile at Preobrajenskoe, where he was allowed to create his own bodyguard trained along western European lines. The new troops proved decisive in 1689 during his successful coup against Sophia, who had been backed by most of the Streltsy. The Streltsy were retained, but the 'foreign' troops were rapidly expanded. Though not always more effective on campaign, new units were politically more reliable. The test came in June 1698 when some Streltsy revolted during Peter's absence on a grand tour of western Europe. The new infantry soon crushed the mutineers, who were tortured, executed or exiled to distant garrisons. A few Streltsy regiments remained, but these were destroyed at the battle of Narva by the Swedes in 1700. The defeat prompted Peter to reform the entire army on a uniform, regular footing, abolishing the remaining traditional formations.

## Siege of Pskov 1581–82

The defence of Pskov by 7,000 Streltsy displayed them at their best. The Poles had counterattacked against Russian incursions into their territory, retaking Livonia, and were now threatening Russia itself. Assisted by 2,000 cavalry and 10,000 militia, the Streltsy held out in the city of Pskov for five months – long enough for Ivan IV to negotiate a compromise peace.

# The Knights of Malta
## A Crusading Order in the Mediterranean

Above: The Cross of Malta on the reverse of a silver sovereign coin of the Order of Malta during the Grand Mastership of Juan de Lascaris-Castellar, 1636–57. Seizures of bullion in raiding provided part of the basis for such coins.

The Knights Hospitaller (see p. 38) of the Order of St John of Jerusalem became known as the Knights of Malta once they had moved their base to that central Mediterranean island. In 1480 their fortress-headquarters on Rhodes had successfully defied the Ottoman sultan Mehmed II, but was then taken in 1522 by the Turks under Süleyman the Magnificent. After this loss, the Knights were given Malta by Süleyman's rival, Emperor Charles V.

In many ways the Knights were a continuation of a medieval crusading order and were clothed and equipped accordingly. Armour and the cross thus played a continuing role in a way that was not the case across the rest of Europe. Organized into national chapters, they lived in Malta in houses belonging to each chapter. Service in their ranks was socially prestigious among Catholics across Europe, a fact which contributed to their high reputation.

### The defence of Malta

On Malta the Knights built major fortifications, especially under their Grand Masters Claude de la Sangle and Jean de la Valette. These stood them in good stead in 1565 when they once again faced Süleyman's forces in one of the great

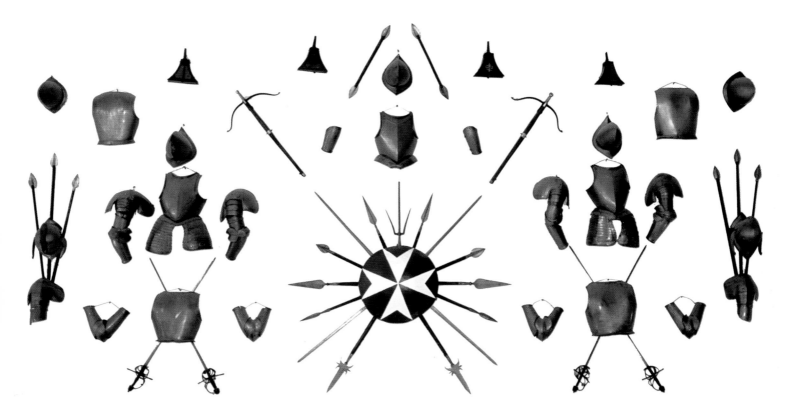

## Key Dates

**1522**
Hospitallers' stronghold on Rhodes falls to the Ottoman Turks under Süleyman the Magnificent. Emperor Charles V gives Malta to the Knights.

**1565**
A Turkish attack on Malta fails after an epic siege.

**1798**
Malta easily falls to Napoleon.

**1800**
French forces driven from Malta, which becomes British territory; the Knights are dispersed.

*Opposite below and below: Displays of arms, armour and weapons in the Armoury of the Grand Master's Palace in Valletta. The Knights of Malta were in many ways a continuation of the medieval crusading order of the Hospitallers. Armour, swords and spears were particularly useful for hand-to-hand combat.*

epics of warfare. To the Turks, Malta – the leading Christian privateering base in the Mediterranean – was a threat to trade, as well as an obstacle to the projection of their power into the western Mediterranean. Transported by 140 galleys, the Turks' 30,000 troops faced about 2,500 trained soldiers on the island, among whom 500 Knights of Malta under the Grand Master, Jean de la Valette, played the key role. Landing on 18 May, the Turks initially focused on the fortress of St Elmo, which they needed to take to obtain a safe harbour.

Having captured St Elmo, the Turks then launched major attacks on the other fortresses, Senglea and Birgu, but, hampered by divided leadership, the summer heat and logistical problems including the supply of drinking water, they could not prevail over the determined defence. The besiegers were held off until a Spanish relief army from Sicily finally arrived on 7 September 1565, at which point the Turks retreated, unwilling to face the new foe. They had suffered perhaps as many as 24,000 casualties, while the defenders sustained about 5,000, including from among their Maltese levies. The Turks never again attacked Malta. Its defence was seen as a great triumph – important both practically and psychologically.

### The Barbary corsairs and Napoleon

Thereafter, the Knights focused on a longstanding conflict with the Barbary corsairs (pirates) of North Africa, who had become Turkish vassals. The Knights played a crucial role in keeping the central Mediterranean free for Christian trade, as well as challenging the Turks in the eastern Mediterranean. Holy War, by what was still a crusading order, was mixed with the search for profit. The profits from raiding Turkish shipping supplemented the benefits from charitable donations by the faithful across Europe, and from ruling Malta.

Having initially relied on rowed galleys, the Knights switched in the 18th century to ships powered by the wind. Improvements in armaments, rigging and sail patterns meant that sailing ships became more significant in

**'If the Maltese Government had performed its duty, if the French Knights [of Malta] had not made sorties with a Militia undrilled ... and had been content to remain behind their ramparts, the strongest in Europe, we should not have gained entrance.'**
**Marshal Auguste de Marmont, on the French capture of Malta in 1798**

## Siege of St Elmo 1565

St Elmo was a key position in the defence of Malta. The Turks launched repeated attacks covered by their artillery, which, in the end, fired about 60,000 shots. The 1,500 defenders of the fortress used their 20 cannon to repel these attacks until, on 24 June, they fought to the death after the walls were breached. This heroic struggle was to be crucial to the subsequent self-image of the Knights of Malta, being seen as equivalent to the Spartan defence of Thermopylae against the Persians.

The siege of St Elmo, showing clearly the well-fortified nature of the defences, and also the Turkish cannons used to breach the walls and cover assaults.

Opposite: Alof de Wignacourt, Grand Master of the Knights of Malta, with his page, by Caravaggio (1608). The painting captures the extent to which the leadership of the Knights involved individual military prowess and prestige.

Mediterranean warfare. Sailing ships were less dependent on a network of local bases, carried more cannon than galleys, and were also less susceptible to bad weather. In 1700, the Knights decided to introduce a squadron of square-rigged men-of-war: the first two were ordered at Toulon and sailed back to Malta in 1704. These ships played an important role in containing the Barbary corsairs, the Turks having now ceased offensive operations in Mediterranean waters.

The Knights held Malta until 1798, when it was occupied by Napoleon's forces en route for Egypt. By then, the Order's military power was of scant consequence and it was bankrupt, in large part because of the confiscation of its sizable French possessions by the Revolutionary government in 1792. In 1798, the French landings were not seriously contested, and the Order's resistance was sapped both by a faction among the Knights favourable to France and by opposition from the Maltese population to rule by the Order. Napoleon's rapidly constructed siege works near Valetta also impressed the defenders. The French forces were soon driven out, however, in 1800, and Malta became a British territory: the Knights were dispersed and did not return.

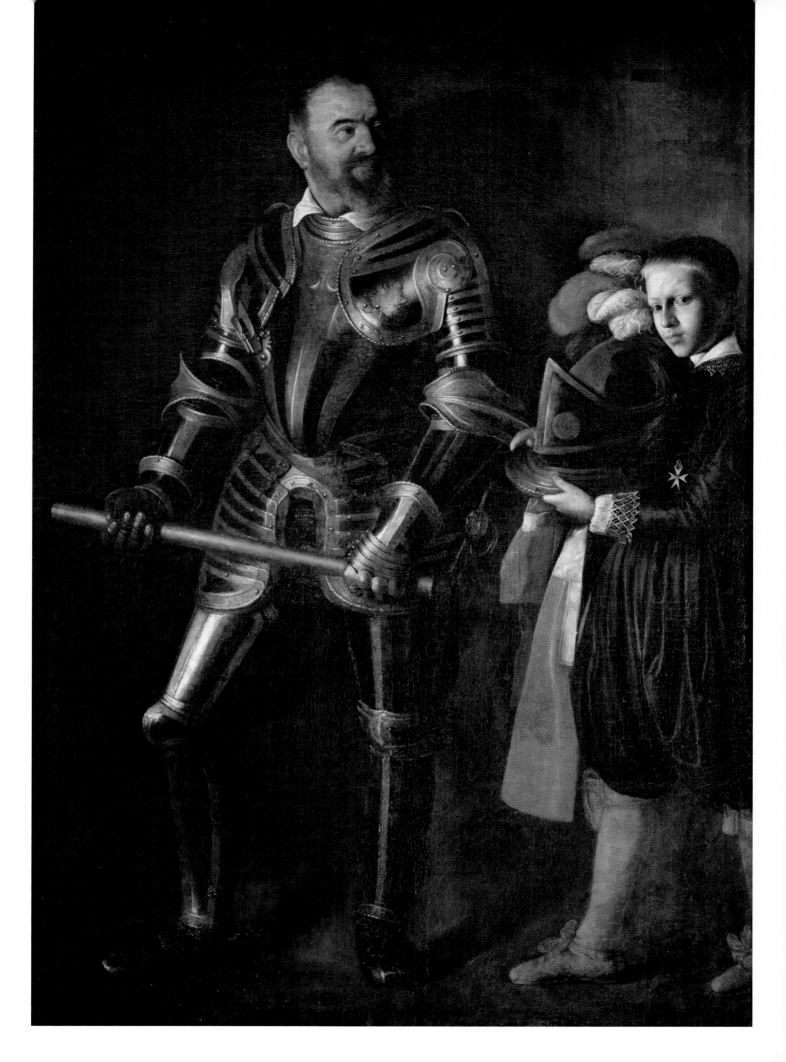

# The Dutch Marine Corps
## Companies of Specialist 'Ship Soldiers'

'all our hearts do now ake; for the newes is true, that the Dutch have broke the chaine and burned our ships, and particularly the Royal Charles ... And, the truth is, I do fear so much that the whole kingdom is undone!'
Samuel Pepys, Diary, 12 June 1667

**S**everal short-lived initiatives were taken to found a permanent corps of marines, or sea soldiers (*zeesoldaten*), in the 17th-century Dutch Republic, but it was only in 1665 that such a corps came into existence with its own command structure. In December 1664 the States-General decided to expand all existing companies of the army by 25 men each; these men, 4,000 in total, were to serve in the fleet. However, this group of marines, the so-called '*Régiment de Marine*' did not have its own command. In 1665, at the initiative of Johan de Witt, the States of Holland dismissed its marines and created instead a new regiment of 'ship soldiers' (*scheepssoldaten*).

Recruited from among former soldiers or seamen, the regiment had its own command and served exclusively at sea, being stationed in cities near the coast. De Witt may have been inspired by the example of England, where a similar unit had been founded in 1664. In 1666 a second regiment of 20 companies was founded, resulting in a total of 8,000 marines paid by Holland. Zeeland and Friesland followed with similar organizations, though on a much smaller scale.

Painting showing the *Royal Charles* being taken into Dutch waters after the Medway Raid, by Ludolf Backhuysen, 1667.

### The Raid on the Medway 1667

The Medway raid was the first occasion when the Dutch Marine Corps participated in an amphibious operation. Their commander, van Ghent, acting as one of the three flag officers, headed a squadron of frigates and light boats that went up the Medway. Marines took part in the occupation of the fortress at Sheerness, the capture of the *Royal Charles* and the burning of several other English warships near Chatham, Kent.

Above: Painting of the Four Days Battle, 1666, by Abraham Storck. At centre left is the Dutch ship the *Seven Provinces*, under de Ruyter, and to the right is the English flagship, *Royal Prince*, grounded on the shoals.

Above: Michiel de Ruyter was a seaman who was appointed captain of a marine company and became one of the most successful admirals in the Dutch navy; portrait by Ferdinand Bol (1667).

Opposite left: Baron van Ghent, by Jan de Baen. In 1667, under de Ruyter, van Ghent commanded the attack on the Medway, briefly capturing Sheerness.

Fighting both on land and at sea, the marines were considered an elite fighting force. They were armed with sabres and *snaphaans*, guns that were lit by sparks instead of fuses, which were less suitable at sea. On land the marines fought in standard infantry formation. At sea they used their low calibre weapons from the deck and from the masts to kill individuals on enemy ships.

Discipline was improved by having officers of their own. Willem Joseph Baron van Ghent, the first commander, had served as an officer in the army for 20 years. To promote their integration in the fleet, some of the Corps' officers also received the command of a warship; conversely, flag officers and captains were appointed captain of a marine company, such as Michiel de Ruyter. Under van Ghent the marines participated in the major battles of the second and third Anglo-Dutch Wars (1665–67 and 1672–74). During the Medway Raid of 1667 they were deployed on the English shore. Under the command of François Palm they fought in the battle near Seneffe (modern Belgium) against the troops of King Louis XIV of France. After the peace of Nijmegen in 1678 one regiment of the Marine Corps was abolished while the other became an infantry regiment. Only in 1699, after the Nine Years War (1689–97), was a new Marines Corps set up, soon consisting of three regiments – two from Holland, one from Zeeland – of 12 companies, 3,600 men in total. During the War of the Spanish Succession (1702–13) the Dutch Marine Corps co-operated closely with its English counterpart in combined amphibious actions in Spain. The most important action was the capture of Gibraltar in 1704 by 1,800 British and Dutch marines.

The Corps was reduced to one regiment after 1713. In the 18th century marines were sent to put down slave revolts in Dutch colonies in South America. Except during the Belgian Revolt, when marines participated in operations along the banks of the River Scheldt and in Zeelandic Flanders, for most of the 19th century and the first half of the 20th century they served overseas. Today, the *Korps Mariniers* still exists as part of the Royal Netherlands Navy.

# The Manchu Bannermen
## Elect Defenders of the Qing Dynasty

**T**he Manchu 'Eight Banners' were the force, mostly cavalry, that enabled the Manchu leaders to unify the lands of Manchuria, conquer China for their Qing dynasty, maintain control of the vast lands and peoples of China, and then expand beyond traditional Chinese borders to incorporate Mongolia, Tibet and East Turkestan (called Xinjiang after its conquest).

Manchuria, inhabited largely by various tribes that later came to be called collectively 'Manchu', was under the very loose supervision of the Chinese Ming dynasty court (1368–1644). However, taking advantage of the growing weakness of China during the 15th and 16th centuries, a dynamic Manchu chieftain called Nurhachi unified Manchuria through war and diplomacy. By the early 1620s he had led his armies to conquer the Chinese areas of Manchuria, adding them to his rule.

### Origins and development of the Bannermen

Nurhachi had created a highly disciplined military arm he named the 'Eight Banners', so called for the different-coloured flags, or banners, that marked each unit. Not only a military, but also a political and social organization, each Banner was required to raise, support and train troops from within its ranks, as well as see to the welfare of the families of the Banner soldiers. The Eight Banner designation was for administrative purposes; for military campaigns several sub-units of the Banners called *niru*, consisting of 200–300 men, were placed under commanders appointed by Nurhachi and his successors. When not on campaign, Bannermen engaged in full-time training or raids into China and Korea. The discipline and experience

Above: Four examples of the ceremonial
armour of the Eight Banners, made of
satin padded with cotton and decorated
with gilt copper studs. The Eight Banners
were organized by colour into different
units to defend Beijing and the emperor.

Opposite left: Imperial painting of the
Meritorious Official, Yan Xiangshi, who
took part in the lifting of the siege of
Yarkand in 1758. Here he carries a bow and
full quiver of arrows behind his back.

Opposite right: The composite bow was
a traditional Inner Asian weapon, used
from horseback to great effect. The quiver
and bow case of this example are covered
with embroidered satin.

gained through these activities provided Nurhachi's successors with a force
that could continue their conquests beyond the borders of Manchuria.

In the 1630s and 1640s Nurhachi's successors created Banners of Mongols,
who served as additional cavalry forces, and Banners of Chinese, who
provided infantry and artillery units. The Manchu Banners comprised a large
majority of the total Banner numbers and proved to be the most disciplined
and effective forces in the conquest of China in the 1640s. The Bannermen
could be utterly ruthless, as demonstrated in the taking of the wealthy
and strategically important city of Yangzhou. The city first put up a stout
resistance to the Manchu attack, decimating the attacking Bannermen with
cannon fire. When Yangzhou finally fell in May 1645, as punishment for its
resistance it was brutally sacked for 10 days. Tens of thousands were
slaughtered and raped; news of the massacre acted as a warning to others in
China of the folly of resistance. However, this ruthlessness and brutality were
calculated, and the disciplined Bannermen obeyed orders to refrain from
sacking those cities, towns and territories that accepted Qing rule.

## Battle of Jao Modo 1696

In June 1696 the Kangxi Emperor led an 80,000-man Qing army to destroy the
Zunghar Mongols, who were threatening to unify and control all Mongolia. At
the battle of Jao Modo, the Zunghar army was held in place by Chinese cannon
fire, while Manchu Bannermen climbed the nearby hills to gain the high ground.
As Chinese infantry troops began an attack, the Bannermen in the hills loosed a
storm of arrows. The decisive blow came from a cavalry charge by the Bannermen
that scattered the Zunghar forces. Many thousands of the enemy were
slaughtered before night fell.

The Kangxi Emperor with his imperial guard. The
emperor used the Bannermen to great effect at Jao
Modo, and later appointed some of its members to run
the affairs of the Manchu homeland and Mongolia.

# 'My Manchu Bannermen are tough and successful because of the hardship of growing up in the north of Manchuria.'

Qianlong Emperor, 1781

Opposite: The Qianlong Emperor in ceremonial armour on horseback, by Giuseppe Castiglione. A successful military leader who expanded the Qing dynasty's territory, the emperor often used the Manchu Bannermen as the spearhead in his campaigns.

Below: Imperial painting of the Bannerman Zha Er Shan. This officer of the imperial guard distinguished himself in the Qianlong Emperor's Xinjiang campaign of 1755–59. The eulogy accompanying the portrait describes him as a courageous and confident warrior.

## Imperial defenders

The long-lasting Manchu Qing dynasty (1644–1911) ruled as a traditional Chinese dynasty, resorting to brutal suppression only when its legitimacy or its control of China appeared threatened. That is where the Bannermen came in. The Eight Banners remained the primary defenders of the dynasty and the fierce military arm of the imperial court. Eight Banner garrisons were placed in Manchuria, around the capital Beijing, and throughout the rest of China in or near key cities and at strategic points along important waterways, such as the Yangzi River and Grand Canal. Kept segregated in walled compounds, the garrisons had their own training fields, exercise yards, stables and gunnery ranges.

The Manchu Bannermen were equipped with a variety of weapons both typical of the Inner Asian lands as well as traditionally Chinese. They carried the Inner Asian composite bow, used by the Mongols and other peoples of the steppes and forests north of China, but were also expected to be skilled in the use of the waist sword – a weapon more identified with Chinese warriors. Each Bannerman was supplied with three to six horses and originally all were trained as horse archers who wore armour and helmets in battle. The strength and durability of the armour improved with Nurhachi's conquests, as skilled Chinese craftsmen were pressed into service. Some Banner units also rode with lances. By the late 17th century all Bannermen in the garrisons were expected to train with matchlock muskets, while the Banner units in Manchuria continued to be primarily horse archers, even in the late 19th century.

Membership in the Banner military force was hereditary, although by the 18th century all officer positions were filled through appointment by the emperor. It was not unusual for a Banner soldier who distinguished himself in combat to be promoted to Banner officer ranks. There were even a few cases of such commoners going on to rise to some of the senior Banner positions.

Military campaigns to expand the territory of the Qing dynasty involved sometimes vast numbers of Chinese soldiers from the Green Standard Army, a native Chinese force of over 900,000. Yet, the campaigns that conquered Tibet, Mongolia and Xinjiang were always spearheaded by Manchu Banner units. Often the Chinese units held an enemy force while the Manchu Bannermen slipped behind the enemy to harass supply lines or prevent relief of the engaged enemy armies.

The Banners succeeded in defending the dynasty and in expanding the borders of the empire during the 17th and 18th centuries, but were woefully unprepared for battle against the British in the First Opium War (1839–42). They fought bravely at the battle of Zhapu, almost to the last man, but were no match for British arms. Throughout the rest of the 19th century the Bannermen resisted reorganization along European lines and as a result ceased to be the main military force of the Manchu rulers.

# The Polish Hussars
## Flamboyant and Feared Heavy Cavalry

**T**he Polish Hussars were the finest heavy cavalry of eastern Europe during the 16th and 17th centuries. Long thought to derive from the Hungarian word for 20th man, the term 'hussar' in fact stems from a Slavonic term for 'bandit'. First applied to the light cavalry that developed in 15th-century Croatia, Serbia and Hungary, from the early 16th century the term was increasingly associated with armoured cavalry using massed charges. Unarmoured light cavalry were usually called 'Croats' or 'Cossacks' regardless of their actual origins.

Armoured hussars appeared in Poland around 1500 and were already a significant factor in the victory over the Russians at Orsza in 1513. By the later 16th century they wore elaborately decorated helmets, breastplates and suits of mail. Each man carried a lance of up to 5 m (over 16 ft) long, a curved sabre hanging from a waistbelt and a longer, straight sword (*pallasz*) suspended from the saddle. A warhammer and a brace of pistols completed the armament, but what really distinguished them was their flamboyant use of leopard and other animal skins worn over the armour, as well as feathers attached to a wooden frame on their backs. Like the metre-long lance pennon, the feathers were intended to scare opponents, especially their horses. The Hussars generally deployed in long lines, five ranks deep, and relied on a massed charge with levelled lances to panic the enemy into running. The pistols, swords and warhammers were used in close quarters against more resolute foes who stood their ground.

The Hussars fully came into their own during the reign of Stephan Bathory, prince of Transylvania, who ruled Poland as one of its militarily most successful kings in 1575 to 1586. Bathory established a permanent force of Hussars as a royal bodyguard and cadre for the national army in wartime. Service in the Hussars became fashionable for Polish nobles, who spent fortunes trying to outshine each other with their lavish dress and superb horses. Leading landowners raised additional units so that the Hussars formed 85 per cent of the army around 1600. The growing effectiveness of disciplined, musket-armed infantry made them less significant from the mid-17th century,

*Above: Karacena, or scale armour, from the late 17th century, including the Polish-style helmet called a zischägge.*

*Right: A set of 17th-century armour, with the famous 'wings' – feathers attached to a wooden frame – on the back.*

'[They] broke into gallop and came down on the vizier's main force like the wind, so that they completely routed them…'
**Philippe Dupont, a French eyewitness at Kahlenberg 1683**

## Key Dates

**1500**
Emergence of hussars as elite heavy cavalry.

**1576**
A permanent hussar regiment is established as Polish royal guard.

**1605**
Victory at Kircholm over the Swedes.

**1621**
Victory at Chocim over the Ottoman Turks.

**1683**
Polish Hussars assist in the victory over the Ottomans on the Kahlenberg hill, breaking the siege of Vienna.

**1795**
The final (third) partition extinguishes Poland as an independent state.

An 18th-century *zischägge* helmet, with decorative metal wings attached. The Polish Hussars wore spectacular armour, often using animal skins and feathers as decoration.

when they accounted for a fifth or less of the total force. Nonetheless, they still proved effective, especially during the wars against the Swedes (1621–29), who developed the tactic of the salvo, or massed single discharge by all ranks, in the hope of breaking the Hussars' feared charge. Hussars continued to serve with their traditional equipment into the 18th century, but increasingly the Polish cavalry discarded their armour and adopted the skirmishing and harassing tactics used by the Cossacks and Hungarians. Retention of the lance as an effective weapon against infantry continued to make the Poles distinctive and other armies added units of lancers from the mid-18th century. By then, the word hussar had become associated with the sabre- and carbine-armed Hungarian light cavalry added to western European armies from around 1700.

## Siege of Vienna 1683

The most significant success of the Polish Hussars was their participation in the combined effort to break the Ottoman siege of Vienna. Three thousand Hussars spearheaded the Polish army on the allied right advancing down the Kahlenberg hill on 12 September 1683 towards the much larger Ottoman force. As the Austrian and German troops in the centre and left wavered, the Hussars attacked, enabling the advance to resume. Once on the plain below, the Hussars launched a massed charge that broke the Ottoman army.

The Polish Hussars smash into the Turkish light cavalry outside Vienna in this near-contemporary painting of the battle.

# The Prussian Grenadiers
## Spearhead Assault Troops

Below: Prussian 1740 smoothbore musket, the main weapon carried by the Grenadiers.

Bottom: Grenadier from Regiment number 1, the oldest unit in the army, which fought in most of the battles of Frederick the Great's reign.

**G**renades have been used in European warfare since the early 16th century, but the first specialist grenadiers date from 1667, when Louis XIV selected four of the fittest and bravest men in each infantry company for this specialist role, adding separate grenadier companies to each regiment in 1672. As France was at that time western Europe's most successful power, French methods were swiftly

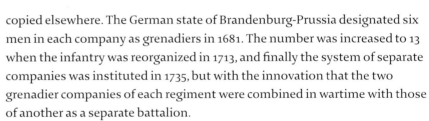

copied elsewhere. The German state of Brandenburg-Prussia designated six men in each company as grenadiers in 1681. The number was increased to 13 when the infantry was reorganized in 1713, and finally the system of separate companies was instituted in 1735, but with the innovation that the two grenadier companies of each regiment were combined in wartime with those of another as a separate battalion.

Grenades were hollow, cast-iron balls filled with gunpowder that was ignited by lighting a fuse. Throwing them required both considerable strength and great courage since the grenadier had to be close to the enemy to hit them. Their main use was in the attack and defence of fortresses, and soon grenadiers were seen as elite assault troops. Apart from their grenades carried in a satchel, they were armed, and trained, as other infantry and so could also employ the disciplined, mass fire tactics that characterized 18th-century European warfare. To allow freedom of movement to throw a grenade, distinctive tall hats were introduced, instead of the tricornes worn by the ordinary infantry. Prussian Grenadier hats were reinforced with brass front plates by the early 18th century, a style soon copied elsewhere, notably Russia.

### An impressive appearance and reputation

The Prussian Grenadiers rose from 10 per cent of the infantry in 1729 to over 17 per cent by 1755 by raising the size of their companies to around 150 men each. Total numbers grew in line with the overall expansion of the army. There were around 16,000 grenadiers during the Seven Years War (1756–63), rising to 22,656 by 1776. In addition to the two companies in each infantry regiment, King Frederick William I created a special three-battalion Guard Grenadier regiment after his accession in 1713. Famed as the 'soldier king'. Frederick William was particularly attached to his Guards, who were known as the 'red grenadiers' after their distinctive breeches, waistcoats and facings to blue coats. Many of the king's ideas were eminently practical, including his demand for particularly tall men for his Guards, giving rise to their nickname *Lange Kerls* ('tall fellows'). In an age of long-barrelled muzzle-loading muskets, it helped to have long arms. However, he took this to extremes, often paying huge bounties to entice giants to enlist, or had his officers kidnap suitable men from across Europe. The Guards saw action only once, at the siege of Stralsund in 1715, but nonetheless enjoyed a Europe-wide reputation for their impressive appearance and the precision of their drill.

Frederick William's son, Frederick the Great, reduced the Guards to a single battalion (numbered sixth) on his accession in 1740, replacing their blood-red distinctions with a more tasteful pale yellow – a uniform they kept till their demise in 1806. However, the new king expanded his own favourite regiment, number 15, to three battalions, and decked its third battalion out as Grenadiers. He also detached the Grenadier companies from other regiments to form seven permanent Grenadier battalions.

The advance of the Guard Grenadiers at Hohenfriedberg, 1745, by the leading 19th-century history painter, Carl Röchling.

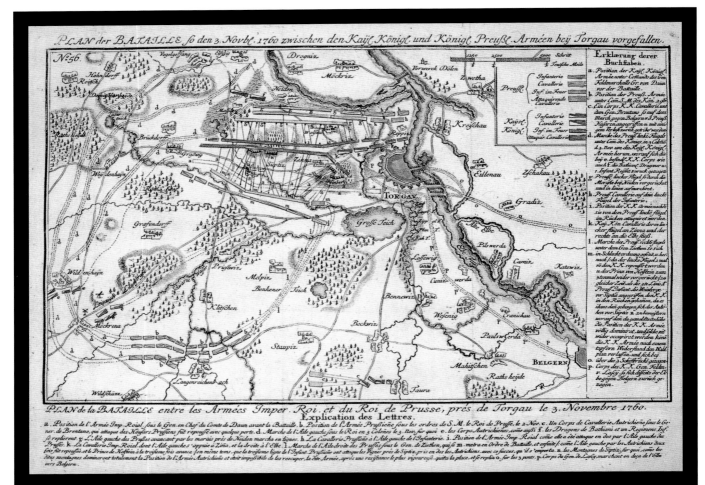

## Battle of Torgau 1760

Both the success and the limitations of the Prussian Grenadiers were demonstrated at the battle of Torgau on 3 November 1760. Frederick planned to pin the Austrian army with a feint attack, while he moved his main force behind them. He mistakenly thought his subordinate had begun the diversionary attack too soon,

and so launched the 10 Grenadier battalions of his own advance guard in a premature, unsupported assault against the main Austrian force. The Grenadiers advanced under withering fire, losing 5,000 men in half an hour, but bought time for the rest of the army to arrive and assist in the eventual costly victory.

Contemporary plan of Torgau, showing the Prussians attacking from the north and south against the Austrians deployed west of the town.

What really cemented the Prussian Grenadiers' reputation were Frederick's victories over Austria in a succession of wars after 1740. These proved the Prussians were not just fine parade ground soldiers, but could deliver their rapid, massed volleys and quick-paced assaults on the battlefield. The Guards and Grenadier battalions were used to spearhead attacks, notably at the battle of Leuthen (1757), when Frederick's prized third battalion stormed a churchyard stubbornly defended by Austrian infantry.

### Strengths and limitations

The Prussian Grenadiers' role symbolized both the strengths and limitations of Frederican tactics and 18th-century warfare in general. Military practice reflected the wider structure of society by assigning specialized tasks to different kinds of soldier. The fittest and best men were reserved for the grenadiers as assault troops. The next best became musketeers, deployed in the first line. Shorter men became fusiliers in the second line, while those

# 'Never in my life did I see anything more splendid ... Their polished weapons shone prettily in the clear sunlight, and their fire rolled like unending thunder.'

**An Austrian officer on the receiving end of the Prussian attack at Mollwitz 1741**

Distinctive brass-fronted Prussian Grenadier hats from Regiment number 2 (left), prior to 1740, and Regiment number 11 (right), of around 1785.

considered less fit or able were relegated to the garrison regiments in the reserve. Foreigners and enemy deserters were considered least reliable and were combined in 'free corps' for raiding or cannon fodder in secondary attacks. Despite various modifications, this thinking continued to dominate Prussian practice after Frederick's death in 1786. It was overtaken by the ideas of revolutionary France which, while still using different categories of infantry including grenadiers, expected all to be able to perform similar tasks if needed.

The old Prussian army paid the price in its defeat by Napoleon at Jena in 1806. A detachment of 27 men from the Guard Grenadier battalion escaped the debacle and became the core of a new guard regiment. This force continued the tradition into later 19th-century imperial Germany when they appeared on parade still with the tall grenadier hats. The tradition was revived in 1920 and again in 1961, when the battalion guarding the federal German defence ministry was designated as successors of the old Grenadiers. Since reunification in 1990 a group of re-enactors parade in Potsdam, dressed as Frederick William's red Grenadiers.

# Rogers' Rangers
## Frontier Irregulars in British North America

Coloured print of Rogers, based on a 1776 engraving by Thomas Hart. Hart's interpretation of Rogers, clad in the distinctive uniform of his command, though not authentic is the best-known image of the famed Ranger commander.

**D**uring the French and Indian War (1754–63), which was part of a larger conflict known in Europe as the Seven Years War, the British crown raised a number of units for service from its subjects in British North America. The most famous was the unit of light infantry organized and led by Robert Rogers of New Hampshire, which won fame operating mainly in upstate New York. Although by no means the first to employ irregular warfare tactics successfully in colonial North America, Rogers' Rangers achieved particular distinction in part due to the fact that their commander wrote down the methods and principles that guided their operations in documents that are still considered seminal works in the field of irregular warfare. Commando units the United States organized during World War II adopted the 'Ranger' name in tribute to Rogers' command and, although there is no direct lineage, modern US Ranger units view themselves as operating in its spirit and carrying on its legacy.

Rogers' military career began as a teenager in a militia ranger company. During the first year of the French and Indian War he was promoted to captain and ordered to raise an independent company of light infantry. This came to consist of some 60 rangers from provincial forces who were encamped in upstate New York, using what is now known as Rogers Island in the Hudson River for training.

### The skills of ranging

Within a few months, Rogers' Rangers had won renown for their ability to operate effectively against French outposts in the region around Lake George and Lake Champlain. Composed of hardy backwoodsmen clad in distinctive green uniforms, Rogers' command demonstrated a flair for long-range reconnaissance missions and conducting small-scale raids in the harsh climate and rugged terrain of upstate New York. Ranger tactics drew heavily on the practices of Native American warriors, emphasizing stealth and living off the land, and they served as auxiliaries to, rather than a central component of, the British regular forces.

Difficulties managing the often undisciplined Rangers, together with the fact that they insisted on higher pay than most troops, however, fuelled tensions between Rogers' command and British regulars. In December 1757 the unit's relationship with British military authorities was severely tested when members launched the 'Whipping Post Mutiny' to protest against the flogging of two Rangers by British regulars. Although Rogers was able to reconcile his men with the British authorities, the incident confirmed a desire on the part of the latter to train their own soldiers in ranging rather than rely on provincials to provide essential scouting and security services in the wilderness. Indeed, several months before the mutiny, Rogers had received directions from Lord Loudoun, commander of British forces in North America, to teach 'Gentlemen Volunteers' from the British regular regiments the skills of ranging. Rogers eagerly went to work training 55 volunteers and, to facilitate his efforts, began writing down the methods associated with Ranger service. In October 1757 he submitted an essay to Loudoun, who responded by asking Rogers to summarize it. Rogers complied with the request, and the end product was a list of 28 'Rules of Ranging' that became better known as his 'Standing Orders'.

Below: Light Dragoon Flintlock Carbine, used in the Seven Years War. Skill in handling firearms and a wide variety of other weapons was essential for members of Rogers' Rangers.

Below: Rogers' Rangers in action. The effectiveness of Rogers' command as a fighting force rested on the ability of its members to endure and adapt to the harsh weather and rugged wilderness of the North American frontier.

'If the enemy is so superior that you are in danger of being surrounded by them, let the whole body disperse, and every one take a different road to the place of rendezvous appointed for that evening, which must every morning be altered and fixed for the evening ensuing, in order to bring the whole party, or as many of them as possible, together, after any separation that may happen in the day; but if you should happen to be actually surrounded, form yourselves into a square, or if in the woods, a circle is best, and, if possible, make a stand till the darkness of the night favours your escape.'

Rule 10, from Rogers' 28 'Rules of Ranging', 1757

However, the British units that were raised ultimately came to operate as adjuncts to Rogers' command rather than replacements. It was with a mixed force of provincial and British Rangers, that Rogers was directed in March 1758 to launch a raid against French Fort St Frederic. The sharp engagement that ensued with a much larger enemy force became known as the Battle on Snowshoes. The Rangers were badly mauled and barely avoided complete destruction. According to legend, Rogers escaped by sliding 120 m (400 ft) down an exposed rock face (now known as Rogers' Slide) to frozen Lake George.

## Later operations

Despite the severe losses suffered at Snowshoes, Rogers' command nonetheless remained actively engaged in operations around Lake George in 1758 and 1759, conducting patrols and reconnaissances, fighting minor engagements and playing a critical role in the operations that led to the British capture of Fort Ticonderoga (Carillon) and Crown Point in July 1759. A few months after these victories, Rogers, now a major whose command had

### Battle on Snowshoes 1758

Frustrated in his hopes of capping a raid along the shores of Lake George with a successful attack on French Fort St Frederic, Rogers decided instead to lay an ambush for the morning patrol from the fort. When a force of about 100 French, Canadian and Native American warriors approached, Rogers ordered his men to spring the ambush. Believing it a success, some of Rogers' 183-man command launched a pursuit, only to find themselves facing a much larger enemy force. The enemy quickly manoeuvred against both Rogers' flanks and the Rangers' position soon collapsed; their commander ordered his men to scatter. Around 130 of Rogers' men were killed, while the French lost fewer than 40.

The second Battle on Snowshoes, also known as the battle of Rogers Rock, as depicted in a painting by Jean Leon Gerome Ferris. Although a near disaster for his command, this sharp 1758 engagement, fought along the shore of Lake George in upstate New York, further added to Rogers' legend.

expanded to nine companies totalling about 200 men, led the Rangers on a raid that culminated in a well-conceived surprise attack on an Abenaki village near St François on 6 October 1759. Despite orders not to harm women and children, an unapologetic Rogers later claimed that during the attack he and his men had killed over 200 natives, making no distinction between combatants and non-combatants, while suffering few casualties themselves.

After supporting British operations against Montreal in 1760, Rogers received orders to transfer to the Great Lakes region. There he and his Rangers won further notoriety, especially for their role in the November 1760 capture of Fort Detroit and their service in the suppression of Pontiac's Rebellion in 1763.

After a difficult postwar period, Rogers offered his services to the Patriot cause shortly after the start of the War of American Independence, but he was not accepted because of well-founded questions about his character and concerns about his loyalty to the revolution. Although a number of veterans of Rogers' command would serve the revolutionary cause with distinction as Rangers, their former commander ended up raising and leading a battalion of Loyalist Rangers that participated in operations around New York City early in the war. But neither Rogers nor the men of his former command would replicate the successes or win the renown as an elite fighting force that they had earlier earned on the frontier.

# Napoleon's Imperial Guard
## Loyal Escort of the Emperor

**T**he French Imperial Guard formed the *corps d'élite* of Napoleon's army. From just 2,000 men in 1800 it grew to a corps of 50,000 by 1812. At its height, the infantry of the Guard was organized into three distinct formations, the Old Guard, Middle Guard and Young Guard. Napoleon employed them as the reserve on campaign and in battle, but increasingly relied upon them after the debacle in Russia in 1812, frequently committing them to combat in 1813 and 1814. Mirroring the character of the French imperial army as a whole, the initial Guard regiments were composed of Frenchmen, but eventually regiments of Poles and Dutch were also formed.

### Veterans of the Revolution

The origins of the Imperial Guard go back to the period of the Consulate (1799–1804). On becoming First Consul of France, Napoleon combined several companies of loyal Guards of the Directory and Legislative Corps who had followed him in the *coup d'état* of 18 Brumaire. He attached to them the company of Guides, who had served him well in Italy and Egypt. The Consular Guard, some 2,000 men in all, consisted of three companies of infantry – two of grenadiers and one of chasseurs; two of cavalry – one *Chasseurs à cheval*, the other *Grenadiers à cheval*; and a company of artillery. They fought with distinction at Marengo in June 1800, and in 1802, after his election as Consul for life, Napoleon expanded the Guard to four battalions, equally divided between grenadiers and chasseurs. The cavalry was enlarged, adding one squadron to the grenadiers and the chasseurs, and one of Mamluks, raised from his Egyptian campaign.

The soldiers of the Consular Guard were drawn from veterans of the Revolution with a minimum of a decade of military service. Their status as palace guard, escort and the elite of the army created much jealousy among the rank and file of the line, as they too were, in large part, long-standing veterans, who believed themselves equal to these cherished regiments. But more than just for show, the Consular Guard represented the continuity of French military tradition, which stretched from the pre-revolutionary *Gardes Françaises* and *Maison du Roi*, to the elite of the new national army, forged on European battlefields in the Revolution. The fostering of martial culture was particularly important to Napoleon, because the soldiers of the army saw themselves as the defenders of the Revolution and Napoleon was its guarantor. Meritocracy was the order of the day in Napoleonic France, and the Consular Guard represented the apex of martial merit. Soldiers of the Guard received higher pay than line troops, and the officers held a distinct position within the social and military hierarchy of the day.

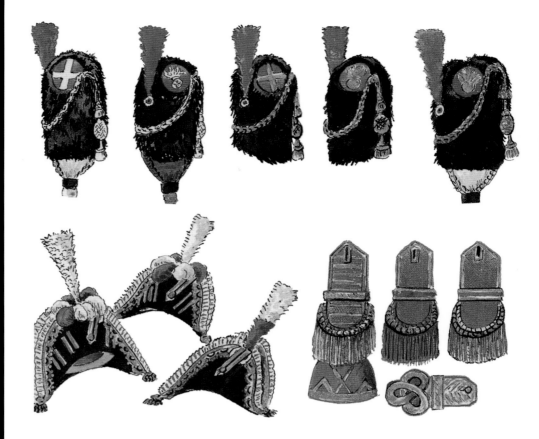

Above: Various hats and epaulettes of the Imperial Guard. The bearskin hat (top row) indicated the elite soldiers of the Guard. The cross on the crown of the hat denoted the *Chasseurs à pied*, while the grenade was used for the *Grenadiers à pied*.

Opposite: The most formidable of Napoleon's Old Guard, the Grenadiers had extensive military service but were employed sparingly by Napoleon. Once committed they always succeeded in achieving their objectives. The Old Guard Grenadiers formed the rear-guard of the French army after the defeat at Waterloo.

## Expansion of the Guard

Napoleon's elevation to Emperor of the French in 1804 meant these elite soldiers of the Revolution would now become an Imperial Guard (though, despite the conscious contemporary parallels between Caesar and Napoleon, this Guard was a far cry from the Praetorians of the Roman emperors; see p. 30). This transformation also meant expansion, and while both infantry regiments retained their organization, Napoleon established two *vélite* battalions, one attached to each regiment. The *vélites* were composed of volunteers from middle-class and well-to-do families, who saw service in the Guard as a fast track to a commission in the imperial army. The cavalry of the Guard was also expanded to accommodate one regiment of *Grenadiers à cheval* and one of *Chasseurs à cheval*, with the Mamluks attached to the latter. The artillery of the Guard consisted of two companies.

The Guard's special nature led to the creation of its own band, hospital and dedicated barracks, and the honour of taking position on the right on the line of march. Napoleon cherished his Imperial Guard, even though he referred to the infantry as *les grognards*, the 'grumblers'. He reviewed the application of every volunteer and recruit for its regiments, and paid particular attention to their military education and grooming.

The uniforms of the Imperial Guard were as diverse as their regiments. The infantry wore the standard French blue coat with white facings. What distinguished the Old Guard battalions from the rest, however, were their bearskins. The *Grenadiers* and *Chasseurs à pied* could be identified by their distinctive hats, and their presence on the battlefield signified that the emperor was in attendance. The cavalry of the guard were the most colourful: regimental uniforms varied from the red pelisses of the *Chasseurs à cheval* with their busbies, to the blue uniform and *chapkas* of the Polish Lancers.

## Significance of the Guard in Napoleon's campaigns

The War of the Third Coalition in 1805 inaugurated the Napoleonic Wars, and the Imperial Guard served in virtually every campaign thereafter. Although Napoleon rarely committed his Guard infantry to combat, the cavalry was often employed. At the battle of Austerlitz, 2 December 1805, the Guard infantry remained in reserve, while the cavalry played a critical role in repulsing the charge of the Russian Imperial Guard cavalry. Napoleon awarded them the *nom de guerre* '*Les invincibles*'.

Right: The charge of Testot-Ferry at the battle of Craonne, 1814, by Pierre Benigni. Commanding the 1st Regiment of the Guard *Éclaireurs* (Scouts), Testot-Ferry twice charged Russian batteries, gaining time for Napoleon to dispatch infantry to secure his position.

Below: The *Chasseurs à cheval* of the Guard were given the title '*Les invincibles*' by the emperor for their charge at Austerlitz. Unlike the Old Guard, they fought in many of the major battles of the Napoleonic Wars.

Napoleon established the Middle Guard during the war against Prussia and the ensuing advance into Poland in 1806. It consisted of one regiment of *Fusiliers-Grenadiers* and one of *Fusiliers-Chasseurs*. Earlier that same year the Empress Dragoons (*Dragons de l'Impératrice*) were added to the Guard cavalry. The campaign in Poland led to the addition of a Polish cavalry regiment. The *Chevau-Léger Polonais* were raised in 1807 and reorganized in 1809 into the 1st Regiment Polish Lancers after their victorious charge at Somosierra Pass in Spain.

The victories of the previous years led to the largest expansion of the Imperial Guard in 1809. Napoleon recruited the best conscripts of the line army into four regiments of Young Guard. Divided equally between *Tirailleurs-Grenadiers* and *Tirailleurs-Chasseurs*, these formations were at full strength by the time of the Austrian war and played a decisive role at the battle of Aspern-Essling in 1809. Just prior to the campaign, two regiments of *Conscrits Grenadiers* were also added to the Young Guard.

The absorption of the Kingdom of Holland into Imperial France led to the merging of the Dutch Royal Guard into the Imperial Guard. The regiment of Dutch Grenadiers formed the 3rd Regiment, the *Grenadiers à pied*, in 1811, and the Dutch Guard Hussars became the 2nd Regiment, the Dutch (Red) Lancers. In preparation for his campaign in Russia Napoleon raised a regiment of *Flanquers Grenadiers* and *Flanquers Chasseurs* for the Middle Guard, and doubled the number of Young Guard regiments by converting the *Conscrits Grenadiers* to *Tirailleurs-Grenadiers*, and then raising an additional four regiments of grenadiers and chasseurs. Napoleon fielded two divisions of Young Guard in 1812.

## Battle of Ligny 1815

After a bloody day of conflict to control Ligny, Napoleon sent in his Old Guard. Fighting was fierce, but the Guard captured the village.

On 16 June 1815 Napoleon led the right wing of the Armée du Nord against Field Marshal von Blücher's Prussian army at Ligny. The fighting raged throughout the day, with the French making little headway against determined Prussian resistance. The villages of Saint-Amand on their right and Ligny towards the centre anchored the Prussian position. Napoleon committed the Young Guard against Saint-Amand at 3 p.m. Fierce fighting compelled the emperor to send in two regiments of the Middle Guard an hour later. Determined to break the Prussian right wing, he ordered up the Old Guard and the Guard cavalry, if needed. The attack succeeded, Saint-Amand fell, but the Prussian centre did not budge. At 7.30 p.m. the battalions of the Old Guard advanced on Ligny, which was now defended by the remnants of 21 Prussian battalions. As the Guard swept in, in columns, a storm broke. Thunder, lightning and torrential rain did not slow the attack, but seemed to unnerve the defenders. Prussian cavalry beyond the village failed to make headway against the Guardsmen as they emerged from the settlement and formed a square. By the time the sky cleared an hour later, Napoleon had broken the Prussian army, sending them into full retreat.

The destruction of the Grande Armée in Russia and its subsequent reconstruction in 1813 led to the creation of more than 26 regiments of Young Guard. The Guard designation, however, was a mere sop to boost the morale of these inexperienced conscripts. Although they performed competently in 1813 and 1814, they lacked the sang-froid of their predecessors. Napoleon also raised three regiments of Guard *Éclaireurs* (Scouts) in 1813 to supplement the meagre line cavalry.

In addition, Napoleon's Imperial Guard also included numerous support troops. In 1804 a regiment of horse artillery was established, followed in 1808 by one of foot artillery. Two squadrons of *Gendarmerie d'élite* provided security details for the emperor and his household. In 1810 an engineer company was formed. A regiment of *Marins de la garde impériale* fought in 1813, and four regiments of *Gardes d'Honneur* joined the Guard that year.

The Guard that fought in 1813 and 1814 was a mere shadow of its former self. However, the regiments raised for the Waterloo Campaign of 1815 ('the Hundred Days') were veterans who returned to their colours after a brief 10-month hiatus. The Old, Middle and Young Guard took the field once more.

# 'The Guard dies, but never surrenders!'

**Reported response of General Pierre Cambronne to the British demand that the Imperial Guard lay down their arms after the battle of Waterloo, 18 June 1815**

On 20 April 1814 Napoleon addressed the Old Guard before going into exile. Veterans recalled the speech: 'For twenty years I have been pleased with you. I have always found you on the path to glory ... Farewell, my children.' This depiction of the event at Fontainebleau was painted by Horace Vernet.

Horace Vernet 1825

# The British Light Infantry
## Mobile Skirmishers and Marksmen

Right: Sir John Moore by Thomas Lawrence (c. 1800–04). A key figure in the development of light infantry, Moore died in battle at Corunna in 1809.

Below: Member of the 90th Perthshire Volunteer Light Infantry, 1832. In the absence of conscription, the British military effort depended on volunteers.

Opposite left: Infantry officers' swords were mostly for show.

**B**ritish Light Infantry are a key example of the light troops developed across Europe in the 18th century in an attempt to ensure greater mobility on the battlefield, as well as to provide a crucial capability in colonial campaigning. Such troops owed much to the example of the Austrian use of light forces in conflict against the Turks, but also drew on the western European tradition of *petite guerre* – irregular conflict, notably skirmishes and raids.

During the 18th century, this form of conflict attracted greater attention from military commentators in Europe. In the case of Britain, an added impetus was provided by the absorption into the regular army after the battle of Culloden (1746) of Scottish Highland units, some of which were well-suited to irregular conflict, as well as the requirements posed by operating in North Africa. The conquest of New France (Canada) in 1758–60 was seen to require troops who could operate in the wooded terrain there, avoiding ambush by the Native Americans allied to the French and, in turn, learning tactics from those Native Americans with whom the British were allied.

These light troops were not popular with conventional British commanders, whose emphasis was on volley firepower and who were apt to believe that fighting from cover was in some respect dishonourable and thus conducive to poor discipline. Within the British army there was a tension between what was termed the 'American' school of officership and the 'German' school. The former drew on British experience in the War of American Independence (1775–83) and the more flexible tactics that it had encouraged. The 'German' school, in contrast, was influenced by British experience of fighting in Germany during the Seven Years War (1756–63) and by the reputation of the Prussian army after the victorious campaigns of Frederick the Great during that war.

David Dundas, the leading figure in the latter school, and British Commander-in-Chief in 1809–11, placed the organized firepower of the close-order line at the centre of military practice, claiming that such a line could resist cavalry in open country. He was much less concerned with light infantry. However, the British disregard for such troops served them ill in conflicts from 1793 on against the armies of Revolutionary France. The French made much of light troops, especially skirmishers, which they sent out in advance of their columns of infantry in order to disrupt the defending line, a tactic that proved particularly effective in the 1790s.

### The development of the Light Division

In response, British reformers promoted the use of light forces. Frederick, Duke of York, the second son of George III and Commander-in-Chief from 1798 to 1809 and from 1811 to 1827, was a keen supporter of the tactic, which was associated in particular with Sir John Moore, an experienced Scottish officer. In 1803, Moore was appointed commander of a new brigade based at Shorncliffe Camp in Kent, a key site in preparations against a French invasion being readied by Napoleon. This brigade was designed to serve as the basis of a permanent light infantry force. Particular emphasis was placed upon marksmanship.

Moore had been much impressed by the system of training and manoeuvring light infantry developed by Colonel Kenneth Mackenzie in the previous decade.

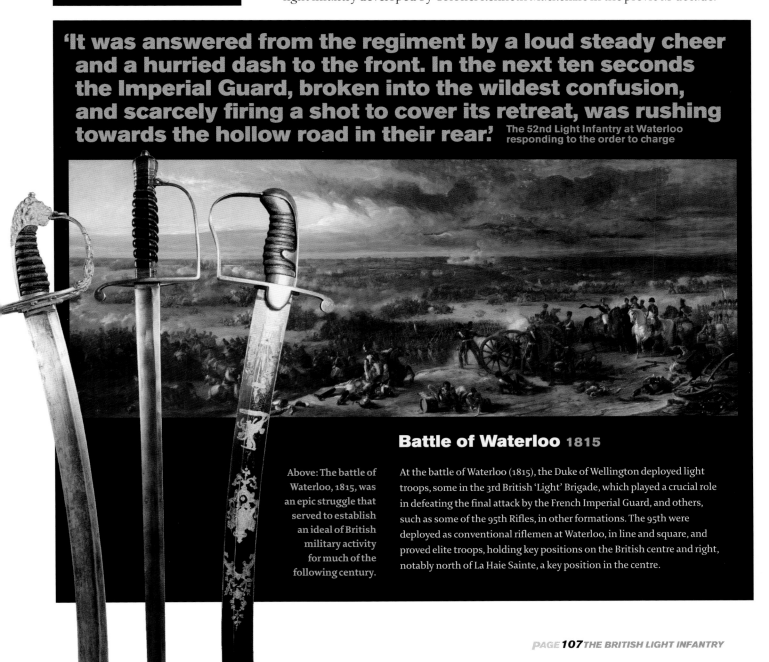

'It was answered from the regiment by a loud steady cheer and a hurried dash to the front. In the next ten seconds the Imperial Guard, broken into the wildest confusion, and scarcely firing a shot to cover its retreat, was rushing towards the hollow road in their rear.' The 52nd Light Infantry at Waterloo responding to the order to charge

## Battle of Waterloo 1815

Above: The battle of Waterloo, 1815, was an epic struggle that served to establish an ideal of British military activity for much of the following century.

At the battle of Waterloo (1815), the Duke of Wellington deployed light troops, some in the 3rd British 'Light' Brigade, which played a crucial role in defeating the final attack by the French Imperial Guard, and others, such as some of the 95th Rifles, in other formations. The 95th were deployed as conventional riflemen at Waterloo, in line and square, and proved elite troops, holding key positions on the British centre and right, notably north of La Haie Sainte, a key position in the centre.

Officers of 90th Regiment Light Infantry officers at the battle of Inkerman, 5 November 1854, photographed by Roger Fenton. British firepower was compromised because the Russians, advancing in darkness and mist, had the advantage of surprise, while the British had experienced overnight rain on the rifles as well as ammunition shortages. As a result, the British relied heavily on bayonet charges and their Enfield rifles to stop the advancing Russian columns.

Mackenzie had trained the Perthside Light Infantry, later the 90th Regiment, and in 1796 he was appointed to command all the flank companies of the British regiments in Portugal as a battalion of light infantry. This was then used as a way to instruct the officers in the army in light infantry tactics. In 1798, the 90th fought with great success against French forces in Egypt, the most significant British victory over the French army that decade. Mackenzie commanded the 52nd Regiment at Shorncliffe.

Moore's force was to become known as the Light Brigade, and, subsequently, as the Light Division. The latter distinguished itself in the British campaigns against French forces in Portugal and Spain in the Peninsular War (1808–13), proving especially mobile on the Duke of Wellington's battlefields. The light forces were also crucial in scouting ahead of the army, screening advances and covering retreats. Many of the troops fought with the effective Baker rifle, and often in pairs, taking advantage of terrain features to fire on their opponents.

The 51st Light Infantry in Afghanistan, 1879. In early 1879, the British appeared in control of the Afghan situation, but that September the newly installed British resident and his staff were killed and a fresh advance proved necessary. The British were victorious at Charasia Ridge and entered Kabul, but it was difficult to win a lasting success, not least because of the fractured nature of Afghan politics.

## A growing reputation

The achievements of the Light Division provided light infantry with an elite reputation to rival that of the Guards. Moreover, the renown of the light troops remained important as the legacy of Wellington's victories dominated British military thought over the following century. These troops were also praised as in some respects indicative of British virtues, notably independence, and were contrasted with the supposedly more rigid formations of autocracies in continental Europe whose troops were presented as if they fought as automatons. In practice, there was always an interplay of dispersed and rigid formations and tactics in the British army of the 19th century, until, with the growth of concentrated firepower, all infantry in effect became light infantry.

The cavalry tradition was separate, with the more nimble, light cavalry providing mobility rather than the shock force of heavier men on larger horses. This distinction underlay that between the Light and Heavy Brigades of British cavalry in 1854 at the battle of Balaclava in the Crimean War.

# The Royal Navy Bluejackets
## From Ship to Shore in the Age of Empire

**B**luejackets, named for the colour of their original high-waisted jackets, were British naval ratings deployed ashore. They have never been a permanent force, but were naval brigades temporarily detached from their ships as and when required – any sailor in the Royal Navy would be a Bluejacket if serving ashore. Once the Royal Navy became established as the world's most successful fighting force, sailors were deployed ashore to exploit British command of the sea. They served as artillerymen in the 17th century, and Nelson, it should be recalled, lost an eye and an arm in operations on shore, leading Bluejacket artillerymen and amphibious infantry.

Reflecting the status of the Royal Navy as the 'Senior Service', sailors were the mainstay of the British empire, with their unique attributes of initiative, daring and agility. After the battle of Trafalgar in 1805 they were trained to work ashore. The speed and élan of their operations earned them the respect of enemies

**Key Dates**

**1814**
Bluejackets are used by Admiral Sir George Cockburn in the capture and burning of Washington, DC.

**1854**
Crimean War Naval Brigade formed.

**1856**
Naval Brigades formed to serve in the Indian Mutiny.

**1858**
Bluejackets provide heavy artillery in the capture of Shah Najaf.

**1899**
Brigades serve in the Second Boer War, including transporting guns to aid in the relief of Ladysmith.

**1914**
Naval Brigades formed by Churchill for the defence of Antwerp, the basis of the Royal Naval Division used at Gallipoli and on the Western Front.

Right: A posthumous portrait of Captain Sir William Peel at the relief of Lucknow, 1858, by John Lucas. Peel, a son of the former British Prime Minister Sir Robert Peel, served as a Naval Brigade officer in the Crimean War – when he was one of the first officers to be awarded the Victoria Cross – and in the Indian Mutiny.

Opposite above: The 'Bellerophon Doves': this contemporary print of sailors from the *Bellerophon* encamped at Sebastopol in the Crimean War shows one of the Bluejackets effortlessly carrying a heavy gun brought in to lift the siege.

Opposite below: Royal Navy officers' uniforms of the 19th century, left to right: undress coat, lieutenant, 1830–43; undress coat of a captain with over three years' seniority; Royal Marine frock coat, 1856–57. Full dress uniform became increasingly old-fashioned and antiquated, influenced by the ceremonial dress worn at court, while undress tended to keep up more with contemporary fashions.

from France to America – where in 1814 Admiral Sir George Cockburn used Bluejackets to spearhead the capture and burning of Washington, DC. With no serious challenge at sea after 1815, Bluejackets operated ashore in almost all British wars down to 1914, from the Crimea to China by way of Sudan, South Africa and India. The list of senior officers who received their baptism of fire ashore stretches from Nelson to Cunningham, and includes most admirals of note in between. Nelson's Bluejackets captured a fort in central Nicaragua, while Andrew Cunningham, Admiral of the Fleet during World War II, began his career as an infantry subaltern at Graspan in the Boer War in 1899.

By the 1850s the Bluejackets were highly trained professionals. In the Crimean War over 1,000 officers and men trained by the naval gunnery school in Portsmouth operated the siege artillery at Sebastopol, earning several Victoria Crosses for courage and daring. During the siege Captain Sir William Peel, RN, threw a live shell out of his battery; he also fought bravely at the battle of Inkerman and was awarded a VC. Peel cemented the Bluejackets' elite status

## Capture of Shah Najaf, Lucknow 1858

In the Indian Mutiny, HMS *Shannon's* Naval Brigade provided the heavy artillery required to demolish the walls of rebel-held fortresses. At the capture of the Shah Najaf compound outside Lucknow in 1858, Captain William Peel deployed a heavy gun and rockets in support of the assaulting infantry, clearing the way for the 93rd Highlanders to storm the position, an irresistible elite combination.

Members of the Naval Brigade from HMS *Diamond* behind their gun battery during the bombardment of Sebastopol; painting by William Simpson, 1854. The officer standing behind the gun is Captain William Peel, VC.

during the Indian Mutiny in the late 1850s, moving massive naval guns across the subcontinent to smash the walls of Indian fortresses. Tragically, he died of smallpox, one of many brilliant young naval officers to die miles from the sea.

The organization of a naval brigade became standard, while training used army drill, doctrine and textbooks. Bluejackets served ashore either as infantry, artillerymen or engineer and logistics support for the hard-pressed British army, which desperately needed supplementing in these areas. As the Navy had to carry the army to the combat zone it was logical for seamen also to reinforce the troops ashore. All naval executive officers were trained to lead Bluejackets as well as Royal Marine infantry and artillery, and could be deployed with or without the army. With the introduction of Continuous Service in 1852, which made service a proper career, naval ratings received a uniform of blue jerseys and bell-bottomed trousers with a straw hat. Combined with army boots, a rifle and infantry equipment this formed the basic dress of the force until 1899. Thereafter Bluejackets fought in khaki.

Under Queen Victoria the Navy had to fill the gap left by the recall of overseas garrisons. Bluejackets became the standard response to any crisis: an accepted element of imperial strategy. How far it was sensible to employ highly trained

Above: Royal Navy Captain Arthur Wilson engages in single combat with only the hilt of his sword at the battle of El Teb. He was awarded the Victoria Cross.

Below: 'Bluejackets to the Front', an illustration published in the *Illustrated London News*, from a sketch made on the battlefield by Melton Prior during the Zulu War of 1879.

and skilled naval ratings ashore when soldiers could be obtained at far lower cost remains open to debate. The classic Bluejackets were long-service volunteer naval ratings, not conscripts, combining the daring and resource of seamen with the disciplined durability of professional warriors. They held the line when others faltered. No one epitomized the Bluejacket spirit better than Arthur Wilson. In the thick of the fighting at El Teb in Sudan in 1884, Wilson used his sword, and when that broke, his fists to hold off Sudanese tribesmen who had broken the infantry square. At Queen Victoria's funeral, it was a party of Bluejackets who pulled her coffin to the grave, a fitting recognition of their status.

In the 19th century Bluejackets served as specialists, but in 1914 Winston Churchill sent entire naval brigades to defend Antwerp. These formations were, however, raw recruits, not the veteran Bluejackets of an earlier age. Over time the brigades lost contact with the sea, becoming an elite unit on the Western Front, distinguished by their naval ranks, beards and a unique *esprit de corps*.

In the world wars of the 20th century Bluejackets seemed irrelevant, but the Royal Navy now makes a massive contribution to operations in Afghanistan: the combination of Royal Marines, naval logistics, medics and support, with Fleet Air Arm Harrier squadrons, means that on occasion the majority of British forces in theatre are Royal Navy and thus, although the title has long since disappeared, they are Bluejackets. So Bluejackets remain an elite force today.

# Cossack Units in the Imperial Russian Army
## Irregular Cavalry from the Steppes

**B**y 1775 the tradition of independent Cossack hosts, or administrative territories (*voiska*), had come to an end. Grigorii Potemkin, Vice-President of the Military Collegium in St Petersburg, assumed command of all Cossack forces in the Don, Iaik, Volga, Orenburg and other hosts, while the Zaporozhian Host was broken up and resettled as a Black Sea Host. The estate privileges of host Cossacks – such as local self-administration through deliberative assembly and their rights to duty-free trade – were preserved, but the host Atamans (leaders) were henceforth appointed by the Military Collegium. Each host was required to maintain a certain number of Cossack regiments for defence of the borders and for service as irregular cavalry in the field army, and Cossacks subsequently predominated among the irregular forces of the Russian army. In 1805 there were about 100,000 Cossacks in service: the Don Cossacks in 80 regiments (each regiment consisting of 560 troopers and 17 officers) the Black Sea Cossacks in 10 foot and 10 mounted regiments; the Ural Cossacks in 10 regiments; 5 regiments of Bug, Orenburg and Chuguev, and Stavropol'-Kal'myk Cossacks; and several thousand Kuban, Greben' and Terek, Khoper, Volga and Siberian Cossacks.

### In action

When Napoleon invaded Russia in 1812 there were initially 36 standing Cossack regiments – totalling 15,000 men – deployed against him in the defence of the western frontier. These were divided between Barclay de Tolly's First Western Army, Bagration's Second Western Army and Tormassov's Third (Reserve) Army. By the autumn of 1812 another 21 regiments (8,000 Cossacks) had been added in reinforcement of the second line of Russian armies, and by October yet another 24,000 Cossacks were mobilized – both Don Cossacks and newly formed militia Cossacks (retired volunteers or men not of Cossack estate origin).

Cossacks were required to provide their own mounts and equipment. Until the army reforms of the 1870s they wore distinctive, coloured kaftans; their basic armaments were lance, sabre, pistols and sometimes a musket (later a carbine). Because they were irregular troops they were not seen as very reliable in holding formation in open battle or in performing reconnaissance, but they did prove extremely effective in 1812 in damaging Napoleon's retreating Grande Armée. Tolstoy's novel *War and Peace*

Above: Don Cossacks in 1814. Cossacks not only had to supply their own horses and weaponry, but also fed themselves and their mounts when in the field.

Opposite: The Cossacks were superb horsemen. The lance, 2.4 m (8 ft) long, was their favoured weapon, but they were also well armed with sabre and pistols and sometimes also a musket. This print is of a galloping Cossack of the Imperial Guard, c. 1870.

celebrated the role they played in these small-unit partisan raids. Cossack forces also supported the operations of the Russian army in Europe in 1813–14.

In 1853 there were 81,476 rank-and-file Cossacks and officers in ten *voiska*. The largest *voisko*, that of the Don Cossacks, contributed 34 mounted regiments and four batteries in peacetime, increasing to 58 mounted regiments and 14 batteries in wartime. Some 82,000 Cossacks served in the Crimean War (1853–56) and 42,000 in the Russo-Turkish War (1877–78). Most of these were Don Cossacks, reflecting the Don Host's greater population, but also the fact that by the late 18th century the Don frontier had been largely secured, allowing more Don Cossacks to be shifted from regional defence to duty with the field army.

## Reforms and changes

Neither Catherine II's Military Collegium nor Alexander I's Ministry of War had gone very far in subjecting Cossack administration, community life or economy to imperial regulation; only those Cossacks on duty in the army had felt the hand of the imperial state very directly. This began to change in 1835, when an Ordinance Concerning the Administration of the Don Host divided Host territory into seven circuits and converted its Ataman into the equivalent of

## The Retreat from Moscow 1812

In the winter of 1812 Napoleon began his retreat from Moscow, his large army constantly raided by Cossacks and attacked by regular Russian formations. Memoirs from French survivors depict the Cossacks as relentlessly harassing the French army's flanks and rear, skirmishing and picking off foragers and stragglers. Cossack raids along the Smolensk road required the French to assign escorts of at least 1,500 to each of their convoys, and Cossack attacks reduced General Sebastiani's division from 3,500 to 800 men; Dr Heinrich von Roos, surgeon to the division, recorded treating one cavalryman for 24 Cossack lance wounds.

The relentless Cossack pursuit of the retreating French soldiers in 1812 greatly contributed to the disastrous defeat of Napoleon's Grande Armée.

'The Cossacks improvised sudden attacks, killing and wounding, robbing all those whose lives they spared, and looting wagons and carriages when they came upon them. It is not difficult to imagine the perturbation spread by such tactics, and their effect on the army's morale. What was worse, they made communications extremely difficult, not only between one corps and another, but between one division and another.'

Armand de Caulaincourt, on the French retreat from Moscow

Cossack pistols typically featured a long slender barrel, *miquelet*-lock, button trigger and large round pommel, and were often richly embellished with silver and other inlays; this example probably dates to the 19th century.

a governor over these circuits. In addition, measures attempted to defuse social tensions by addressing the issue of land seizure by the Cossack officer corps and establishing a minimum land entitlement for each adult male Cossack. The Ordinance also began to regulate the administration of Cossack settlements and the functioning of their communal deliberative assemblies, and systematized Cossack military service obligations. Don Cossacks were now required to serve in the army for 30 years, with men of serving age rotating between field army service and local defence service every few years. The 1835 Ordinance was susbequently applied to the other hosts.

The emancipation of the serfs in 1861 and local government reform in 1864 raised the question of whether the large Cossack establishment and the anachronism of Cossack estate privileges should be maintained. By the 1870s it had been decided to raise Cossack service obligations: Cossack manpower might be needed to deter German aggression against the empire's western domains and to reinforce the police in suppressing village and urban disorders, and the practice of rotating Cossacks between field army and local defence duty was thought to harmonize well with the War Ministry's aim to reduce the size (and costs) of the standing army by creating a reserve system. In 1875 the Ministry introduced new Cossack service obligations, which in practice often exceeded the capacity of many Cossack households, and this has been seen as a factor politically radicalizing the Cossack population by the late 19th century.

Right: A parade of Cossack regiments in 1853 at the unveiling of a statue of Ataman Platov, leader of the Don Cossacks, who distinguished himself in the Napoleonic Wars in Russia. The statue was erected in Novocherkassk, a city founded by Platov; painting by Carl Peter Mazer.

Opposite: Photo of a Kuban Cossack in early 1900s, still bearing his sabre and dagger. Cossacks were always greatly feared by enemy troops.

# The Zulu Impis
## Warriors of the King

*mpi* is a Zulu word meaning simply a body of armed men, but European observers used it to refer more specifically to a Zulu army or to one of its constituent age-regiments. Shaped by King Shaka in the early 19th century, Zulu impis waged war against neighbouring African societies with great success. Defeated enemies were either absorbed into the expanding Zulu community or forced to migrate elsewhere, often taking their own versions of impis to other parts of Africa.

'[W]e drove them before us; we carried them on our assegais, we brained them with the poles of our shields, we walked over the brook on their bodies!'
Description of a battle with the Swazi by one of Shaka's veterans

Age-regiments originated in the late 18th century, when, for reasons that are still being debated, there was a marked increase in conflict throughout southeastern Africa. Political and military structures of Bantu-speaking peoples in the region changed dramatically as leaders struggled for scarce resources. One of the most significant changes was the transformation of age-class systems. Previously, groups of teenagers had been initiated into manhood together, forming guilds which then performed various duties for local chiefs. As pressures grew, the guilds took on more of a military function. Shaka carried the process further: young men from across the realm now provided service directly to the king, rather than just chiefs. While their service continued to include civic duties, the age-sets became essentially conscripted military regiments.

A newly formed impi might number 1,000 men commanded by a hierarchy of officers and subdivided into constituent companies. The corporate identity of a regiment was facilitated by a distinctive

Right: Zulu impis overwhelm British troops at the battle of Isandhlwana during the Anglo-Zulu War of 1879, in a painting by C. E. Fripp.

Opposite: A Zulu broad-bladed assegai, or stabbing spear, an ox-hide shield, and a warrior in 'full-dress' ceremonial uniform.

Below: Ntshingwayo kaMahole, senior commander of Zulu armies in the war of 1879.

## Gqokli Hill 1818

Although outnumbered two-to-one, well-drilled Zulu impis crushed the Ndwandwe, their main rivals, at Gqokli Hill. The Zulu enveloped and destroyed them in fierce hand-to-hand combat, demonstrating the superiority of Shaka's new system.

ceremonial uniform of decorations, furs, feather headdresses, and common colours and patterns for ox-hide shields. Each had its own anthems and battle-cries. Communal rituals bound the men together with a sense of spiritual well-being. All this imparted a proud *esprit de corps*; on campaign, while some impis might be brigaded together temporarily into 'corps', others stayed apart so that simmering rivalries did not escalate into armed brawls. By postponing their right to marriage until middle age, Shaka lengthened his control over the warriors, whom he quartered in individual barracks scattered throughout the kingdom. The new system centralized his hold over the state, facilitated the incorporation of outsiders and strengthened the kingdom's unity. Logistical problems limited the time impis could remain in the field, however, so warfare often took the form of cattle-raiding rather than prolonged campaigns.

Before being drafted into age-regiments, Zulu youths led hardy lives as herd-boys in a rugged environment, gaining skill with weapons and aggressive self-reliance. Instead of the old, tentative style of fighting in which light throwing spears had been hurled back and forth, Shaka made his warriors engage in ferocious mêlées in which they slaughtered enemies with lethal underhand thrusts of broad-bladed assegais, or stabbing spears. Whenever possible, he favoured a disciplined 'Horns of the Beast' tactical formation, in which impis would catch the enemy in a double envelopment. His armies also possessed an astonishing mobility – marches of 80 km (50 miles) per day were commonplace. Such a mode of combat inculcated new ruthlessness into warfare in the region.

When impis were confronted by foes employing Western technology – mounted Boer commandos and imperial British forces – they were less successful. Although some Zulu acquired firearms, they could not match Western firepower. In the Anglo-Zulu War of 1879, impis obliterated a British column at Isandhlwana, but were subsequently decimated by the fire of laagered, or entrenched, enemy troops. With their defeat, the regimental system was abolished, and, after attempts to resurrect it in rebellions in 1888 and 1906 failed, the impis disappeared entirely, remaining only as a potent symbol for resurgent Zulu nationalism in recent times.

# The Sikh Khalsa
## A Powerful Military Force in 19th-Century India

Two members of the Sikh bodyguard of Ranjit Singh dressed in brightly coloured robes, riding horses draped with sumptuous cloths and armed with muskets; painting c. 1838–42, perhaps by Kumar Singh.

**T**he Sikh Khalsa, a community of baptized Sikhs, was formed in 1699 by Guru Gobind Singh, the tenth leader of the Sikh religion. A major reason for the Khalsa's formation was to ensure that all males received military training to enable them to protect the community from Mughal persecution. The Khalsa's military wing was instrumental in establishing Sikh hegemony in the Punjab after the Mughal empire's collapse. However, Sikh power was not centralized and the Khalsa's military power was divided among many Sikh *misls*, or clans. The Khalsa army's infantry comprised landlord militias which were used for garrison duties. The light cavalry or the *ghorchurra* held pride of place and dominated the clan chieftains' armies.

It was during the reign of Ranjit Singh that the disparate Khalsa army emerged as a unified force, evolving under his control into one of the subcontinent's most powerful military forces. In 1799 Ranjit Singh, then a powerful Sikh chieftain, defeated the invading Afghan army of Zaman Shah and captured Lahore, declaring himself Maharaja of the Punjab and supreme military leader of a unified Khalsa army in 1801. He immediately set about subduing recalcitrant Sikh *misls* and in 1804 seized Multan from the Afghans. By 1808 he turned his attention to the Malwa region on the Sutlej River. This resulted in a confrontation with the British. A force of Ranjit's Khalsa infantry was easily defeated by a smaller force of British-led Indian sepoy soldiers. This defeat convinced Ranjit that to succeed he would have to modernize his army along European military lines. Having signed the Treaty of Amritsar in 1808 with the British, he set about transforming his army. He initially used deserters from the ranks of the sepoys and men from the disbanded armies of the Maratha chieftain, Mahadji Sindhia.

In 1822 Ranjit Singh hired two former Napoleonic officers – a cavalry officer, Captain Jean-François Allard, and an infantry officer, Colonel Jean-Baptiste Ventura – who dramatically overhauled the Sikh forces. New regular infantry and cavalry units trained along French lines were established and Sikh artillery was substantially upgraded, with gun foundries being established to manufacture contemporary designs. This initial force of 10,000 men was dressed in western-style uniforms. By the 1820s the regular infantry alone had swelled to 20,000. The discipline, reputation and élan of

'There was nothing cringing in the manner of these men in laying down their arms ... they are undoubtedly a fine and brave people.'

**General Sir Colin Campbell describes the Sikh Khalsa's surrender at the end of the Second Anglo-Sikh War**

Left: An exquisite Sikh helmet, probably made in Lahore c. 1820–40; steel overlaid with gold and with a neckguard of iron and brass links. It is designed to accommodate a Sikh turban or topknot.

Below: Ranjit Singh unified and transformed the Sikh army. He hired ex-French army officers to train his troops along Napoleonic lines, though their uniforms often showed British influence. This watercolour of two Sikh soldiers is probably by Imam Baksh, c. 1840.

the regular infantry began to attract Sikh recruits. Traditionally the infantry was seen as a poor brother to the dashing cavalry, and most recruits favoured the latter. This attitude changed, however, and by 1835 Sikh recruits manned the entire regular army. By the time of Ranjit Singh's death in 1839, the Khalsa's military strength stood at 150,000 men, with some 65,000 men in the regular army. It was easily the most formidable non-British army in the subcontinent.

Ranjit's death unleashed great instability within the Sikh empire. The assassination in 1840 of his son and successor Kharrack Singh led to a power struggle. The army had begun to govern itself through elected councils and was courted by different political factions. The British, sensing an opportunity, unilaterally broke the treaty of 1809 and declared all Sikh territory south of the Sutlej under its 'protection'. The Sikh army crossed the Sutlej in December 1845, triggering the First Anglo-Sikh War. The British had secretly acquired the services of two Sikh leaders, the prime minister Lal Singh and the army commander Tej Singh. Their treachery enabled the British to eke out bloody victories in the battles of Mudki, Ferozeshah and Sobraon. The Second Anglo-Sikh war broke out in 1848. Once again the British narrowly prevailed after the battle of Chillianwalla. The British annexed the Punjab on 30 March 1849 and disbanded the Khalsa army.

## Battle of Chillianwalla
### Second Anglo-Sikh War, 1849

The British commander General Gough launched an infantry attack on the Sikh positions at Chillianwalla on 13 January 1849. The Sikh Khalsa infantry fought back fiercely and successfully defended their gun positions, inflicting heavy losses on the attacking British/Indian infantry. Sikh irregular cavalry also gained an unexpected victory when they charged and scattered the British 2nd Cavalry Brigade. British reinforcements, however, saved the night and the Khalsa army withdrew towards the Jhelum River.

# Garibaldi's Redshirts
## A Volunteer Army in the Unification of Italy

**T**hey were enthusiastic and always ready for the call, they were careless of their lives and health, they fought as if they were playing a game: they were Garibaldi's volunteers – the Redshirts. Their training consisted of a brief instruction and a large amount of direct experience in action in order to learn and exploit Garibaldi's particular South American guerrilla warfare tactics – their winning card.

Their origin lay in Uruguay, where Garibaldi founded the Italian Legion in 1842, and where they adopted their famous red shirts. When the First War of Italian Independence in the long struggle for the unification of Italy began in 1848, a proportion of them followed Garibaldi back to Italy. They arrived too late to play a significant role in the campaign, but many more volunteers joined this small initial group, and in 1849 they went to the aid of the newly declared Roman Republic, formerly part of the Papal States. The French and

## 'Here we make Italy or we die!'
### General Giuseppe Garibaldi, Calatafimi, 15 May 1860

the Neapolitans sent expeditionary forces to quash the republic, but Garibaldi's forces forced the French both to retreat from Rome and to seek a truce; the Redshirts then marched south and defeated the Neapolitans at Palestrina and Velletri. However, the republic was forced into a surrender on 30 June 1849. Garibaldi fled Italy and the Redshirts disbanded, waiting for their next opportunity.

In 1859 the Second War of Italian Independence broke out; by now the Redshirts were a regular brigade and dressed in grey. But their spirit and style of guerrilla warfare had not changed, and, commanded by Garibaldi, they defeated the Austrians at Varese and San Fermo, in spite of being heavily outnumbered.

Their finest hour came in May 1860, when 1,000 of them – 'the Mille' – landed in Sicily to liberate the island and southern Italy from Bourbon control. They won their first clash at Calatafimi, captured Palermo and other key towns, and then entered Milazzo after a bloody victory before crossing the Strait of Messina to the mainland. Thousands of volunteers flooded to join them from Italy, as well as some from Hungary, France and Britain. After entering Naples, they defeated the Bourbon army on the Volturno River on 1 and 2 October 1860. They were now ready to march on Rome.

But international policy prevailed and the Piedmontese army arrived from the north and took the war upon itself – the Redshirts had to choose between returning home or joining the regular army; many of them did the latter, as the 'second of the Mille', such as Nino Bixio, Giacomo Medici and Istvan Türr, and reached the highest ranks. So when in 1862 Garibaldi attempted another march on Rome, only a few veteran Redshirts joined him, and they were disbanded by regular Italian troops.

In 1866, during the Third War of Italian Independence, the Redshirts grouped again under Garibaldi's command as a part of the regular army. They campaigned in Trentino province, defeating the Austrians six times in 18 days, notably at Bezzecca. In 1867, 6,000 of them followed Garibaldi in his new march on Rome, but pro-papal French troops defeated them at Mentana on 3 November.

Their last campaign was in autumn 1870, when Garibaldi went to defend the newly declared French Third Republic. Again volunteers came from all over Europe to join him, and his men composed the Army of the Vosges, the only army never defeated in French service and which captured an enemy flag.

The spirit of the Redshirts continued. After the unification of Italy, many veterans sat in the Italian parliament in the following years and some served as ministers and premiers while others reached the top ranks of the army. Their spirit played a major role in Italian affairs and greatly contributed to positioning Italy on the Allied side in World War I.

Opposite: Giuseppe Garibaldi, photographed here in his late 40s, learnt his successful guerrilla tactics fighting for various independence causes in South America. He passed these on to his volunteer Redshirts, many of whom were fiercely loyal to their leader.

Below: Garibaldi leading the Redshirts of 'I Mille' ashore at Marsala in May 1860, at the start of their campaign to liberate Sicily and southern Italy from Bourbon control and gain Italian independence. This was the Redshirts' finest hour.

## Battle of Calatafimi 1860

Having landed at Marsala in Sicily on 11 May 1860, the Redshirts began their 'Expedition of the Thousand' against the Bourbon Kingdom of the Two Sicilies, gaining their first victory at Calatafimi on 15 May. This defeat of the Bourbon forward army, numbering about 2,000, was a blow to the morale of their enemy and was instrumental to the success of Garibaldi's Sicilian campaign.

# The Iron Brigade in the American Civil War
## Hard-Fighting Union Troops

**S**everal units during the American Civil War at one time or another claimed the moniker 'Iron Brigade'. But by far the most famous was the one that, in a series of sharply fought engagements between August 1862 and July 1863, demonstrated its right to occupy its place as the First Brigade of the First Division of the First Army Corps in the Union army order of battle. In addition to its exceptional performances on some of the war's bloodiest fields, this Iron Brigade was set apart from its sister units by the high-crowned, black felt

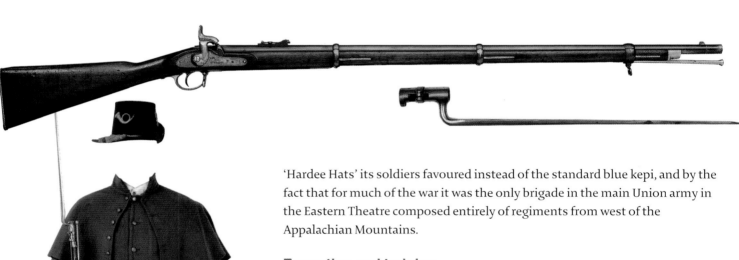

'Hardee Hats' its soldiers favoured instead of the standard blue kepi, and by the fact that for much of the war it was the only brigade in the main Union army in the Eastern Theatre composed entirely of regiments from west of the Appalachian Mountains.

### Formation and training

In October 1861, the 2nd Wisconsin Volunteer Infantry Regiment, which had seen hard fighting earlier at the battle of First Manassas, was combined with the new 19th Indiana and 6th and 7th Wisconsin to form a brigade commanded by Brigadier General Rufus King. The brigade spent the winter of 1861–62 receiving instruction under King's rigorous direction. When King was promoted to division command, direction of the brigade passed to Brigadier General John Gibbon, who took command in May 1862. While King had been a capable commander, it was under Gibbon that the brigade developed the sense of distinctiveness, physical and moral toughness, and *esprit de corps* that made it an elite fighting force. It was also under Gibbon that the entire brigade adopted the distinctive headgear that inspired its first nickname, the Black Hat Brigade.

Along with the rest of King's division, Gibbon's command spent the spring and summer of 1862 in northern Virginia. During this time Gibbon kept up a demanding programme of drill, marching and adherence to regulations that led one officer in July to declare his commander a 'regular old fire on strict discipline … He attends to his troops very closely, knows all that is going on.'

Above: Brigadier General Rufus King, the first commander of the Iron Brigade.

Opposite above: An Enfield 1853 rifle-musket. The Civil War was the first major war in which both sides were equipped with rifled weaponry, which contributed to the heavy casualties units such as the Iron Brigade regularly suffered in battle.

Opposite below: Unlike the rest of the Army of the Potomac, the men of the Iron Brigade eschewed the kepi in favour of the high-crowned black 'Hardee Hat' at the insistence of its second commander, John Gibbon.

## Into battle

The unit's baptism of fire came during the afternoon of 28 August 1862, when it took on veteran Confederate units led by Stonewall Jackson in what one man described as 'a fair square stand up face-to-face fight' at the Brawner Farm near Gainesville. A little over two weeks later, the members of the Black Hat Brigade distinguished themselves again while assaulting a strong Confederate position defending Turner's Gap in South Mountain. On 17 September, Gibbon's brigade once more found themselves battling Jackson's redoubtable command at Antietam, spearheading the morning attack of Brigadier General Abner Doubleday's division along the Hagerstown Pike. A brutal fight for control of the Miller Cornfield and West Woods left the brigade's ranks thinned by a third.

Even though another unit in Doubleday's division was already known as the 'Iron Brigade' and had done nothing in the campaign season of 1862 to warrant any slight, by October of that year Gibbon's command had appropriated the nickname. That same month, the newly raised 24th Michigan Volunteer Infantry was attached to the brigade. A few weeks later command passed to Brigadier General Solomon Meredith, the imposing former commander of the 19th Indiana. He was soon replaced by Colonel Lysander Cutler of the 6th Wisconsin. Aided by his strong political connections, however, Meredith was quickly reinstated and would lead the brigade through the May 1863 Chancellorsville Campaign, where it was not heavily engaged.

# Battle of Gettysburg 1863

In one of the most brutal engagements of the entire war, the Iron Brigade stabilized the situation west of Gettysburg by shattering one Confederate brigade and assisting in the rout of another during the morning of 1 July. However, in the afternoon the brigade was outnumbered, outflanked and driven from positions on McPherson Ridge and Seminary Ridge in a brutal fight. By the end of the day, over 1,200 of the 1,900 men who reached the field that morning were dead, wounded or missing.

The battle of Gettysburg and its horrific aftermath. The Iron Brigade never recovered from the heavy casualites it suffered at this battle, often seen as the turning point of the Civil War.

## The turning point

The Iron Brigade was once again in the thick of the fighting on 1 July 1863. That morning, it arrived on McPherson Ridge west of Gettysburg and, along with another brigade commanded by Cutler, took over from Brigadier General John Buford's cavalry in what was developing into the largest and bloodiest battle of the war. Four of Meredith's regiments then advanced into McPherson's (or Herbst's) Woods to rout a Confederate brigade and make its commander the first general officer in the Army of Northern Virginia to be captured in over a year. Meanwhile, in a railroad cut north of the woods the 6th Wisconsin helped Cutler's brigade destroy another enemy brigade.

The afternoon, however, brought disaster. The Confederates resumed their attack against the Iron Brigade's position with overwhelming numbers of fresh troops and in the course of a brutal battle in the woods and along Willoughby Run managed to envelop its position. Meredith's decimated command made a fighting retreat back to Seminary Ridge, but were forced to retreat further after another bitter struggle. Of the nearly 1,900 men who had arrived on the field, over 1,200 fell, including Meredith, who

'They are equal to the best soldiers in the world. It is not the numbers of men but the right kind of men that makes the "IRON BRIGADE".'

George B. McClellan

The battle of Antietam, 1862, by Thure de Thustrup. This 1887 painting of the battle shows the Iron Brigade spearheading the Union advance towards the Dunker Church early on 17 September, which remains the bloodiest single day of combat in American military history.

was seriously wounded and passed command of the brigade to Colonel William W. Robinson of the 7th Wisconsin.

Gettysburg marked the end of the Iron Brigade's all too brief history as an elite unit. A little over two weeks later, a Pennsylvania unit was added to the brigade, ending its status as an all-western unit. The brigade saw further action between Gettysburg and the end of the 1863 campaign season, after which it was transferred to the Fifth Corps, and forced to relinquish its proud designation as the First Brigade, First Division, First Corps. As part of the Fifth Corps, first under the command of Cutler and then Colonel Robinson, the brigade saw significant fighting in the opening engagements of the 1864 Overland Campaign, suffering heavy casualties.

By August 1864, the Iron Brigade, now commanded by Brigadier General Edward S. Bragg, was but a shadow of its former glory and it was decided to end its existence as an independent unit. By the time the war in Virginia ended in April 1865, of the brigade's regiments only the 6th and 7th Wisconsin were still in the field. In all, about 8,200 men had served in the ranks of the Iron Brigade over the course of the war. Over 1,700 of those who wore the 'damned black hats' had fallen, most in just the 10 months between August 1862 and July 1863 in which the Iron Brigade proved itself one of the truly elite units of the American Civil War.

# Mosby's Rangers in the American Civil War
## Bold Confederate Guerrilla Band

**D**uring the American Civil War numerous partisan or guerrilla units operated in the occupied South, with the most famous being that commanded by John Singleton Mosby. The exploits of Mosby's unit distracted and diverted many times their number of Fedral, or Union, troops from the task of defeating the main Confederate armies in Virginia. Although about 1,570 men served in the unit over the course of the war, at no one time did it number more than 400, while most operations were undertaken by fewer than 150 men. Around 640 of Mosby's Rangers were killed, wounded or captured during the course of the unit's existence, while it inflicted roughly 3,000 Federal casualties.

A lawyer by training, Mosby's performance as a cavalry officer during the first year of the war so impressed General James E. B. Stuart that in January 1863 he authorized the creation of a unit of partisan rangers for Mosby to command. Mosby quickly recruited a band of men whose operations in northern and western Virginia won them fame as 'Mosby's Rangers'. On 10 June 1863, the unit was formally christened the 43rd Battalion, 1st Virginia Cavalry.

Mosby's band quickly won renown for the skill and boldness with which they harassed Union operations. They also provided protection and an incalculable boost to morale for pro-Confederate residents of northern Virginia, who gave support to the rangers. Although their operations were distinguished largely by traditional guerrilla tactics, Mosby's men often wore regular Confederate army uniforms when in action. Preferring firepower and shock, Mosby equipped his men with short-range revolvers rather than sabres, and emphasized closing with the enemy quickly through vigorous mounted charges.

In March 1863 the unit's fame increased tremendously as a consequence of a raid deep behind Union lines on Fairfax Court House. Throughout 1863 Mosby's command harassed Union outposts, raided supply lines and fought spirited engagements with Union forces at such places as Aldie and Miskel's Farm. So successful were Mosby's operations that when the Confederate Congress decided in February 1864 to repeal the law under which partisan units were authorized, an exception was made for his command. During the first eight months of 1864 Mosby's Rangers continued to pose a seemingly insoluble nuisance to Federal authorities and fought significant skirmishes at Loudoun Heights, Blackley's Grove and Mount Zion Church. Union commanders then adopted a harder tone, with their frustration further exacerbated in August, when Mosby's men conducted a

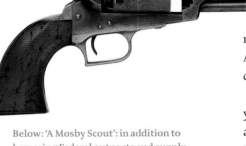

Because of their effectiveness at short range, revolvers, such as this Colt, were the preferred weapon of Mosby's Rangers.

Below: 'A Mosby Scout': in addition to harassing Federal outposts and supply trains, Mosby's men gathered invaluable information for Confederate military authorities in Virginia.

*Mosby's Rangers Returning from a Raid*, by E. Armand-Dumaresq (c. 1868). Mosby is the clean-shaven officer astride his horse on the right side of the painting.

# 'Hurrah for Mosby! I wish I had a hundred like him.'

Robert E. Lee

This photograph of Mosby wearing the rank of full colonel was taken near the end of the war when his fame as a partisan leader was at its height.

skilful raid against a Union wagon train at Berryville. A little over one month later, members of George Custer's command executed six of Mosby's men at Front Royal, hanging a placard on one of the dead proclaiming, 'Such is the fate of Mosby's men'. This did little to hamper Mosby, as was evident on 14 October, when, in what became known as the Greenback Raid, his men seized $173,000 from two Union paymasters after derailing a train near Duffield's Station.

Then, on 6 November and with the approval of authorities in Richmond, Mosby retaliated by executing some of Custer's men and sending a note to the Union commander in the region explaining why he had considered it necessary. Although they executed no more of Mosby's men, Federal authorities did conduct a punitive raid in late 1864 against the resources in Loudoun County that sustained Mosby's command, an operation that became known simply as 'the Burning'.

After the main Confederate army in Virginia surrendered at Appomattox Court House on 9 April 1865, Mosby quickly realized that continuing the struggle was pointless. Unable to reach terms with Union military authorities that he deemed satisfactory, Mosby never officially surrendered his command. Instead, he simply gathered his men at Salem on 21 April 1865 and announced: 'I disband your organization in preference to surrendering to our enemies … The vision we cherished of a free and independent country has vanished.'

## Fairfax Court House Raid 1863

During the night of 8–9 March 1863, Mosby and 29 of his Rangers managed to make their way through a Federal picket line and enter Fairfax Court House. Without losing a man or firing a shot, they then captured two officers – including a general officer who was seized from his bedroom by Mosby personally – 30 men, a civilian and 58 horses, before escaping to Culpeper Court House, which they reached on 10 March.

# The French Foreign Legion
## The World's Premier Mercenary Corps

Two examples of insignia of the Foreign Legion: (top) the emblem of the Legion as used between 1962 and 1990; (bottom) the snail and eagle of the 1st Regiment.

*T*he *Légion étrangère* did not begin life as an elite force. On the contrary, it was founded on 9 March 1831 as a temporary organization to sweep up refugees who had crowded into France from failed revolutions elsewhere and ship them to North Africa, because French law barred foreign nationals from serving in French ranks. Indeed, so eager was Paris to offload this experimental force that in 1835 the Legion was transferred into Spanish service. But the demands of imperial policing combined with the attractiveness of Paris as a refugee destination served to transform this temporary military experiment, over time, into the world's premier mercenary corps. The Legion served in North Africa, the Crimea, Italy in 1859, in Mexico (1863–67) and in the Franco-Prussian War of 1870–71 with some distinction, despite – or perhaps because of – its reputation as a congregation of cut-throats who required strict, at times pitiless, discipline.

### A romantic reputation

The Franco-Prussian war behind them, France's post-1871 imperial expansion inaugurated the Legion's golden age. The corps, which numbered around 10,000 legionnaires, saw action principally in North Africa and Indochina. In this period the Legion matured its reputation as a band of romantic misfits, a myth inspired by the *anonymat* – the requirement to enlist under an assumed name – and soon picked up by literary works beginning with *Under Two Flags* by Ouida in 1864, and peaking with P. C. Wren's *Beau Geste* in 1925.

This imperial idyll came to a thudding halt in 1914. Idealistic volunteers, nationally homogeneous units and murderous offensives beginning in 1915 led to problems with morale and discipline, until legionnaires on the Western Front were organized into the *Régiment de Marche Légion étrangère* (RMLE), which became the most decorated unit in the Legion and, as the *3ème étranger*, disputes the title of the most decorated unit in the French army with the French marines.

The post-World War I years brought more imperial campaigns in Syria and Morocco. By 1933, the Legion numbered over 30,000 soldiers, and, organized eventually into six infantry and one cavalry regiment, had carved out an organizational niche under an Inspector General based in Sidi bel-Abbès in Algeria. Many of the Legion's 'traditions' date from the inter-war years, when its first Inspector General, Paul Rollet, adopted the white kepi, red and green epaulettes, and blue cummerbund as the standard uniform. Rollet also showcased Legion exceptionalism with a series of regimental rituals at its headquarters at Sidi bel-Abbès that culminated on 30 April 1931 with the adoption of the 1863 battle of Camerone as the Legion's official feast day. The official version of *Le Boudin*, the Legion march, was also adopted in this

# 'Voici la Légion! L'affaire est dans le sac!' – 'Here's the Legion – it's in the bag!'

### General MacMahon, at Magenta in the Italian War of 1859

period, although the Legion's distinctive slow march appears to date from 1945. Popular films such as *Beau Geste* (which went through three remakes in the inter-war years), *Morocco* (1930), *Le grand jeu* (1934) and *Under Two Flags* (1936) made the Legion a household name.

## World War II and Indochina

The year 1939 offered in many respects a reprise of 1914, with foreign volunteers – central European Jews and Spanish Republicans prominent among them – directed both into the Legion and into three regiments of foreign volunteers, whose heroic but doomed performance in 1940 was later incorporated into Legion annals. A *13ème demi-brigade Légion étrangère* rallied to Charles de Gaulle in Britain in June 1940 and spearheaded the Gaullist conquest of French colonies in sub-Saharan and North Africa and also in Syria, where it fought against Legion units loyal to the collaborationist Vichy government. Political rancour between pro-Gaullist and ex-Vichy Legion units, stoked by Syria, continued through the Italian campaign, where the Legion participated in the

The flag of the Foreign Legion is decorated with the Legion d'Honneur at a ceremony at Sidi bel-Abbès, 1906. This town in Algeria was the headquarters of the Legion until 1962, and was where many of its traditions and rituals were formalized.

## Battle of Bir Hakeim
### 1942

Of the 3,700 men of the 1st Free French brigade group under General Pierre Koenig who occupied Bir Hakeim, a desert outpost which anchored the southern extremity of the British line in eastern Cyrenaica in February 1942, 957 were legionnaires. On 26 May, Rommel launched an attack to circumvent the British position and race into Egypt. The refusal of the garrison to surrender over 16 days of assaults by artillery and air lengthened Rommel's supply lines and delayed his advance. This was the first fight between Free French troops and Axis forces which Gaullist *Radio Londres* elevated into a '*rendez-vous d'honneur*'.

Legionnaires race across the desert during the battle of Bir Hakeim, Libya, 9 June 1942.

The insignia of the 2nd parachute regiment (*2ème REP*) of the French Foreign Legion.

Opposite: The modern Foreign Legion, photographed marching down the Champs-Élysées in Paris during the annual Bastille Day parade.

breakthrough at Monte Cassino in May–June 1944, and during the hard fighting in Alsace in the winter of 1944–45 under Marshal Jean de Lattre de Tassigny.

The Legion contributed roughly 8 per cent of the 235,000 troops in the French Expeditionary Corps during the Indochina War (1946–54), in which the Legion fielded paratroop and motorized cavalry units, as well as their standard infantry formations. However, even a heroic performance by five Legion battalions at the battle of Dien Bien Phu in early 1954 could not salvage Indochina, whose defence cost over 10,000 Legion dead. Hardly had the smoke cleared at Dien Bien Phu before the Legion was repatriated to Algeria for another doomed defence. The *1ère REP*'s (*Régiment Étranger de Parachutistes*) association with the military rebellion against de Gaulle in April 1961 caused it to be disbanded.

### The modern Legion

After 1962, the Legion headquarters was transferred to Aubagne, a suburb of Marseille, where its essential traditions continue to be nurtured. Aubagne, classified as the *1ère étranger*, receives prospective recruits who enlist for five years. The Legion's once exceptional status as a professional unit in a conscript army has somewhat diminished as the French army abandoned conscription in the 1990s. All Legion officers are French born or naturalized citizens. While the Legion maintains the *anonymat* and shields every legionnaire's privacy, each prospective recruit is thoroughly interrogated by the *Bureau des statistiques de la Légion étrangère* (BSLE). Care is taken to have a mix of nationalities, including Frenchmen, in the units. Following basic training at the *4ème étranger* based at Castelnaudary, legionnaires are sent to one of eight units stationed in France or in the overseas territories. It is possible to become a corporal after two years' service. However, NCO rank is reserved for re-enlisted legionnaires.

With slightly fewer than 8,000 officers and men, the Legion now spearheads France's overseas interventions. It saw action in the Gulf War of 1990–91, and has served in many African missions, in Cambodia, the Balkans and in Afghanistan.

# The
# Modern
# World

1900 –

# The Red Baron's Flying Circus

## German Air Aces in World War I

The insignia of the Order *Pour le Mérite* (above), popularly known during World War I as the Blue Max – as seen worn by Manfred von Richthofen in this photograph taken in 1916 (below).

**T**he Flying Circus was a nickname given to the most famous aerial fighting unit of World War I, Jagdgeschwader 1, or JG 1– the 1st Fighter Wing of the Imperial German Air Service. JG 1 existed from June 1917 to November 1918 and was disbanded at the war's end. Much of JG 1's fame comes from its identification with its best-known commanding officer, Rittmeister Freiherr Manfred von Richthofen (known as the Red Baron), World War I's top ace, with 80 victories.

At the outbreak of World War I the ability to conduct aerial reconnaissance was key to obtaining clear intelligence of enemy forces and in directing artillery fire. It soon became clear that the side that could carry out reconnaissance while denying that ability to the enemy had a major advantage. Soon, fast and manoeuvrable aircraft were developed with the mission to shoot down enemy aircraft. The German Fokker I monoplane, first fielded in 1915, was the first purpose-built fighter and was followed by British and French fighters. By the end of 1916 both the Allied and Central Powers fielded fighter squadrons with the aim to win air superiority over the battlefield. This new arm of aviation required pilots who were not only competent, but also extremely daring and aggressive and who had to be willing to get within 50–100 m (160–330 ft) of an enemy – the best ranges to be sure of a kill – and shoot him down.

Aviation was already an elite force within the armed forces as all pilots were volunteers who possessed the good eyesight, physical fitness and skill to fly the dangerous open-cockpit aircraft of the era. So the fighter force soon became an elite force within an elite force.

### Enter the Red Baron

In January 1917 the recently formed German Fighter Squadron 11 (Jasta 11) was not regarded as anything special within the Air Service. However, that month it welcomed a new commanding officer, Lieutenant Manfred von Richthofen, who already had 16 aircraft hits to his credit. In 1916 von Richthofen, a former cavalry officer who transferred to the Air Service in 1915, was serving as an observation pilot when Oswald Boelcke, the legendary top German ace, spotted something special in the 23-year-old officer and had him transferred to his fighter squadron. Under Boelcke's guidance, von Richthofen began an impressive career in shooting down Allied aircraft. He followed Boelcke's advice on the

Right: A Fokker triplane of the type flown by von Richthofen on display in Berlin in the 1930s.

Below: A German squadron on the ground, 1917. Sheltering the planes in tents made the fighter squadron a highly mobile organization, easily moved to critical sectors. The tents inspired the 'flying circus' nickname.

best way to fight the enemy, 'I approach the enemy until about 50 metres behind him, take aim carefully, and then the opponent falls'.

When von Richthofen took over Jasta 11 he demonstrated the leadership qualities that Boelcke had noted. Richthofen insisted that his pilots train constantly and he personally flew with his pilots on training missions which included live fire at towed targets. He disdained what he called, 'fancy flying', insisting that the best thing was simply to get close to the enemy and shoot well. Richthofen wanted only the most aggressive pilots, and those who did not meet his standard were transferred out. Good marksmanship was also expected and this was reinforced by constant gunnery practice.

In April 1917 the British began a major offensive at Arras and put the greater part of the Royal Flying Corps (RFC) over that sector of the front. The Germans met the challenge: although they were outnumbered by the RFC,

> **'The German leader showed great acumen in his choice of pilots and was stern and patient in his schooling of them ... they became one of the most efficient fighting forces of the war.'** H. A. Jones, 1934

they were equipped with new Albatross D.III fighters that were far superior in manoeuvrability, speed and firepower to the mostly obsolescent British aircraft. The air battle over Arras became known as 'bloody April' when the German Jastas shot down 151 planes for a loss of only 66 of their own and Jasta 11 won fame as the top-scoring German fighter unit on the Western Front.

When he became squadron commander von Richthofen had his aircraft painted bright red. As he led from the front, his red plane made it easy for the squadron to follow their leader; other squadron members followed suit, painting parts of their planes red. In the spring of 1917 von Richthofen proved the worth of his system of tactics and training by shooting down more than 20 British aircraft. Promoted to captain and awarded Germany's *Pour le Mérite* (popularly known as the 'Blue Max') medal, he became a national hero – called the 'Red Baron' by the Allies and the 'Red Battle Flyer' by the Germans.

### 'Fighter Wing'

In June 1917 the British began an offensive in Flanders and the Royal Flying Corps, now equipped with better aircraft, flew over the front line in mass formations to drive the Germans from the sky. The Germans responded by organizing four of their best fighter squadrons – Jastas 4, 6, 10 and 11 – into

## Battle of Arras 1917

In April 1917, during the major air offensive initiated by the British Royal Flying Corps, Jasta 11, now flying the superior Albatross D.III aircraft, accounted for 89 British planes, more than half of the British losses on the Western Front that month. It was in this battle that von Richthofen, commander of Jasta 11, became famous as an air leader.

Richthofen (in the cockpit) in 1917, with pilots of Jasta 11, his first command.

Above: This painting by Claus Bergen depicts Richthofen, in the foreground, leading JG 1 in patrol formation, as they would have appeared in early 1918.

Below: A line of Fokker Dr.1s. The Fokker was highly manoeuvrable but was outclassed by the main Allied fighters by the time of Richthofen's death in April 1918. However, in the following month German fighter units received the Fokker D VII, often called the best fighter plane of World War I, which was chosen for production at Richthofen's urging.

a single unit, a Jagdgeschwader, or Fighter Wing, under the command of von Richthofen. JG 1, as the new organization was called, was to be a highly mobile elite force. Equipped with vehicles for ground support and large tents to shelter the aircraft, JG 1 could be quickly moved to the most threatened sector of the front. The large tents gave the wing the nickname of 'flying circus'.

By the end of 1917 von Richthofen, now flying a Fokker triplane, had more than 60 aircraft kills to his credit, and many of the pilots he had recruited to JG 1, such as Ernst Udet and Werner Voss, also became top aces. Richthofen was killed in April 1918, but under other commanders, including the Luftwaffe's future leader Lt Hermann Goering, JG 1 continued as an elite force, taking on the British, French and, finally, the Americans over several sectors of the Western Front in 1918. By the end of the war JG 1 had 892 aerial victories for a loss of 125 pilot casualties.

# The German Stormtroopers of World War I
## Assault Units on the Western Front

'The turmoil of our
feelings was called
forth by rage,
alcohol and the
thirst for blood ...
And therewith
beat the pulse of
heroism – the godlike
and the bestial
inextricably mingled.'

**Ernst Jünger, 1924**

*T*he developing trench systems and the huge casualties suffered in the mass attacks of 1914 demanded a new approach to fighting the war on the Western Front. The German army's response took the form of the Stormtroopers. These innovative units began to take shape when junior officers of the infantry and pioneers developed concepts in good part borrowed from siege warfare. Small detachments, directly supported by light mortars and machine guns, flamethrowers and modified artillery pieces, would approach a position by stealth, break into it by surprise and exploit the breach using hand grenades.

Successfully tested on a small scale in 1915, the new methods proved well suited to the raids and counter-raids characteristic of trench war. Stormtroops were so effective at Verdun in 1916 that their strength and numbers were rapidly increased to 18 battalion-strength units, mostly volunteers. Attached by ones and twos to the field armies, assault battalions spent little time in trench routines or route marches. Instead they were brought to the front by truck, committed for sudden attacks and quick withdrawals, then returned to their bases. Their external distinctions were not obvious: breeches instead of boots, sacks of grenades slung over the chest. What set stormtroopers apart was their swagger.

In addition to an operational function, the assault battalions also had a training one. Their ultimate mission was to make themselves redundant by training the entire infantry in stormtroop tactics. Their success was incomplete – inevitably in the context of a mass army of poorly trained conscripts. The original stormtroop concept of well-prepared, limited-objective attacks nevertheless increasingly affected German tactics in general during 1917, most notably at Cambrai. Stormtroop methods were also enhanced by the infiltration tactics developed at Verdun and refined in Russia. Instead of keeping in touch with units on their flanks and securing objectives to their front,

German stick grenade and ball grenade –
the weapons of the Stormtrooper. Men
for these assault units were carefully
selected: they were the fittest, keenest
and most aggressive, able to act
independently and make swift decisions.

**1915**
German High Command authorizes
an experimental force combining
infantry, pioneers and artillery.

**1916**
Armies ordered to send picked
officers and NCOs for training as
Stormtroop instructors.

**1917**
General application of Stormtroop
methods allows Germans to break
through the Italians at Caporetto.

**1918**
Stormtroop formations spearhead
the final German offensive on the
Western Front.

# Day of the Stormtrooper 1918

The opening day of the German Operation
Michael on 21 March 1918 is known as the Day
of the Stormtrooper. The assault battalions
were the first to follow the German barrage.
In general they were employed in company-
strength *Sturmblocks*, armed with rifles,
grenades and light machine guns. Like rising
water they infiltrated British forward positions,
probing for gaps and weak spots, isolating
centres of resistance, stopping for nothing.

But the Stormtroopers' shock power was not
matched by their staying power. They were
expected to drive as far as the British gun
positions on the first day – a distance of up to
8 km (5 miles). Few of them made it. None did so
in enough strength to achieve a breakthrough.
Their infiltration tactics transformed closed
fists into outspread fingers.

Advancing, 1918: Stormtroopers focused on
slipping between pockets of resistance.

assault units pushed into enemy rear zones on their own, bypassing defended
obstacles. The combination of assault and infiltration offered a possibility of
converting break-ins to breakthroughs. A German army committed to staking
the war's outcome on one desperate final offensive looked increasingly to the
Stormtroopers as its cutting edge. They would make the initial penetrations,
then keep going. Consolidation and exploitation of their victories would be left
to ordinary infantry – every man of which, according to the High Command,
was to be trained as a Stormtrooper. In fact, only around a third of the divisions
on the Western Front qualified as 'attack' formations, and even the best of them
were well below the assault battalions in their levels of skill.

That point became clear from the beginning of the German offensive of
March 1918. Within hours the assault became a battle of attrition – exactly what
the Stormtroopers had been created to avoid. Expected to fight for as long as 10
days without relief, assault battalions saw their casualties mount alarmingly,
and they could not be readily replaced, except by cannibalizing companies. Nor
did Stormtroops have supply trains: what they needed, they carried on their
backs. Stress and fatigue combined to dull the cutting edge of the will to fight,
and diminish effectiveness based heavily on individual judgment and initiative.
Standard infantry could not apply consistently and successfully the Stormtroop
tactics of fire and manoeuvre on a larger scale. By November 1918 the assault
battalions had become defensive fire brigades in a losing war, plugging gaps
almost at random. As a final irony, one of them was assigned as headquarters
guard to protect the now-discredited High Command against mutineers and
revolutionaries. Total war, it seemed, could not be won by elite forces alone.

Opposite below: German
Stormtroopers practising assault
tactics, including throwing stick
grenades and breaking through
barbed wire, at their training school
at Sedan, May 1917.

Below: A German World War I poster
to boost the war effort, using an
idealized portrait of a Stormtrooper.

# The Italian Arditi of World War I
## The Daring Ones

The official insignia of the Arditi was an upright Roman sword, the *gladius*, in the centre of a wreath of oak and laurel leaves (below), but their own preferred emblem was a wreathed skull with a dagger clenched between its teeth (above).

**A**n elite troop established in the Italian army in World War I, the Arditi, 'the Daring Ones', were volunteers who already had war experience. They had no care for their lives and no fear of any enemy, while they in turn were feared and killed if – and it happened only rarely – they were taken prisoner. Their weapons of choice were hand grenades, daggers, pistols, flamethrowers and, less often, machine guns and rifles. The Roman *gladius* (sword) in a wreath of oak and laurel was their official insignia, but the skull was the unofficial and most loved one, because they were so close to death; black was the corps' colour on their collar patches.

## 'All heroes, or all killed'
### Sentence painted on a wall by an unknown officer, 'P', 1918

The Arditi's official name was *Reparti d'assalto* – assault units. Established by Colonel Bassi in 1917, their function was to carry out surprise assaults, open the way for massive infantry attacks and to make raids on Austrian lines, capturing positions or prisoners. Their training was conducted under live fire – using real bullets and hand grenades from the very first exercise – and included hand-to-hand combat, the use of the bayonet and continuous physical exercise. This, added to their previous war experience, rendered them fast and dangerous combatants, as the Austrians discovered.

Below: A romantic image of the Arditi, reflecting their reputation for bravery and ferocity. Their name comes from the Italian word *ardire*, 'to dare'.

Initially, each army corps had an Arditi company – four platoons, a machine gun section and a flamethrower section – which was later increased to an assault unit – three companies and three machine gun sections. In June 1918 the Italian general staff organized two Assault Divisions, including also sections of Bersaglieri, cavalry and carabinieri, which were later grouped in the Assault Army Corp, under General Francesco Saverio Grazioli. Their contribution to ultimate victory was significant, especially in late spring and summer of 1918, when they were instrumental in halting the last Austrian offensive, sustaining very high losses. They soon came to be regarded as a kind of symbol and exemplar. One of their most celebrated unit commanders, Major Giovanni Messe, began his career as a private, was made a general, then commanded the 1st Italian Army in Tunisia in 1943 and became the Chief of Staff of the Italian army after World War II.

In early 1918 assault units were sent to France, where as an element of the Italian II Army Corps they took part in the operation in the valley of the River Ardre, especially in Bligny, and on the Chemin

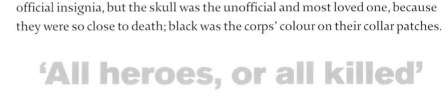

Right: A newspaper report dated February 1918 illustrating a group of Arditi bursting into an enemy command post – note the daggers between their teeth and the raised hands holding grenades.

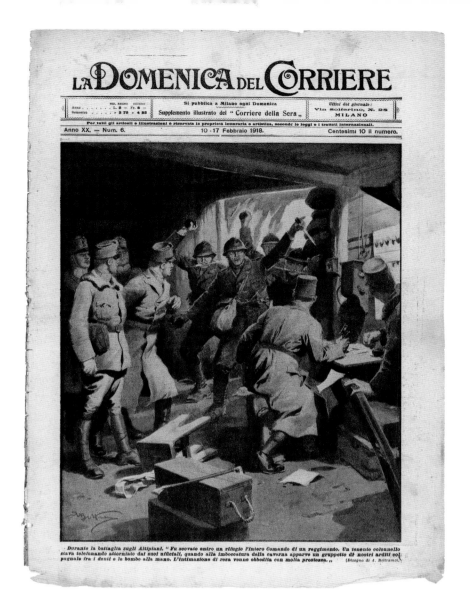

LA DOMENICA DEL CORRIERE

Si pubblica a Milano ogni Domenica
Supplemento illustrato del " Corriere della Sera „

Anno XX. — Num. 6.     10 - 17 Febbraio 1918.     Centesimi 10 il numero.

- *Durante la battaglia sugli Altipiani. " Fu scovato entro un rifugio l'intero Comando di un reggimento. Un tenente colonnello stava telefonando attorniato dai suoi ufficiali, quando alla imboccatura della caverna apparve un gruppetto di nostri arditi col pugnale fra i denti e le bombe alla mano. L'intimazione di resa venne obbedita con molta prestezza. „*     (Disegno di A. Beltrame).

The Arditi were established in 1917 as assault units with the role of breaching enemy defences to prepare the way for infantry attacks, as seen in this postcard of an Arditi crossing barbed wire with the Italian flag in his hand.

des Dames, successfully resisting – as did all their army corps – the German offensive in June and July 1918.

After the end of the war, the Arditi organized a veteran association, which soon gave political support to the recently formed Fascist party. At the same time, in October 1919, two Arditi batallions deserted the Royal Army and joined Gabriele D'Annunzio's government in its occupation of Fiume. It was for this reason that the Italian government, which had already in January 1919 reduced the Arditi to just one Assault Division – the 1st – and in February had sent it to Libya, decided to post them overseas again as soon as they returned to Italy in late May. So four assault units, IX, X, XXI and XXII, landed in Albania to fight against local partisan bands. The peak of the fighting was around Valona in summer 1920, after which the Arditi returned to Italy in August 1920 and the process of officially disbanding the units began.

Arditi remained as platoons in infantry regiments until the end of World War II, after which they survived – and still exist – as a specialization in Italian army units. Whoever passes the training period in the Corso d'Ardimento at the Infantry School is still allowed to wear the old and glorious badge featuring the Roman *gladius*.

# The French Chasseurs of World War I
## The Steadfast Blue Devils

**T**he term 'Chasseurs' (literally 'hunters') goes back to the French army of the 17th century and originally designated light infantry or light cavalry specializing in reconnaissance or rapid action. A royal order of 27 October 1840 officially created the *Chasseurs à pied*, who went on to distinguish themselves during operations in North Africa in particular. The battle of Sidi-Brahim (22–25 September 1845) – in which five Chasseur companies were surrounded by an enemy who outnumbered them by ten to one but refused to surrender and were reduced

> 'Verdun imposed on our Chasseurs all the hardship of a struggle with none of its exhilaration. Step by step advanced the combat, the carnage against the massed human sacrifice, against weapons of destruction which technology had borrowed from the Dark Ages and made yet more cruelly efficient.'
>
> **History of the 21st Battalion of Chasseurs**

to just 15 survivors – became one of the most important landmarks in French military tradition. The Chasseurs came to be an elite corps, famed for their steadfastness in combat and their utter devotion to duty, to the point of sacrifice. The *Chasseurs alpins* were created on 24 December 1888 as a specialized unit for mountain combat, although they were later deployed on all fronts.

At the start of World War I, the *Chasseurs à pied* were a subdivision of the infantry. With their strong fighting spirit, they were marked by an individuality evident in their uniforms as well as their attitude. The blue uniform features yellow piping on the trouser leg, giving them the nickname the *bleus-jonquille*, the 'Daffodil Blues'. They also wore a type of wide beret tipped to one side, known as a *tarte*. During World War I the Chasseurs had frequent opportunities to demonstrate their style of heroism in action. The battles of Vosges (1915) and Verdun (1916) are symbolic of their attitude – a relentless tenacity when on the defensive and an unstoppable drive when on the offensive. In the Vosges mountains the Chasseurs distinguished themselves in the fighting at Vieil-Armand or Hartmannswillerkopf: at a height of 956 m (3,136 ft), this was a key observation point on the Alsace plain which both sides fought to control. On 26 March 1915, the 1st brigade of Chasseurs (7th, 13th, 27th and 53th battalions of *Chasseurs alpins*) retook the summit from the Germans. It subsequently changed hands several times until December

## Key Dates

### 1845
Battle of Sidi-Brahim: Chasseurs of the 8th battalion face 10,000 Algerian troops; after a charge through enemy lines 15 survive.

### 1915
*Chasseurs alpins* fight against the Germans for the possession of Hartmannswillerkopf.

### 1916
The Chasseurs of Lt Colonel Driant hold out against the Germans at the Bois des Caures, Verdun.

### 1917
Battalions of the *Chasseurs alpins* retake Monte Tomba, Italy.

### 1940
The 10th Chasseurs are encircled by the Germans at Blaregnies; short of munitions they charge with bayonets, with 70 per cent losses.

### 1947
Encircled at Dat Do Phong (Indochina), Captain Dessertaux falls at the head of his company.

Above: The 26th battalion of Chasseurs marching to the front line in 1918.

Opposite: The blue uniform of the Chasseurs of World War I distinguished them from other soldiers, as did their fighting spirit. On the left is a uniform of a *Chasseur à pied* of the 8th battalion and on the right an illustration by Maurice Mahut of a Chasseur of the 30th battalion.

1915, after which it remained under German control until 1918. The Chasseurs earned the nickname of 'Blue Devils' from the German troops in tribute to their courage.

The Chasseurs fought in many areas during World War I: the 6th battalion of the *Chasseurs alpins* were in Corfu in spring 1916; the 51st, 70th and 115th retook Monte Tomba on the Italian front in December 1917. In November 1918, Chasseur units were deployed across the entire front. Chasseur units were, and still are, deployed in all the French army's theatres of operations, from the Ivory Coast to Chad, from Beirut to Bosnia and Afghanistan. Within the French forces, the Chasseur battalions proudly maintain the tradition of the blue uniform and the values of combat and camaraderie that it represents to this day.

## Battle of Verdun 1916

At Verdun, the Chasseurs of Lieutenant Colonel Driant met their collective fate in the Bois des Caures after a German attack on 21 February 1916. The 56th and 59th battalions held the north of the defensive sector, which the Germans had to take if they were to march on Verdun. The systematic bombardment of the Bois des Caures began at 7 a.m. on 21 February. The German infantry began its attack at 5 p.m., their barrage devastating the woodland. The resistance of the Chasseurs was desperate. Each company was attacked by a battalion of the 18th German army corps. The 56th Chasseur battalion lost 518 men out of 1,100, while the 59th lost 668, leaving only six officers and 266 troops. The 9th company of the 59th battalion was reduced to 20 men, with no officers or NCOs. This sacrifice by Driant's Chasseurs slowed down the German advance by one day, allowing the French to send urgently needed reserve forces to Verdun.

Portrait of Colonel Driant, 1914; in reality he would have worn the traditonal blue uniform of the Chasseurs.

# The Gurkhas
## Bravest of the Brave

**T**he name 'Gurkha' is synonymous with the distinctive courage and tenacity of the hill men of Nepal and their characteristic curved-bladed knife, the *kukri*. A fiercely competitive selection system into British army service has always ensured that only the very best recruits are able to serve, and their history is replete with countless stories of individual and collective acts of valour.

The Gurkhas are in fact a collection of tribal groups, which includes the Thakurs, Chettris, Limbars and Rais in eastern Nepal, and the Magar and Gurung in the west; their name is derived from Guru Goraknath, the 8th-century Hindu warrior saint. They rose to prominence through the 18th century, eventually taking control of the Kathmandu Valley and the modern state of Nepal in 1804, coming into conflict with the British East India Company in 1814. After a two-year war the Gurkhas were defeated, but the British, immensely impressed by the fighting qualities of the Gurkhas, had raised three battalions in British service while the war was still in progress. Although the Treaty of Segauli (1816) ended conflict between India and Nepal, the Nepalese government officially disapproved of the recruiting of Gurkhas. However, Gurkhas were attracted by the rates of pay and the terms of service and were soon a feature of the British Indian forces in every campaign of the 19th century. Gurkhas were also recruited by the Punjab state of Lahore and by the short-lived Afghan regime of Shah Shuja.

It was during the Indian Mutiny (1857–58) that the Gurkhas excelled as the most valued colonial troops of the British empire. Alongside regular units of Nepal, Gurkha battalions stayed loyal to the British against the mutineers and they showed particular devotion

Above: Gurkhas acting as QRF (Quick Reaction Force) in Helmand province, Afghanistan; their adversaries, the Taliban, are said to fear these fierce soldiers more than any other unit of the British army.

Opposite centre: The *kukri* – despite the advent of modern weaponry, the iconic curved fighting knife of the Nepalese warrior still adorns every Gurkha's uniform and is even, occasionally, used in battle.

Opposite below: The Gurkhas have served in every theatre of war since entering British service. This photograph shows them in Tunisia in North Africa, in 1943, where they acted as the mountain warfare experts of the Eighth Army.

to duty during the siege of Delhi. The 2nd Sirmoor Rifles, for example, lost 327 out of 490 men in the successful defence of Hindu Rao's residence in that city. The Gurkhas were regarded as brilliant light infantry, particularly in mountain warfare, and they were often the favoured troops for leading assaults against tribesmen and Afghans on the North West Frontier of India.

They were accorded the honour of wearing Rifle Green uniforms with a Kilmarnock cap (later replaced by the slouch hat) to reflect their special status, but on campaign khaki became the standard camouflage dress from the 1880s. Their association with highlanders meant their band featured drums and bagpipes as well as the bugles of light infantry formations. While Scottish regiments claim a close bond with their Gurkha counterparts, it is true to say that every British soldier has a close affinity with their comrades from Nepal and they have always been accorded a great deal of affection and respect.

At the outbreak of World War I in 1914, there were 26,000 Gurkhas in British service, divided between 10 two-battalion rifle regiments in their own Gurkha Brigade, formed in 1903. By the end of the war, over 200,000 men had served in France, Gallipoli, the Middle East and India, with 50,000 riflemen in the Gurkha Brigade alone. In World War II, there were no fewer than 43 battalions, with over a quarter of a million personnel. The Gurkhas distinguished themselves by winning nine VCs and 2,725 other gallantry awards. The Gurkhas fought with their usual skill and determination against both the Axis powers in Europe and North Africa, and against the Japanese in Burma.

Tul Bahadur Pun exemplified the exceptional fighting spirit of the Gurkhas: he won the Victoria Cross in June 1944 for a single-handed attack against a reinforced Japanese machine gun post that had killed and wounded almost all his section. Alone, he advanced across a cratered and exposed area of open

During World War II, British lines of communications near Bishenpur on the India–Burma border were threatened by a Japanese offensive. The Japanese had captured two commanding hill features, and were prepared for a counterattack. A single company of the 5th Gurkha Rifles had to retake the hills in the teeth of heavy machine gun and mortar fire. Having suffered significant losses in the opening stages of the attack on 26 June 1944, the Gurkhas refused to yield. Led by Naik Agansing Rai, they fought their way up the slopes. Rai led two attacks, hurling grenades and firing his submachine gun at close quarters. The two hilltop positions were taken, and Rai was subsequently awarded the Victoria Cross. Subedar Netrabahadur Thapa also earned the highest gallantry award that day, holding off Japanese attacks and launching his own charge to drive them off.

ground, killed three Japanese gunners at close quarters and put to flight a further five, seizing two light machine guns before covering the advance of his comrades. In numerous other battlefields, eyewitnesses testify that the war cry 'Jai Mahakali, Ayo Gurkhali!' ('Glory to the goddess of war, here come the Gurkhas!') has echoed with similar selflessness and bravery.

In 1947 the British withdrew from India and it was decided to split the Gurkhas, six regiments being allocated to India (where they are known as Gorkhas) and just four to Britain (the 2nd King Edward VII's Own Gurkha Rifles; 6th Queen Elizabeth's Own; 7th Duke of Edinburgh's Own; and 10th Princess Mary's Own), each of two battalions. The British Gurkha battalions were first deployed to Malaya, before being garrisoned for some years in Hong Kong and, after 1997, in the United Kingdom. The officer corps was always traditionally provided by British personnel, but Queen's Gurkha Officer Commissions (formerly Viceroy's Commissions) were available from World War II onwards.

The Gurkhas saw service in both conventional and counter-insurgency operations after 1945, taking part in the Malayan Emergency, the Borneo Campaign and the Falklands Conflict, as well as in Afghanistan. Controversy

Men of the 2nd and 9th Gurkha Rifles training in the Malayan jungle, October 1941. As well as conventional warfare, the Gurkhas have also taken part in counter-insurgency operations.

A Gurkha on patrol in Afghanistan – note the badge of crossed *kukris* on his beret. The Gurkhas have earned a reputation for rugged endurance and great tenacity in combat – a reputation that is both hard-won and richly deserved.

'Bravest of the brave, most generous of the generous, never had country more faithful friends than you.' Sir Ralph Turner, MC, 1931

surrounded their claim for the same pay and pensions as British servicemen in the 1990s, and it was not until 2009 that they achieved equal status and the right to residence. Despite severe cuts in their numbers (there were just two battalions in British service in 1995), they have retained their reputation for dash and courage in action, and continue to provide an integral element of the British infantry's order of battle.

# The Few
## RAF Fighter Pilots in the Battle of Britain

The RAF wings cloth badge (above) and two RAF cap badges (below). The badge on the right below is made of a form of bakelite and is intentionally dark and matt in order not to reflect sunlight.

**W**inston Churchill famously celebrated the achievement of the pilots of the Battle of Britain in his remark that: 'Never in the field of human conflict was so much owed by so many to so few'. Over the summer and autumn of 1940, a total of barely 3,000 airmen were able to check the more numerous and experienced Luftwaffe, and thus helped prevent any chance of a German invasion of Britain. Without air and naval superiority, Hitler had to concede that 'Operation Sealion' was impossible. The fact that the survival of the last European state still resisting Nazi Germany rested on such a small contingent earns them the accolade of a special force in the annals of war.

The defence of British airspace cost the lives of 510 pilots, representing a sixth of their strength, but they shot down between 1,700 and 2,000 German aircraft. Fortunately, the Luftwaffe, under Hermann Goering's direction, diluted its efforts by attacking convoys, airfields, the aircraft industry and radar stations, thus giving the British an opportunity to avoid a mass air battle that would soon have depleted their ranks. RAF Fighter Command instead carefully marshalled their precious 'Few', fighting with the minimum strength to neutralize a particular attack and ensuring that pilots who were forced to bale out were returned to duty as soon as possible. The systematic radar tracking of German formations, in some cases before they had even crossed the coast of France, enabled Fighter Command to co-ordinate their response, but squadrons in southeast England still had to be prepared to get into the air at a moment's notice. Pilots might enjoy a few hours on the ground in relative peace only to be suddenly 'scrambled' and pitched into battle.

Around 188 pilots reached five 'kill' claims, making them an 'ace'. Not all the pilots were British – a significant minority came from Australia, Canada, New Zealand, Poland, Czechoslovakia, Jamaica, Ireland, France, Belgium and the United States. Indeed, a Polish pilot, Antoni Glowacki, and a New Zealander, Brian Carbury, both achieved the status of an ace in a single day's fighting.

Above: A Hurricane (foreground) and a Spitfire, with markings as they appeared in Guy Hamilton's film *Battle Of Britain*, 1969. This Spitfire was built in 1940 and took part in the Battle of Britain, serving with 266 Squadron and 603 Squadron. The Hurricane was built in 1944 and is thought to be the last Hurricane to enter service with the RAF. Both aircraft are still flying with the Battle of Britain Memorial Flight.

Opposite below: Scrambling in full kit to get airborne in order to intercept German aircraft. Although it proved difficult accurately to ascertain the number of kills, it is clear that even though the RAF pilots were invariably outnumbered in the Battle of Britain they were able not only to survive the German air assaults of 1940, but also to inflict significant losses.

Below: The Spitfire (left) is perhaps the fighter aircraft most closely associated with the Battle of Britain in popular imagination, while in fact greater numbers of the Hawker Hurricane (right) were flown and were probably responsible for destroying more enemy aircraft in the Battle of Britain.

These feats seem all the more remarkable since, day after day, these pilots were hurled into dogfights against forces much stronger than their own. Churchill was genuinely moved by the inexhaustible courage of the pilots and felt that the RAF offered an inspiration to the rest of the country as it endured continuous bombardment from waves of German aircraft. After the British army's retreat from France, the losses caused by U-boats and the defeat of Britain's European allies, the success of the RAF offered a glimmer of hope.

## Courage and experience

The RAF pilots had to contend with more than just the prowess of the German Luftwaffe, however. RAF tactical doctrine placed great emphasis on a tight three-plane V formation, known as the 'vic', but this reduced the pilots' ability to observe the skies for enemy aircraft. Individual 'weaver' planes flying between vics were supposed to alleviate the problem, but too often they were isolated and shot down. Experiments continued during the Battle of Britain and a four aircraft 'line astern' formation offered manoeuvrability and mutual support in the initial moments of a dogfight. Nevertheless, it was the courage and growing experience of the pilots that won the battle.

# Battle of Britain 1940

The Battle of Britain developed through four critical phases. In the first phase, from mid-July to mid-August 1940, the German Luftwaffe tried to wrest control of the Channel airspace from the RAF. Here the Germans held the advantage since their massed formations of aircraft could attack convoys of surface ships and yet still parry the British fighters. It was also clear the some British aircraft were inadequate in dogfights with their German counterparts. The second phase, until the end of August 1940 saw the Germans shift their emphasis to attacks on coastal airfields, and in the third phase they began attacking RAF airfields further inland. The critical days were 16–18 August, when the largest numbers of aircraft took to the skies. The RAF pilots performed well, and better than the Germans had expected, such that they were forced to provide stronger fighter escorts for their bombers and they also scaled back their attacks on radar stations. More importantly, in the final phase, from early September, the Luftwaffe switched to the bombing of cities, which gave the RAF a crucial respite and enabled them to destroy large numbers of German bombers.

A flypast of World War II fighter aircraft. Both the Spitfire and the Hurricane flew in many different theatres.

Opposite: Despite losing both his legs before the war, Douglas Bader was able to rejoin the RAF. A fearless leader, he became a living legend during the Battle of Britain.

Below: Enjoying a hair cut; pilots and ground crews were in a constant state of readiness awaiting the signal to scramble. Behind the scenes, an efficient apparatus of early warning, tracking, analysis and direction was in place, bringing the British fighters to the precise point to engage German formations.

The spirit of the fighter pilot is exemplified by Group Captain (Sir) Douglas Bader. Having lost his legs in a flying accident in 1931 after a brilliant sporting career, Bader rejoined the RAF at the outbreak of war and fought with distinction in the Battle of Britain, initially as part of 222 Squadron, where he achieved two kills. Then, as Squadron Leader of 224 Squadron, he destroyed a further eight aircraft. He went on to notch up a total of 22 kills before the end of the war, a sum that would no doubt have been higher had he not been shot down and captured in 1941. His force of personality, fearlessness and hatred of red tape made him a popular figure with his fellow pilots and won the admiration of all his enemies.

## Turning the tide

The main fighter aircraft used by the RAF in the Battle of Britain were the Hurricane and, although fewer in number, the Spitfire. The Hurricane and Spitfire were comparable with the main German fighter, the Messerschmitt 109 and the RAF pilots could hold their own against greater numbers of more experienced adversaries. They enjoyed their greatest success against the slower moving German bombers, the Stuka dive-bomber in particular. The limited range of the German fighters meant that their bombers often had to proceed over their targets with limited support, and gave 'The Few' a chance to even the odds against them. Nevertheless, a shortage of RAF pilots at the beginning of the campaign, the need to continue to run training establishments and the manpower demands of the British bomber fleet meant that many personnel in the fighter squadrons were inexperienced. This makes their achievements all the more remarkable. Despite the fatigue, the loss of their comrades and the relentless need to take to the skies against greater numbers every day, 'the Few' demonstrated that fighting spirit and determination can turn the tide of war.

'. . . the Battle of France is over, I expect that the Battle of Britain is about to begin. Upon this battle depends the survival of Christian civilization. Upon it depends our own British life, and the long continuity of our institutions and our Empire.'

Winston Churchill, 18 June 1940

Above: An RAF officer's badge. For the RAF of 1940, the airman's wings symbolized a deserved reputation of excellence in air combat.

# The Commandos of Britain's Royal Marines
By Sea, By Land

Above: Royal Marine Commando badges: worn by all Commandos the one immediately above illustrates the three sections, consisting of airforce, army and navy, represented by the eagle, gun and anchor.

Below: The Royal Marines' landings in Normandy on D-Day, 6 June 1944, helped to open the way for the liberation of Europe. Marines had long specialized in amphibious operations, seizing port facilities, securing beachheads and raiding enemy coasts, and, as such, they were often the spearhead formation in combined land-sea actions.

**C**ommandos is the title adopted all over the world to designate the elite of the armed forces, and more specifically to describe troops who emphasize specialist skills, great physical endurance and clandestine tactics. The British associate the name commandos with the Royal Marines, but during World War II, there were also army commando companies who were trained and deployed in much the same way as the Royal Marines of today.

The idea of commandos has a longer history: in the South African War of 1899–1902, the British were confronted by fast-moving, independent companies of 'Boer' fighters known as *Kommandos*. The Boer commandos made use of camouflage and cover as a way of making up for their inadequate numbers. It was also necessity that forced them to use irregular tactics to evade the larger British formations that pursued them. Their mobility and raiding techniques, such as hit-and-run guerrilla attacks on railways, patrols and outposts, impressed the colonial authorities, but it was some time before the British decided to raise their own version of such a force.

The other 'root' of the Commandos was the Royal Marines. Sending footsoldiers aboard ships to fight boarding parties or capture enemy vessels and ports can be traced back to medieval times, but organized units appeared in 1664 during the British wars with the Dutch. The seaborne nature of the British empire meant that the demand for troops able to operate both on land and at sea was high. Throughout the 19th century they acted as skirmishers ahead of naval landing parties and their title was altered to Royal Marine Light Infantry (RMLI) in 1855. The Light Infantry always tried to select the fittest men of the army and those who could use their initiative to fight independently. The Marines thus established themselves as a *corps d'elite*, often tasked with reconnaissance work and therefore usually the first to encounter the enemy.

In World War I, the Royal Marines made a significant contribution to the landings at Gallipoli in 1915. The Marines provided raiding forces

Above: The Commando raid on Vaagso, 1941, with the oil refinery burning in the background, taken by a War Office official photographer. The Commandos sought to disrupt and deny Norwegian ports to German invaders, earning the enduring gratitude of the Norwegian people.

against Turkish shore batteries in the Dardanelles in the follow up to a naval bombardment, but they also took part in the main attack, coming ashore under intense fire. The Marines then took their place in the trenches of the Western Front, but they also led the remarkable Zeebrugge Raid in April 1918, earning two Victoria Crosses in an attack on the German shore defences of a U-boat harbour. After the war, the RMLI and RMA were amalgamated into the Corps of Royal Marines. However, the outbreak of World War II brought further changes, not least the designation of Commando.

## Formation and operations

In 1940, when faced with the prospect of Nazi invasion and occupation, the British government organized special units of volunteers who would carry out raids and assassinations of Nazi personnel. They were to be concealed in secret bunkers and would form the nucleus of a nationwide resistance movement. However, ideas quickly turned to a more aggressive counter-force that would be entirely self-sufficient and could carry out reconnaissance, sabotage and more substantial raids on German-held territory on the continent of Europe. Elements of these Special Forces eventually went on to become the SAS and Paras, but the Commandos were a combination of selected army personnel and Royal Marines. The Royal Marines had already fought as an amphibious force in Norway and Crete, but in 1943, they were brought together with specially selected army commandos to form the Special Service Brigade, with their own landing craft support. Four brigades were raised and the RM Commandos were given the numerical titles 40 to 48.

The Commandos made several opposed landings, including Sicily, Salerno, the Dieppe Raid and the D-Day invasion in Normandy. They conducted raids on the French coast and in Norway, where in December 1941 they single-handedly sank eight German ships. On D-Day, Commandos took part in the fighting on each of the British and Canadian beaches. They also fought in operations in Burma. Much was learnt from each of the early operations, so that, by the end

Right: Commandos of the 1st Special Service Brigade go ashore at Sword Beach, Normandy, under the command of Lord Lovat, who reportedly ordered the brigade's piper, seen here in the foreground, to pipe the men ashore.

Opposite: A column of 45 Royal Marine Commandos march towards Port Stanley. The Commandos were keen to recapture the Falkland Islands' capital in 1982 because a small detachment of the Royal Marines had been overwhelmed by an Argentine invasion force earlier that year. In a succession of battles, and in spite of tough climatic conditions, the Commandos fought their way over the mountains and secured the port, raising the Union Flag once again.

of the war, the Commandos were fighting as highly effective and flexible formations. A total of four Commando Brigades were eventually formed. Their training was tough and realistic, with live ammunition used throughout. Specialist skills involved signals, climbing, endurance, survival and unarmed combat. A costly but successful raid, Operation Frankton, took place in December 1942, involving 10 canoeists attempting to lay charges against the hull of German ships in Bordeaux. Such was their fear of this sort of sabotage that the Germans issued orders that all captured Commandos were to be shot. After the war, the designation of Commando was retained by the Royal Marines.

After 1945, the Royal Marine Commandos were involved in all Britain's military operations, including Malaya, Korea and Suez, often because of their high state of readiness. In the Indonesian Confrontation (1964–65), Lima Company Royal Marines rescued local hostages in an amphibious operation at Limbang (Sarawak, Borneo). In the Falklands Conflict (1982), because a single platoon of the Royal Marines had fought the initial Argentine invasion, it was a point of pride for the 'bootnecks' to retake the Islands. By May of that year, all three Commandos, 40, 42 and 45, were 'yomping' and fighting their way back to Port Stanley. An iconic image of the war is of a Royal Marine wireless operator with a Union Flag striding across a windswept and desolate battlefield.

The RM Commandos also served several tours in Northern Ireland, attempting to keep the peace between warring sectarian factions and combating terrorist groups. In the 1990s and early 21st century, they have

## St Nazaire Raid 1942

Perhaps the greatest epic for the Commandos was the St Nazaire Raid in March 1942. Having rammed the lock gates of the French port with an obsolete warship, *HMS Campbeltown*, 600 Commandos fanned out to assault shore defences under heavy fire from over 5,000 defenders. The desperate fighting led to the award of five VCs. Only a handful of the raiders escaped, but their mission was a success – a delayed charge in the bow of *Campbeltown* detonated as planned, denying the use of the port to all German vessels.

Above, left and right: Commando training exercises at Bickleigh, southern England, and Scotland. Commando training is among the toughest of the United Kingdom armed forces. High standards were set during World War II as the Commandos were expected to carry out deep raiding in enemy territory.

Left: The Fairbairn-Sykes knife is carried by all Commandos. A double-edged knife developed by William Ewart Fairbairn and Eric Anthony Sykes in Shanghai before World War II, it was made famous during the war when issued to British Commandos, including the SAS.

Opposite: A Royal Marine at Bagram. The Royal Marine Commandos were among the first to deploy to Afghanistan, and were also called upon to act as the spearhead for operations in Al Faw, Iraq, in 2003. The Royal Marines were tasked with suppressing pro-Saddam resistance, securing the country's vital oil assets in the process. They were also able to quell civil unrest, protect reconstruction efforts and defeat insurgents.

deployed on peacekeeping missions to Kosovo, Sierra Leone and East Timor. In the overthrow of the Taliban, an SBS unit was soon augmented by elements of 40 Commando and then by 45 Commando, but attention was then diverted to Iraq where, in 2003, 3 Commando Brigade served alongside the Marine Expeditionary Force of the United States to take the Faw Peninsula. Also in Iraq 42 Commando seized the port of Umm Qasr, while 45 Commando ensured the security of oil installations vital for the country's reconstruction. In 2006, the Royal Marines rotated through Helmand province in Afghanistan as part of Operation Herrick, often taking the fight to the Taliban.

## A highly trained and effective force

Royal Marine Commando selection and training remain as rigorous and gruelling as ever. A total of 25 weeks is spent in basic training, followed by a six-week Commando course. Emphasis is placed on carrying considerable loads at great speed, regardless of terrain, temperature and weather conditions. Successful entrants are entitled to wear the distinctive green beret and are at the peak of their physical fitness. From this point, Commandos may specialize in particular roles, such as the Commando Helicopter Force, Amphibious Ready Group, Fleet Protection or the Assault Group, alongside the Commando gunners and engineers. Within each Commando group there are further specialist divisions, including fire support, snipers and Close Combat Troops.

The Royal Marine Commandos are a highly trained, professional and effective fighting force, able to deploy, as their motto suggests, with equal agility *per mare, per terram* ('by sea, by land'). They can be seen mounting patrols using light raiding craft, bringing down sophisticated fire support from surface vessels, jumping into action from helicopters or operating from their own armoured vehicle supports. Whatever the situation, they have lost none of the toughness and courage established by their forebears. It is appropriate that the Commando Memorial is located near Spean Bridge in the Scottish Highlands, where so many men trained prior to their service in World War II.

'Indifference to personal danger, ruthless pursuit of success, and for resourceful determination in adversity.'

Attribution to 3 Commando Brigade in Southeast Asia after halting Japanese counteroffensive in February 1945

# Paratroopers of the Third Reich
## Disciplined and Fearless

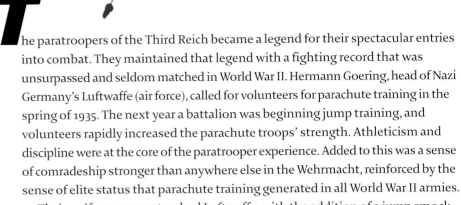

**T**he paratroopers of the Third Reich became a legend for their spectacular entries into combat. They maintained that legend with a fighting record that was unsurpassed and seldom matched in World War II. Hermann Goering, head of Nazi Germany's Luftwaffe (air force), called for volunteers for parachute training in the spring of 1935. The next year a battalion was beginning jump training, and volunteers rapidly increased the parachute troops' strength. Athleticism and discipline were at the core of the paratrooper experience. Added to this was a sense of comradeship stronger than anywhere else in the Wehrmacht, reinforced by the sense of elite status that parachute training generated in all World War II armies.

Their uniforms were standard Luftwaffe, with the addition of a jump smock designed to keep clothing and equipment from getting caught in the parachute shroud lines. The paratroopers' armament included a high proportion of machine pistols and machine guns. Since the larger weapons had to be dropped in separate canisters, pistols, knives, and grenades were the jumpers' initial

Right: German paratroopers landing in southern Norway, north of Oslo, in April 1940. This was one of the first operations of the paratroopers in World War II and they proved their effectiveness.

Opposite above: German Fallschirmjaeger parachuting into Crete, May 1941. The operation was a triumph of air assault, defeating the British, Greek and New Zealand defenders, but at a cost. After this, the highly trained paratroopers were used mostly as infantry shock troops.

Opposite below: A German World War II smock of the type worn by paratroopers. It is reversible, one side with the normal camouflage pattern, the other white for action in snow.

tools – a fact that encouraged the aggression and ferocity emphasized as the core of small-unit paratroop tactics.

## Air assaults

By September 1939 a three-regiment division and a separate assault detachment were part of the Luftwaffe's order of battle. That reflected Goering's success as an empire-builder, but also made military sense: paratroopers and transport crews were part of a single command. The system proved itself in 1940, when parachute units played roles out of all proportion to their numbers in the overrunning of Norway and the Netherlands. Employed in companies and battalions, their psychological impact outweighed their tactical one – and the two together were sufficient to earn the Fallschirmjaeger no fewer than 26 of the prized Knight's Crosses to the Iron Cross, plus the creation of their own corps headquarters to plan and control future operations.

The paratroopers' evaluation of their performance was that their success had depended heavily on surprise and that the troops deployed were individually too weak to force decisions by themselves. Those observations dovetailed neatly with Adolf Hitler's idea of using the paratroopers against geographically limited targets – like islands. The overrunning of mainland Greece in spring 1941 left the island of Crete still in Allied hands. With its naval base and airfields, Crete was an obstacle to future Axis operations in the eastern Mediterranean.

Its capture was a triumph of air assault. But the losses convinced Hitler that such large-scale parachute assaults represented excessive risk – not only for the paratroopers, but also for the valuable transport aircraft that carried them. For the rest of the war the Fallschirmjaeger would do their serious fighting on foot.

## Fighting on foot

That second operational career began in September 1941, when 7th Parachute Division was transferred to the Russian Front's hard-pressed Leningrad sector. In six weeks the paratroopers repulsed 146 Russian attacks. By November over 3,000 of them had been killed or wounded. Until summer 1942 the division's component elements were used to plug gaps the Russians tore in even 'quiet' sectors. They made no combat jumps, but their successes were such that in November 1942 another division was organized. Eventually renumbered 1st and 2nd, they were assigned to France as part of the theatre reserves.

In the Mediterranean, proposals for a German-Italian airborne attack on another island fortress, Malta, had reached the advanced planning stage when Hitler changed his mind. Instead, an improvised parachute brigade was sent to North Africa to reinforce Erwin Rommel's hard-pressed forces. Another regiment went to Tunisia after the Allied landings in Operation Torch. Initially used in detachments to seize and hold crucial ground while awaiting reinforcement, they finished the campaign as an elite reserve before being taken captive in May 1943.

The Allied invasion of Sicily brought both parachute divisions into Italy. The 2nd Fallschirmjaeger seized Rome in the aftermath of Italy's surrender. Elements of the division performed spectacular small-scale parachute operations: the rescue of Mussolini; the capture of Elba; the jump on to the island of Leros in the Aegean. A newly organized 4th Fallschirmjaeger Division played a key role containing the Allied beachhead at Anzio in Italy.

But it was 1st Fallschirmjaeger that epitomized the paratroopers' redefined mission as infantry shock troops by its epic defence of Monte Cassino against

## Battle of Crete 1941

On 20 May 1941, the Fallschirmjaeger division, reinforced by a glider-borne assault regiment, struck Crete from the air. The Royal Navy blocked initial efforts to support the attack by sea. British, Greek and New Zealand defenders resisted bitterly on the ground. Hundreds of men died in their chutes. The survivors had to seek out separately dropped weapons canisters. But the paratroopers rallied and held. They captured and held Maleme airfield. Men and supplies, including an entire mountain division, came in by air. Ten days later the island was in German hands. The paratroopers had earned 23 Knight's Crosses; they had taken 17,000 prisoners. But 3,350 of them were dead. The Luftwaffe had lost almost 400 aircraft, many of them the invaluable JU 52s. Crete was a spectacular victory – but it proved a Pyrrhic one.

*Victorious German paratroopers ride through the streets of Crete after the fierce 10-day battle to capture the island from the air.*

# 'Calm and caution, vigour and determination, valour and a fanatical offensive spirit will make you superior in action.'

**From 'The Parachutist's Ten Commandments' carried by a German captured on Crete**

some of the best troops in the Allied armies during the spring of 1944. British and New Zealanders, Gurkhas and Punjabis, Americans and Poles – for five months the Fallschirmjaeger defied them all. The 1st abandoned Monte Cassino only on direct orders.

By D-Day (6 June 1944), the Luftwaffe included five parachute divisions. None would ever jump into battle. Parachute training was minimal, but the new formations were built around strong cadres of old hands in key positions. The 3rd and 5th were formed in France and cut to pieces in Normandy. Five more low-strength or improvised divisions took the field at various stages of the final campaigns in east and west. Two corps headquarters and, eventually, a 1st Parachute Army complete the order of battle.

In Crete and Russia actual or suspected partisans might be summarily executed. In combat it was kill or be killed. But against uniformed opponents the German paratroopers earned a reputation as hard fighters who played mostly by the rules: respectful in victory, courteous in defeat. Reminiscing decades later, one veteran recalled (probably hyperbolically) each man of his captured unit being assigned two guards. 'They were scared to death … We were the paratroops.'

In 1943, after Mussolini had been deposed and arrested, Adolf Hitler ordered a mission to free him from imprisonment on Gran Sasso, in the Apennines in Italy. The successful operation was undertaken by German paratroopers, as seen here, who landed gliders in the mountains and rescued Mussolini.

# The British Paratroopers
## Spearhead Troops 'Ready for Anything'

**T**he Paras are the spearhead infantry regiment of the British army, whose primary function is to assault the enemy aggressively wherever found and whatever the circumstances. Selection is rigorous and the training regime is physically among the most demanding, ensuring that the Paras are prepared to go into action at a moment's notice, to drop behind enemy lines if necessary and to take the battle to the enemy.

Impressed by the performance and agility of the German Fallschirmjaeger in 1940–41 in Norway, the Low Countries and Crete (see p. 160), the British government ordered that a British equivalent be established. On 10 February 1941, a team of 50 parachutists from what was then the Special Air Service carried out a successful raid in Italy known as Operation Colossus. No 2 Commando was then reassigned to become the Parachute Regiment, which eventually grew to a strength of 17 battalions, and formed into the 1st and 6th Airborne Divisions and the independent 2nd Parachute Brigade.

The Paras soon established a reputation for daring, despite some setbacks caused by the hazards of making landings during combat. In northern France they carried out a brilliant raid on a German radar station at Douvres-la-Déliverande in February 1942, but suffered significant losses because of strong winds in their air assault over Sicily in 1943, when a number of men and gliders were blown into the sea. Despite casualties, they created havoc

Top: All British airborne forces wore the Pegasus badge on their sleeves.

Above: A set of World War II wings with the parachute symbol, as seen on the men's uniforms, right.

Right: Men recruited to the Paratroopers in 1941 assisting in fixing parachutes. The Paras expected to be inserted behind enemy lines and they always anticipated the stiffest resistance, consequently their training was gruelling.

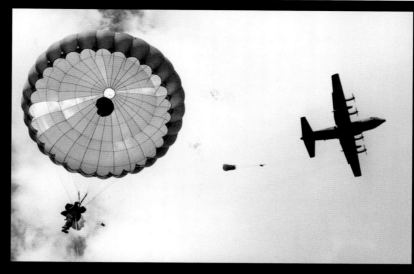

# D-Day Landings 1944

Among the Paras' most famous exploits were the landings in Normandy on D-Day. High winds scattered their formations and some were drowned in flooded country to the east of the landing beaches, but the remnants rallied in small groups and fought doggedly against German formations. At Merville Battery, a fortified German gun emplacement, Lieutenant Colonel Otway of 9 Para managed to gather just 150 of the original 650 assault group. His tiny force made an assault across a minefield and barbed wire directly into the German position. The German defence was determined, with massed machine gun fire and artillery and mortar fire. However, the Paras continued to press on, and, having blown open the doors of the casemates with explosives, they used grenades, rifles and bayonets in the hand-to-hand struggle. Eventually the German defences were entirely overcome at the cost of 65 killed and wounded.

A re-enactment of the D-Day invasion on the 50th anniversary.

A British Paratrooper in Iraq, securing a Landing Zone (LZ). Paras today are more frequently deployed from helicopters than by parachute.

The Lee Enfield rifle and the SA80 Individual Weapon and their associated ammunition, the .303 and 5.56 mm rounds. Air insertion and rapid deployment means that heavy weapon support has to be sacrificed and the Paras are therefore dependent on their speed and their own resources, including the weapons and ammunition they carry into battle.

behind enemy lines. German troops, who had experienced their tenacity in battle in North Africa, christened them 'Red Devils', a nickname that has stuck.

The uniform and equipment of the Paras were also distinctive. The 'denison smock' was more suitable for jumps than standard battledress, and they wore proudly their Para Wings and red berets – symbols that denoted both their ability to parachute into a war zone and their elite training. Paras were lightly equipped and had to operate without the sort of heavy weapon support enjoyed by ground units, but this also served to reinforce their ethos of self-reliance and the necessity for rapid, aggressive assaults.

The hardest fighting of the war for the Paras fell to the 1st Airborne Division at Arnhem, as they tried to secure the vital bridge across the Rhine. Meeting unexpected resistance, the Paras were isolated, and, although they briefly held one end of the bridge, they had to fight for nine days without support until gradually reduced to a pocket around Oosterbeek. The survivors were evacuated back across the Rhine. Although a reverse, the Paras once again established their reputation as a tough and aggressive force that could take tremendous punishment and yet retain both cohesion and fighting spirit. Urban combat, which characterized the regiment's fighting in September 1944, still forms a core component of today's training programmes.

After World War II, elements of the Paras served in Malaya (1954–57), in Suez (1956), and in the Indonesian Confrontation (1964–65). In each of these theatres, although there only relatively briefly, the Paras were able to deploy rapidly, carry out effective fighting patrols and assert themselves over their adversaries. At Plaman Mapu in Borneo in March 1965, B Company of 2 Para inflicted over 50 casualties in close-quarter fighting during the defence of their patrol base.

A very different approach was needed in the peacekeeping duties in Northern Ireland and tragically, on 'Bloody Sunday' in 1972, the Parachute Regiment opened fire on a crowd, killing 14 civilians. Personnel of the Paras have always maintained that they were targeted by gunmen on that day, but official enquiries have failed to confirm this either way. During the 'Troubles' the Paras lost 40 men to bombing and sniping attacks.

The Paras were a spearhead force in the Falklands Conflict of 1982 and distinguished themselves particularly at Goose Green. Colonel 'H' Jones was killed in the assault on Argentine positions, characteristically leading 'from

Top: A British Para in the Falklands on Sussex Mountain, prior to the Goose Green attack in 1982. After an eight-hour firefight, the Paras overwhelmed the Argentine troops in a close-quarter battle.

Above: The cap badge of the Paras, worn with their distinctive red berets.

the front' and was awarded the Victoria Cross. A second VC was won by Sergeant Ian Mackay at Mount Longdon when his patrol came under heavy machine gun fire. He led an assault under the very muzzles of the guns and destroyed the nest with grenades and rifle to save the lives of his comrades.

The Parachute Regiment was in Iraq in the first phase of Operation Telic, the British element of the overthrow of Saddam Hussein's regime in 2003. Their skills in peacekeeping were tested to the limit, while still retaining an instinct to react quickly to insurgent ambushes. In Afghanistan, the Paras were deployed in 2002 to assist in the ousting of the Taliban. In June 2006, they were tasked to drive the Taliban out of Helmand province in Operation Herrick. They found themselves under sustained attack, but inflicted heavy losses and were part of the operation that extended the control of Western forces and the Afghan government at Musa Qala and, in 2009, into the 'Green Zone' of central and southern Helmand. The Parachute Regiment thus maintains its long and formidable tradition of hard fighting, fully living up to its motto: *Utrinque Paratus* ('Ready for Anything').

# Panzerkorps Grossdeutschland
## The German Army's Foremost Armoured Formation

**G**rossdeutschland was the elite armored formation of the German army of World War II, but it was not until 1942 that it received its first tanks. Though it became the nucleus of a Panzer corps, Grossdeutschland kept its Panzergrenadier title to honour its infantry origins. The division's insignia remained a steel helmet in white – the infantry's branch colour. The roots of this elite formation lay in the Weimar Republic's Berlin Security Force. Renamed Wachregiment Berlin in 1934, in April 1939 it was expanded into a four-battalion regiment retitled Grossdeutschland (Greater Germany), drawing its personnel from throughout the Reich. Uniforms were army standard, the principal difference being a cuff band bearing the formation's name. But physical and educational requirements were stringent and training was rigorous. Equipment was ample and the best available, from machine pistols to some of the first assault guns.

The regiment first saw action in May 1940 as part of the armoured force that battered its way across the River Meuse. Its next major commitment came in June, when it participated in the final overrunning of France, reaching Lyons before being sent back to Paris for the victory parade. Now with an established reputation for tenacity in close combat and great skill in mobile war, Grossdeutschland was increased by a fifth battalion of light anti-aircraft guns, armoured cars, motorcyclists and pioneers, and by an artillery battalion.

## Key Dates

**1939**
Grossdeutschland Regiment is activated from Wachregiment Berlin.

**1940**
Battle of Stonne.

**1942**
Grossdeutschland is expanded to a motorized infantry division.

**1943, 23 June 23**
Redesignated Panzergrenadier Division Grossdeutschland, though it is organized and equipped as an elite panzer division.

**1943, August–December**
Earns nickname the 'Fire Brigade' for its performance in south Russia.

**1944**
Reinforced and reorganized as Panzerkorps Grossdeutschland.

Above: Oberst Karl Lorenz, in the foreground, was commander of the Grossdeutschland towards the end of World War II, between September 1944 and May 1945, when the tank corps was fighting its last actions – ultimately without tanks.

Opposite: Tiger (Panzer VI) tanks of the Panzergrenadier division Grossdeutschland in combat position near Jassy in northeastern Romania in 1944. This offensive saw ferocious fighting as the German army attempted to hold the Russian advance.

## Battle of Stonne 1940

Grossdeutschland established its elite status in its first action, at the French village of Stonne in 1940, where it faced two excellent French divisions desperately seeking to reach the German bridgeheads over the Meuse. Stonne changed hands 17 times between 15 and 17 May. Outnumbered and outgunned, Grossdeutschland prevailed, taking over 500 casualties in a battle compared by both sides to Verdun.

Grossdeutschland had a brief opportunity to settle into its new order of battle in Yugoslavia before joining Heinz Guderian's Panzer Group 2 for the invasion of Russia in June 1941.

### In action in Russia

In Russia Grossdeutschland further enhanced its reputation in the battle for the Minsk Pocket and the fighting for the Yelnya salient, where it took heavy losses from Red Army counterattacks. It accompanied Panzer Group 2 during the move south and the encirclement of Kiev, returning to the central front in October for Operation Typhoon, the final drive for Moscow. First mud, then freezing temperatures and heavy snows, slowed movement to a near standstill. As tank losses mounted, more of the burden fell on the infantry. Through October and November Grossdeutschland played a leading role in both attack and defence. With the full-scale Russian counterattack that began on 5 December, the regiment was split into detachments to reinforce vulnerable sectors.

The front held. But since the start of the campaign, Grossdeutschland had lost 900 killed and over 3,000 wounded. In the spring of 1942 Grossdeutschland was expanded to a larger motorized division: two regiments each of three infantry battalions, an assault gun battalion and its own tank battalion of medium Mark IVs, with the guarantee of more and better to come.

Beginning in June 1942, the reconfigured Grossdeutschland took part in Operation Blue, the Stalingrad campaign. It crossed the Don River, took Voronezh, and was then transferred north to meet the Soviet offensive around Rzhev, taking heavy losses. It suffered more when used as a 'fire brigade' against the northern sector of the Russian encirclement of Stalingrad itself. By the year's end Grossdeutschland's casualties amounted to almost 12,000.

Whether from faith or desperation, Grossdeutschland began 1943 by participating in the recapture of Rostov. Its reward was a few weeks in reserve, and re-equipment and reinforcement with half-tracked armoured personnel carriers, a second tank battalion, and a company of newly manufactured Tiger tanks. By this time the division's replacement of troops was drawn from across the spectrum of the Reich's depleted manpower. But a hard core of veterans remained to instruct newcomers on the honour of wearing Grossdeutschland's insignia, and on the customs of war in Russia.

In June Grossdeutschland was officially retitled a Panzergrenadier division. In July it was committed to the battle of Kursk. As part of 4th Panzer Army it

Members of the Grossdeutschland taking a short rest in the 'big bend' in the Don in July 1942 after the capture of Voronezh and before returning to action.

clawed its way through the layered Russian defence until the massive Soviet counterattack around Orel forced the cancellation of the German offensive. For the rest of the year Grossdeutschland played a key role in the German retreat from the Ukraine.

In the first half of 1944 Grossdeutschland remained the southern sector's 'fire brigade' of choice as the Russians drove through the Ukraine and into Romania. The division's high priority for replacements and equipment enabled it to maintain its strength and cohesion while other mobile formations shrank. By 1944 Grossdeutschland was stronger than most panzer divisions – army or SS – with an authorized strength of over 22,000 and over 200 medium and heavy tanks – Mark IVs, Panthers and Tigers.

## The end of the war

Transferred to the Baltic sector in July, Grossdeutschland fought to near extinction in East Prussia and around Memel against a Red Army whose numerical superiority was enhanced by increasing tactical sophistication. Evacuated by sea, Grossdeutschland became part of a new formation, *Panzerkorps Grossdeutschland*. In autumn 1944 an Army High Command seeking to economize manpower began creating permanent panzer corps: two stripped-down divisions with service and support troops concentrated at corps level. The organization was never completed and the corps never fought as an entity.

Grossdeutschland made its final attack in January 1945 as part of a quixotic effort to relieve the besieged city of Koenigsberg. Again pushed into a defensive pocket on the Baltic, it was ferried to Pillau at the end of March. The price was the division's vehicles. The army's foremost armoured formation spent the rest of its war fighting as infantry.

Opposite: The vanguard of a German tank corps on the Eastern Front in the Caucasian steppe in 1942. The tanks were alerted to the positions of the Soviet troops by radio messages from the Luftwaffe plane in the air above them.

# Soviet Shock Armies
## Fighting for Russia in World War II

The military elites of the Soviet Red Army of World War II conform only loosely to the usual definition of such forces. There were no large units manned by selective recruiting that required specialized training or equipment to perform their mission. The men wore no special uniforms or insignia, and were armed similarly to other, ordinary soldiers. There were units, however, that were given particular tasks and were sometimes augmented by additional fire support and received an individual title to make the men feel as though they had elite status. These were the five shock armies (*udarnye armii*), numbered one to five. Comprising mostly ordinary infantry brigades and divisions, often strengthened by extra artillery and tank brigades, their primary purpose – reminiscent of World War I shock troops – was to create breaches in the enemy's lines which follow-on forces could exploit to penetrate into the enemy rear.

The PPSh-41 (Pistolet-Pulemyot Shpagina) submachine gun, named after its designer, Georgi Shpagin. Produced in huge quantities, it became a standard weapon of the Red Army, being reliable and low maintenance. The drum magazine held 71 rounds.

### The First Shock Army

Four of the five shock armies were formed towards the end of 1941. The First was created in November 1941 by renaming and augmenting the already existing 19th Army. Its immediate task was to defeat the attack by the Germans on Moscow and throw them back, not only to save the city but also to prepare the way for a general counteroffensive. Having succeeded in the battle of Moscow in stopping the Germans, the First Shock Army's next major mission was the Demiansk Operation. Between January and March 1942, the Army broke the German lines and encircled nearly 100,000 enemy soldiers. However, the First Shock Army, along with the Third and Fourth, and two other 'regular' armies, ultimately failed to crush the Axis forces trapped in the 'Demiansk Pocket' and the German forces escaped. For the remainder of the war the First

Shock Army was assigned to the liberation of Leningrad and the re-conquest of the Baltic States.

## The Second and Third Shock Armies

The Second Shock Army was formed in December 1941 by renaming and strengthening the 26th Army. Throughout the war it was assigned to the northwest theatre of operations around Leningrad and the Baltic. It is most noted for the disastrous Liuban Operation – the spring offensive in 1942 to lift the siege of Leningrad. The initial advance by the Army succeeded in punching through the German lines, but as it progressed it became surrounded by a German counterattack. The Soviet high command refused to allow the Army to break out for two months. When it finally received permission to do so it was virtually annihilated in the attempt. As a result, its commander, General Andrei Vlasov, who felt that the Army had been abandoned, defected to the German side and agreed to form and become the leader of the Russian Liberation Army composed of Soviet soldiers who joined to fight against the Soviet Union. The Second Army was reformed and again destroyed and once more reconstituted later in the year. It ended the war participating on the north flank of the Berlin operation, but did not fight in the city.

The Third Shock Army was formed in December 1941 by renaming and reorganizing the 60th Army. Its first major operation was in January 1942 when

## Battle of Moscow 1941

The First Shock Army was formed in November 1941, first to stem the German attack on Moscow and then spearhead the counteroffensive to roll back the Nazis from the capital. In its first action in late November, the First Shock Army not only stopped the German advance on the city's northern flank, but also succeeded in throwing the enemy back across the Moscow-Volga Canal, ending the threat of encirclement from that direction. The First Shock Army then, in mid-December, along with two other armies, led the counteroffensive on Moscow's northern flank and broke through the German forces, forcing them to retreat nearly 32 km (20 miles). Later, in January, the First Shock Army resumed the offensive, pushing the Germans even further from Moscow in conjunction with a general offensive along the front north and south of Moscow in which the Third and Fourth Shock Armies also participated. By the end of January, Moscow was finally secured and the threat of capture by the Nazis permanently ended.

*Russian tanks and infantry advance in the snow in the battle of Moscow, 1941.*

Above: A poster of 1943 celebrating
the Russian counteroffensive against
the Germans following victories at
Stalingrad, in which the Fifth Shock
Army took part, and Kursk.

Above right: A famous image of a soldier
of the Third Shock Army raising the Soviet
flag over the Reichstag after the capture
of Berlin, 8 May 1945.

it spearheaded the breakthrough on the southern flank of the German defences
in the Demiansk Operation. Its drive took it all the way to Kholm, deep in the
German rear, which it encircled but ultimately failed to take. During the battle
it unsuccessfully defended the western approaches to the Demiansk Pocket,
yielding a corridor to relieving German forces into the pocket, and ultimately
allowing the besieged forces to escape. The remainder of the war saw the Third
Shock Army serving in northwest Russia, the Baltics – and eventually the battle
of Berlin. One of its soldiers hoisted the Soviet flag over the Reichstag during
the capture of Berlin.

### The Fourth and Fifth Shock Armies

The Fourth Shock Army was also formed in December 1941, from the basis of
the 27th Army. Its first major battle was fighting on the left flank of the Third
Shock Army in the battle for the Demiansk Pocket and Kholm. Thereafter the
Fourth Shock Army fought primarily in northwest Russia until being diverted
into Belorussia in 1944. Finally, in 1944 and 1945 the Fourth Shock Army helped
push the Germans out of the Baltic States and besieged the Nazi forces in
Courland, but was unable to crush them.

'No imagination can recreate what was happening in the Valley of Death. A continuous wall of fire, unceasing howling and roaring, a stupefying stench of burnt human flesh ... and thousands of people rushing into this fiery corridor. We all thought that it would be better to die in fire than be captured by the Germans.' E. Klimchuk, 1990

Above: A Soviet victory medal with the head of Stalin, which was issued to all soldiers after the war. The inscription reads: 'Our cause was just, Victory is ours'.

Below: A Russian offensive on the northwest front (3rd and 4th Armies). Soldiers of the Red Army clamber up the banks of the Lovat River after crossing it with boats, around March 1942.

The Fifth Shock Army was the last to be formed, being created in December 1942 on the basis of the reconstituted 10th Reserve Army. Its first action was in the battle of Stalingrad where it fought in the successful counteroffensive that surrounded the German Sixth Army in the city. Driving back German and Axis forces southwest, away from Stalingrad, it forestalled and then defeated relief efforts. Its next campaign was in the Don basin where it participated in the eviction of German forces from that part of southern Russia in early 1943. It then fought in the liberation of the Ukraine in 1943 and 1944. The Fifth Shock Army's wartime service culminated in the forcing of the Oder River and marching on Berlin alongside the Third Shock Army. It ended the war fighting in the suburbs of the German capital.

In the end, the shock armies performed and fared the same as ordinary Soviet armies. Their rate of success at breaking through enemy lines using shock action was equal to similar types of formations. Being given command of a shock army was not considered a special honour, and few commanders stayed at the helm for more than a few months. The first four shock armies were concentrated in the north and all participated to some degree in the attempts to relieve the siege of Leningrad. The most successful shock army was the Fifth, which fought in south Russia and the Ukraine. There the Soviets committed the bulk of their resources and reaped the rewards accordingly.

# American 'Top Gun' Pilots of the Korean War
## Jet Air Aces Battle for Air Superiority

Of all the military elites, few have received more attention than successful fighter pilots, specifically the aces – those credited with downing five or more enemy aircraft. During the Korean War, of the 433 American fighter pilots credited with aerial victories, only 40 achieved ace status – 39 flying jet fighters, and the last a Navy night pilot on a prop-powered aircraft. Many of these men had flown in World War II – 58 had scored victories in that war, 21 of whom were aces. The most notable was probably Francis Gabreski, the top-scoring US fighter pilot in Europe (with 28 credits), who added 5.5 Korean War credits to his victory log. He was one of eight who achieved ace status in both wars. Since the Korean War saw the largest number of air-to-air actions since World War II, clearly that conflict's aces form an elite within an elite.

The 'uniform' of the American aces was similar to that of the World War II flyers – simply a flying suit. The two major advances were the adoption of an anti-gravity ('g'-) suit (just coming into use towards the end of World War II) and the hard flight (more commonly called 'crash') helmet fitted with an oxygen mask. In contrast, the pilots of the opposing Communist forces lacked both the 'g'-suit and the helmet, wearing instead soft leather headgear.

### Opposing fighters

The Korean War broke out in June 1950, and after initial setbacks the United Nations saw successes in the autumn. However, victory was thwarted by the massive intervention of Chinese Communist forces in November 1950, crucially including the introduction of Soviet MiG-15 fighters, which were on the cutting edge of aviation technology and markedly superior to the UN's jet- and prop-powered aircraft. The MiGs drew first blood in early November and forced the US to respond with new equipment. In mid-December the North American F-86 Sabre, the West's best fighter, entered combat, scoring its first victory and sustaining its first loss. This jet air war raged for the next two and a half years.

1950, 25 June
North Korea invades South Korea, initiating the Korean War.

1950, 1 November
First appearance of the MiG-15, attacking a formation of UN aircraft but inflicting no damage.

1950, 8 November
First MiG claim by 1st Lt Russell Brown flying an F-80.

1950, 5 December
First F-86 Sabre combat mission.

1950, 17 December
First American jet claim by LTC Bruce Hinton flying an F-86.

1950, 22 December
First F-86 lost in combat to a MiG-15, Capt Lawrence Bach is shot down and captured; he survives captivity.

1951, 20 May
Captain James Jabara claims and is credited with two MiG-15s to become the first American ace (a total of six credits) of the war.

1953, 18 May
Captain Joseph McConnell destroys three MiG-15s, bringing his total to 16, the highest scoring American ace in the war.

1953, 27 July
Captain Ralph Parr downs a Il-12, the last American aerial claim of the war, and his 10th credit of the war, hours before a truce brings the conflict to an end.

Opposite above: The F-86 could turn quicker and dive faster than the MiG-15, while the Russian fighter had a higher ceiling and better rate of climb. The American pilots also had the advantage of 'g'-suits and more accurate radar-ranging gunsights. Most significant to the American victory, however, were the better-trained pilots.

Opposite below: The MiG-15 was a Soviet fighter designed to intercept and combat American strategic bombers. Using a British designed engine, the aircraft surprised the world with its performance, which was superior to all western fighters with the possible exception of the F-86 Sabre.

Takeoff of an F-86 of 51st Fighter Group in June 1953. This was the second Sabre air superiority unit to fight in Korea.

# The First MiG Credit by an F-86 in the Korean War 1950

Led by LTC Bruce Hinton, a flight of four F-86s took off from Kimpo airfield on 17 December 1950. The newly arrived Sabres concealed their identity by mimicking the radio traffic and flying performance of the much less capable F-80. They spotted four MiG-15s below, dropped their wing tanks and dived on the hostile fighters. Hinton opened fire on the second MiG-15, observed hits, closed to 240 m (800 ft) and saw smoke, flame and pieces streaming from the aircraft's fuselage. Although the MiG was not observed to crash, the Air Force awarded Hinton credit for its destruction, the first of over 800 American MiG credits in the Korean War.

The two opposing fighters, the American F-86 and Communist MiG-15, were both swept wing and jet powered, with nose intakes. The American fighter could dive faster and was more stable at higher speeds, but being heavier had inferior acceleration, rate of climb and ceiling performance compared with the Soviet fighter. The F-86 was armed with six 0.50-calibre machine guns that had a superior gunsight and higher rate of fire, but less punch than the MiG's armament of one 37 mm and two 23 mm cannons. Although the Americans improved the F-86, it was at best the equivalent of the MiG.

Measured in aerial victories and losses the Korean air war was much smaller than World War II: in the former, F-86 pilots were awarded credits for 866 aerial victories compared with 15,800 Army Air Forces (AAF) credits in the latter, and 39 American jet aces compared with 692 AAF aces. But Korea was the first and the largest jet-versus-jet fighter campaign of all time. Russian fighter units, and later Chinese and North Korean units, slugged it out against a relatively small number of mostly USAF pilots. In the battle for air superiority the Sabres and their pilots established a special place in history by downing more aircraft than any other jet fighter. This is the more remarkable since the Communists had the advantage of numbers, combat close to their bases, radar support and in theory a sanctuary, in addition to the MiG's slight performance superiority over the F-86.

Nevertheless, the American forces won a decisive victory, due primarily to the quality of the Sabre pilots. The first American jet ace was James Jabara who downed his fifth (and sixth) MiG in April 1951. He returned for a second tour in 1953 and added nine more victories to end the war as the second highest scoring American with 15 credits. Top honours went to Joseph McConnell who tallied

16 credits. Success in air-to-air combat requires a number of factors, but one key element is aggressiveness. Whereas Communist pilots were considered unaggressive and in many cases described as students, American pilots were eager for combat, perhaps to a fault. They engaged in a number of practices that made them both more effective and more vulnerable. One technique used by a number of pilots to maximize flying time depended on exploiting the prevailing westerly winds and the Sabre's gliding ability to enable them to get back to base without engine power after exhausting their fuel. This was successful most, but not all of the time. Another practice was to penetrate into Chinese air space and hunt Communist aircraft in their own, supposedly inviolate territory, in some cases over their airfields, despite the hazards and the rules of engagement. These intrusions ran up American victory scores, demoralized Communist pilots, and maintained UN initiative and air superiority.

# 'The second MiG manoeuvered towards me and I found myself about 1,000 feet from him looking right down his gun barrels as he blazed away at me.' Cecil Foster (9 credits)

## Victory in the air

As with aces in other wars, those of the Korean War had a disproportionate impact on the aerial battle. The 39 Korean war jet aces represented perhaps 3 per cent of the F-86 pilots who saw air-to-air combat in Korea and 9 per cent of those who scored victories, yet went on to post 35 per cent of the total victory credits. In achieving this total the USAF admits to the loss of 78 F-86s in air-to-air combat, with another 26 Sabres listed as lost to unknown causes. According to American (USAF) figures, the F-86s achieved an 8 to 1 victory to loss ratio over the MiGs. The Communists dispute these figures, asserting that they downed some 800 to 900 F-86s, about 70 per cent at the hands of Russian pilots. The Communists claim that some 43 to 60 Soviet, 6–9 Chinese, and 2–4 North Korean pilots achieved ace status. The top Soviet aces were Evgeny Pepelyaev with 15 to 20 victories and Nikola Sutyagin with 21 credits, of which 15 were F-86s.

Whatever the exact figures, which probably will never be settled, the impact of these few Sabre pilots was clear and profound: the UN had air superiority and the air-to-air battle was fought deep in North Korea, over Communist territory, far from the ground front lines. Although other factors in the air-to-air battle essentially offset one another, the training, experience, aggressiveness and abilities of the Sabre pilots were the most important elements in achieving aerial victory and air superiority. Victory in the air battle was one of the few bright spots for UN forces in the Korean War and gave them a huge advantage. Air superiority allowed the massive use of air power: the reconnaissance, close air support, interdiction and air transport that provided a major boost to UN ground forces. This assistance increased Communist casualties as it reduced UN casualties. Therefore the Sabre pilots' contribution, especially that of the aces, certainly made a difference in the final outcome.

Opposite: Captain Joseph McConnell stands on the wing of his Sabre with helmet in hand and wearing both parachute and life vest. He needed the last two when he was forced to bail out into the Yellow Sea; he was rescued and went on to become the leading American ace of the conflict with 16 credits.

Below: John Glenn, future astronaut and US senator, was one of a number of Marines on exchange duty who flew USAF F-86s. Glenn's Sabre was appropriately painted with three stars under the cockpit, indicating his three aerial victories.

# The SAS and SBS
## Who Dares Wins

Above: The SAS winged badge with the famous motto 'Who Dares Wins' – symbols recognized throughout the British armed forces, and the world, as the epitome of an elite fighting force.

**T**he Special Air Service or SAS is regarded as the *corps d'elite* of the British army and perhaps the pre-eminent Special Forces organization in the world. Its selection process and training are among the most demanding, but this merely reflects the extreme nature of the operational duties it has to perform. Designed for insertion deep behind enemy lines, the SAS collect intelligence, carry out raids and sabotage, and train local insurgent forces. They are also tasked with counter-terrorism, both in the United Kingdom and overseas, but the precise nature of their work is never discussed publicly. The SBS carry out similar functions, but are more closely linked with the Royal Marines and Royal Navy.

The SAS were formed by Lt Col. David Stirling during in World War II in July 1941 to carry out raids on Axis convoys and bases in the North African desert. The reference to 'Air' in the name reflected an expectation that insertion from the air could be one of their modes of deployment, but in fact a variety of methods was used to get behind enemy lines. Driving deep behind the lines in North Africa in adapted jeeps, the men were expected to be entirely self-reliant and to cause maximum disruption to German forces. In 1943, A Squadron was re-designated Special Raiding Squadron (SRS) for service in Sicily, while B Squadron became the Special Boat Squadron (later changed to 'Service') and was deployed to the Aegean. In April that year, a 2nd

Above: Malaya 1953, a British SAS team is dropped off in the jungle by helicopter to counter CTs (Communist Terrorists). The SAS ambushes required total self-reliance, painstaking endurance and great courage.

Right: The famous 'Pink Panther' combat vehicle has now been superseded, but its colour proved remarkably effective as camouflage in the desert.

Opposite below: Armed with an M16 assault rifle, this SAS trooper forms part of the vanguard of the UK's assault ability. Speed, stealth and ruthless efficiency and aggression are the hallmarks of the SAS in combat, but they are also experts in living off the land, befriending locals to build up auxiliary forces, intelligence gathering and great mobility.

SAS Regiment was raised and also fought in the Mediterranean theatre. In 1944, SRS and 2nd SAS were united under Lt Col. Paddy Mayne to form the SAS Brigade, fighting in France, the Low Countries, Germany and Scandinavia until their disbandment at the end of the war.

In 1946, the SAS were reformed as a Territorial Army unit known as the 21 SAS (Artists') Regiment, a title subsequently shortened to 21 SAS, but the escalation of the Malayan Emergency meant that a party of volunteers from 21 SAS, augmented by a selected group of regular soldiers called the Malayan Scouts, were formed into a new regular force called 22 SAS in 1952. In 1959, a second Territorial SAS Regiment, 23 SAS (TA), was raised and combined in the early

The SAS in Malaya evacuating one of their own injured team members. The SAS pride themselves on their resilience and toughness, whatever the conditions; small, close-knit teams are able to achieve results out of all proportion to their size and strength.

SPECIAL AIR SERVICE REGIMENT

Above: Badge worn by all members of the SAS in World War II.

Below: The SAS Wings, awarded on completion of the SAS parachute training.

'The relentless pursuit of excellence; ... strict discipline; ... there must be no sense of class, only merit counts; ... humility; ... humour.'
Brigadier Stirling's principles for the SAS, 1941

1960s with a Headquarters SAS Group and two signals squadrons. Eventually all UK Special Forces, including the Royal Marines' SBS (Special Boat Service), have come under the direction of the SAS HQ.

There are various specialisms across the SAS, but each operational troop, part of the 'Sabre' Squadrons, consists of small teams that have a balance of individuals with particular skills, such as demolitions or signals. The SBS have similar structures, but often focus on coastal operations. Given the need to be inserted behind enemy lines, personnel have to be proficient in mountain warfare, parachuting, waterborne deployment and all forms of transport, and specialized troops are established for different environments. The stealthy entry methods are attended by great risk: the HALO (High Altitude, Low Opening) parachute jump for example, requires the SAS trooper to free fall until just 600 m (2,000 ft) from the ground, while helicopter insertions might entail an abseil from the aircraft into a jungle canopy or leaping into the sea from 15 m (50 ft) above the water.

Special Forces around the world have modelled themselves on the SAS. The New Zealand SAS were formed during the Malayan Emergency, while C Squadron SAS went on to become the Rhodesian 1st SAS Regiment until its disbandment in 1980. The 1st Australian SAS Company (later the Australian SAS regiment or SASR) was formed in 1957 and went on to fight in Borneo and in Vietnam. The SASR and SAS have served together in Bosnia and in the Iraq War, and both co-operate closely with US Special Forces. However, the SAS is capable of independent operations, as they proved in the Dhofar Insurgency in southern Oman in the 1970s, and in the Falklands Conflict of 1982. In Dhofar, the SAS assisted not just in fighting

# Iranian Embassy Siege, London 1980

One of the most celebrated and professional insertions took place on 5 May 1980 against a terrorist group which had taken over the Iranian Embassy in central London. A number of hostages were taken, one of whom was shot dead during the negotiations. In Operation Nimrod, the SAS were called in to seize the building, neutralize the terrorists and rescue the hostages. Using detailed plans and rehearsing the assault in a nearby barracks, the SAS used explosives to break through the bulletproof glass and abseiled through windows or jumped through roof entry points. Five of the six terrorists were killed; one was captured masquerading as a hostage. Only one civilian was lost in the operation. The assault proved to be an inspiration to counter-terrorist forces around the globe and established a magnificent reputation for the SAS.

The Iranian Embassy siege, London: hostages were rescued with textbook efficiency.

Below: Abseiling into action, from buildings or helicopters, typifies the SAS reputation for rapid and stealthy insertion, followed by explosive aggression, engaging the enemy with a great range of weapons systems.

rebel 'Adoo' guerrillas, but also trained local security forces and established bases deep inside rebel-held territory. Small detachments found themselves having to hold off large-scale rebel attacks, but they provided cover while development schemes and political reforms were carried out behind them.

In the Falklands, the SAS made a textbook raid on Argentine ground-attack aircraft at Pebble Island on 14 May 1982 and acted as the spearhead of infantry operations, calling in air strikes and providing vital battlefield intelligence. As befitting their clandestine role, little of their work was ever broadcast. The flurry of books in the 1990s, a combination of both factual memoirs and fictional works, was eventually brought to an end with special disclosure terms, but they did no harm to the reputation of the force. The SAS and SBS both operate in Afghanistan and have taken part in raids on Taliban headquarters, and are reportedly much feared by insurgents.

The permanent staff of the SAS consists of soldiers and NCOs, the officers being lent on attachment. The return of SAS officers to their units has fast-tracked their promotion – for example, General Sir Peter de la Billière served as General Officer Commanding British forces in the First Gulf War (1990–91), and General Sir Charles Guthrie became the Chief of the General Staff. However, every member of 'The Regiment', regardless of rank, wears their sand-coloured beret and cap badge with considerable pride. The flaming sword Excalibur, sometimes referred to as a 'winged dagger', is adorned with the famous and apt motto, 'Who Dares Wins'.

# The US Navy SEALs
## Sea, Air and Land: Amphibious Commando Force

The Special Warfare insignia, also known as the SEAL Trident (or more popularly 'The Budweiser'), consisting of a golden eagle clutching a US Navy anchor, trident and pistol.

**I**n World War II the large number of complex amphibious operations conducted by the US Navy posed a whole new set of challenges. To land entire divisions on a defended enemy shore required a careful intelligence analysis of beach conditions and fortifications. Since most defended beaches were protected by a belt of underwater obstacles designed to rip the bottoms out of landing craft, in order to land forces safely on a beach the attacking force would have to clear lanes through them in advance. Without good intelligence and obstacle clearance, amphibious operations would probably fail. And even if the landings still succeeded, they might only be at the cost of excessive casualties. Here was a problem that required a solution.

The US Navy's answer to the dilemma was to create a specially trained force that could use the new technology of small inflatable boats and underwater breathing apparatus (the forerunner of today's scuba equipment) to sneak quietly ashore to gather intelligence before the landing, or to destroy the underwater obstacles immediately before the main forces landed. Such units

Above: The Colt M16 automatic rifle is a lightweight assault weapon; this one is mounted with an M203 grenade launcher. SEALs are expert in a wide variety of US and foreign weapons.

Right: The Heckler & Koch MP5K submachine gun was designed for close-quarters battle use by clandestine operations and special services. It is not used by US regular forces, but SEALs are equipped with many specialist arms.

Above: SEAL team members participating in tactical warfare training. Becoming a SEAL today requires more than a year of intensive training, during which most applicants are 'washed out'.

would have to operate with stealth and in small teams. Because they might face enemy defenders, they had to be able to fight as soldiers with light weapons. Because they operated from small boats and often swam to the objective, they had to be superb small boat handlers and swimmers. Because their primary job was to blast a path through obstacles, they had to be expert in demolitions.

## Underwater Demolition Teams

In June 1943 the US Navy began training its first Underwater Demolition Teams (UDTs) in such skills. From the first, the UDTs were designed to be an elite force. Volunteers were accepted from the army and navy, and the initial weeks of training were designed to weed out all but the toughest and hardiest individuals. UDTs were then given extensive training in demolitions and small boats, and were organized into companies of 16 officers and 80 men. The companies were further organized into smaller assault teams that would be responsible for clearing a particular sector of a landing beach.

The UDTs were first used in support of the landing at Kwajalein Atoll, part of the Republic of the Marshall Islands, in January 1944, and were a great success. Unable to get their small boats over the reef, the UDTs left them behind and swam in close to bring back accurate intelligence of the Japanese beach defences. From that time on, all the major landings in the Central Pacific were preceded by UDTs. By the time of the Okinawa campaign in April 1945, the US

On 13 April 1945 a formidable Allied amphibious landing took place at a beachhead at Okinawa, preceded by UDTs to clear the obstacles ahead of the larger craft and to reconnoitre and gather intelligence. Okinawa was the biggest operation of World War II for the UDTs, the predecessors of the SEALs.

Navy would employ more than 800 UDT sailors in support of the Marine and army landings – this was the biggest UDT operation of World War II.

In Europe the UDTs played a vital role in the D-Day landings in Normandy in June 1944. Teams went ashore at both Utah and Omaha beaches to blast gaps through the extensive German beach defences. At Omaha Beach the UDT sailors managed to open 13 lanes for landing craft through the German obstacles, but at a price of more than 50 per cent casualties for the 175 UDT men deployed.

After World War II the UDTs were almost all demobilized, but the force was employed again during the Korean War (1950–53). During this war the UDTs carried out their usual missions, but they also added commando training and techniques to their repertoire of small-boat skills and emphasis on swimming. Trained in stealth and explosives handling, the UDTs executed raids all along the North Korean coast, coming ashore at night and blasting essential rail lines and tunnels and coastal installations. Another mission they took on in this region was the training of the South Korean Navy's UDTs.

## Battle of Mogadishu
### 1993

Several SEALs were part of the US Special Forces raiding team that took part in a dramatic battle in Mogadishu on 3–4 October 1993. The operation, also referred to as 'Black Hawk Down', was against Somali militias and their warlord. In the course of the action, two US Black Hawk helicopters were shot down and many of the American raiding force were trapped, taking heavy casualties before the team was rescued. The Somali guerrillas, as well as civilians, suffered hundreds of casualties.

A still from the film *Black Hawk Down* highlights the fact that, although they are Navy SEALs, the teams can undertake multiple roles and types of operation.

US Navy SEALs on a night mission to capture Iraqi insurgent leaders on 27 July 2007, near Fallujah, Iraq. In the current conflicts against terrorist and insurgent groups around the world, a vital SEAL mission is to target key terrorist leaders.

## The next evolution

Now firmly a part of the naval force, the next evolution of the UDTs was their designation as SEALs in 1961. SEAL is an acronym for SEaAirLand, which fitted the navy's requirement that the force's members would be equally capable of fighting at sea and on land, and could also be trained to parachute into battle. Like the old UDTs, the SEALs remain a volunteer force and receive more than a year of specialist training as demolition experts, small boat handlers, scuba divers, light infantry soldiers and paratroopers. The training is both physically and mentally demanding, and is regarded as among the toughest anywhere. The SEALs became, and are today still recognized as, one of the top commando forces in the world.

The SEALs served in Vietnam between 1962 and 1970. Their first mission was to train the South Vietnamese Navy commandos, but their main focus became the 'brown river' operations through the Mekong Delta. As experts in small-boat war and fighting at night, the small navy SEAL teams carried out raids and ambushes in Viet Cong-held areas and became feared as a very lethal anti-guerrilla force.

Following the Vietnam War the SEALs were brought under the Special Operations Command, which incorporates the elite branches of the US navy, army and air force, and they continue in their role as special reconnaissance and commando forces. Navy SEALs have served in all American conflicts since the 1980s. Today the US navy has more than 1,000 SEALs organized into 15 teams. All the US fleets have SEAL teams at sea, ready to carry out a variety of unconventional operations that range from training host nation forces to fighting pirates along the Somali coasts. Most recently, SEALs saw action in Afghanistan and Iraq's Al Anbar province, one of the toughest regions in the guerrilla war in Iraq. In Iraq, the SEALs also carried out successful raids against terrorist headquarters and leaders and were responsible for the successful capture of one of the top al-Qaeda leaders there in 2009.

A team of Navy SEALs
operating in Afghanistan
in support of Operation
Enduring Freedom against
al-Qaeda and the Taliban.
SEAL teams conducted
special reconnaissance
missions in caves used by
terrorists, capturing many
fighters and destroying
huge quantities of enemy
weapons and explosives.

'They're the titans. They're impossible men doing an impossible job, and they did the impossible with me ... They're at the point of the sword every day, doing an impossible job every day.'

Ship's Captain Richard Phillips, rescued by US Navy SEALs from Somali pirates, 2009

# The Green Berets
## The US Army Special Forces

**T**he US Army special forces have their origin in World War II, when several units were set up with the mission of organizing and training partisan groups fighting in occupied countries or carrying out reconnaissance deep behind enemy lines. In the European theatre 15-man teams of specially trained soldiers, called Jedburgh Teams, were inserted into occupied France to help the French Resistance forces and lead them in sabotage missions and in collecting intelligence against the Wehrmacht. In the summer of 1944 resistance forces led by Jedburgh Teams destroyed hundreds of rail bridges and helped cripple the

'I will maintain myself, my arms, and my equipment in an immaculate state as befits a Special Forces soldier. I will never surrender though I be the last. If I am taken, I pray that I may have the strength to spit upon my enemy. My goal is to succeed in any mission — and live to succeed again.' Special Forces Creed

**1942**
The Office of Special Services (OSS) begins organizing special groups to operate behind Axis lines. These become known as Jedburgh Teams or 'OGs' (Operational Groups).

**1944**
19 Jedburgh Teams deployed to France support French Resistance operations.

**1944–45**
OSS Detachment 101 leads a force of Kachin tribesmen behind Japanese lines in northern Burma that grows to nearly 11,000 men.

**1952**
US Army allocates 2,500 men to the Special Forces. In June the 10th Special Forces Group is formed.

**1961–73**
Special Forces serve in Vietnam.

**1991**
Special Forces are deployed in support of the Gulf War in Iraq.

**2001**
Green Berets are the first Western forces into Afghanistan and play a central role in defeating the Taliban government.

**2003**
Special forces serve in Iraq to train Iraqi security forces.

Above: An exercise in combat surface swimming and marsh ambush. Special forces soldiers must be certified in two or three specialist skills. The teams often operate independently and far from the main force, so a range of skills within each team ensures that they can carry out their mission, even in the harshest conditions.

Opposite: US Green Berets in training at Fort Bragg, illustrating five of the specialist skills and areas of operation of paratroopers of the special forces (left to right): combat, high flight, mountain, underwater and forest.

Germans' ability to move supplies and troops to the Normandy front. The Teams also conducted raids and ambushes to disrupt German communications and the 19 Jedburgh Teams in France killed more than 900 Wehrmacht soldiers for the loss of only seven of their own.

The Jedburgh Teams that worked for the Office of Special Services (OSS), the forerunner of the CIA, required a special kind of soldier – highly trained in military skills and able to operate as part of a small team cut off from the regular support resources of the army. The teams were usually inserted behind the lines and supplied by airdrop. To function effectively, the soldiers had to have a variety of skills and also needed to know the language of the country they were operating in. In every way, these highly independent soldiers proved their worth.

Although most of the regular US army disdained such irregular soldiers, post-war Chief of Staff General Dwight Eisenhower saw their value and made sure that a small cadre of special forces was kept in the army organization. During the Korean War the value of small teams who could operate behind enemy lines became clear, and the Army Special Forces as we know them today began to take shape.

In 1952 the US army set aside 2,500 personnel slots for the special forces and organized the 10th Special Forces Group. The green beret, often worn unofficially in the 1950s, was made official and the special forces became known as 'Green Berets'. The essence of the special forces soldier was established at this time and has not changed dramatically since. All Green Berets are volunteers, normally junior NCOs who already have a good record in the infantry or Airborne. Parachute qualified, many also go through the rigorous Ranger training. All special forces soldiers have training in a primary skill, as well as a secondary one such as medicine, heavy weapons, communications

In July 1964 Special Forces A Team 726, under the command of Captain Roger Donlon, was assigned to the village of Nam Dong in central Thua Thieu province. The team organized a local defence force for the 5,000 Montagnard villagers. On 6 July 1964 a Viet Cong battalion attacked Nam Dong under cover of a massive mortar barrage. The Viet Cong fought their way through the first line of camp defences; Captain Donlon, although wounded, helped the Montagnard defence force and his team to retreat without heavy losses to the inner stronghold. Despite heavy fire and enemy attacks all night, the camp's inner stronghold held out against superior forces and the Viet Cong withdrew from the battle the next day. The Viet Cong had hoped for a great propaganda victory in overrunning a Montagnard camp. Instead, special forces had shown that the Viet Cong could be defeated.

or demolitions. Fort Bragg, North Carolina, became the centre of the Army Special Forces and remains so today. Green Beret soldiers are normally assigned to special forces groups, brigade-size organizations that operate in a particular region of the world. In addition to military training, each special forces soldier is therefore normally trained in one or two foreign languages common to his group's assigned geographic area.

In 1961, with the Kennedy administration's interest in counter-insurgency warfare and with the increased commitment of the US in Vietnam and Laos, the special forces were enlarged and reorganized. As in World War II, the special forces normally operated in 10–15 man teams and were deployed to remote areas, leading the local defence forces against the Viet Cong and North Vietnamese forces. Thousands of Montagnard villagers were organized into defence forces by the Green berets. At an epic battle at Nam Dong Camp in July 1964, Captain Roger Donlon won the Medal of Honor for holding out against a major Viet Cong attack. With actions such as these, the Green Berets soon became the most famous of the US forces in Vietnam. To meet the requirements of the war there the Green Berets were increased to over 10,000 men by 1966. The Green Berets served in Vietnam from 1961 to 1973.

After Vietnam, numbers of Green Berets were dramatically cut back, but small special forces detachments were especially useful in training allied indigenous forces facing insurgents in El Salvador and other Central American countries. Through the 1980s Green Berets served as the cutting edge of the US military in helping small allied nations meet unconventional threats.

In the Gulf War of 1991 the Green Berets, with their language and training expertise, served very effectively as liaison teams to support allied Arab forces in the war against Iraq. From 1992 to 1994 they were part of the US forces in Somalia supporting UN peacekeepers facing opposition from the Somali militias. In late 2001 the Green Berets won worldwide attention when special forces teams were deployed in Afghanistan to support the Afghani Northern Alliance forces fighting the Taliban government that had provided support and shelter to the al-Qaeda terrorists who attacked America on 11 September 2001.

Opposite: Green Berets abseiling from a helicopter. Special Forces soldiers are trained to operate behind enemy front lines and in isolated areas – they can be inserted by parachute, helicopter or small boat.

Below: US Army Special Forces MK 44 Minigun in use on patrol in Iraq in 2007.

Special forces soldiers wearing Afghani garb and riding horses fought with America's Afghani allies and called in US air strikes that devastated the Taliban forces. Within weeks the Taliban were routed and the Northern Alliance took control in Kabul. From 2001 on, the Green Berets have played a key role in the NATO campaign in Afghanistan by training Afghani government soldiers, a role they have also fulfilled with the Iraqi security forces since 2003. Special forces teams have also been working with the Philippine armed forces since 2001 to help counter the Islamic insurgency in the southern Philippines.

As the Western nations face a wide variety of unconventional threats, the Green Berets are more important than ever. Today there are approximately 20,000 Green Berets in the US army.

# India's National Security Guard
## The Black Cats

*I*ndia's National Security Guard (NSG) was established in 1984 in the wake of the assassination of Indian Prime Minister Indira Gandhi. Modelled along the lines of the British SAS and the German GSG-9, the unit is responsible for taking on all anti-terrorism roles in the country. Its mandate is broad, including anti-hijacking operations and hostage rescue, as well as counter-terrorism support for state and central police forces.

The unit is divided into two formations: the Special Action Group (SAG), with recruits drawn from the army, and the Special Ranger Group (SRG), with recruits drawn from federal and state level paramilitary and police units. The NSG training centre is a large complex in Manesar, Haryana, 50 km (31 miles) from the capital, Delhi. Hand-picked from thousands of applicants, volunteers undergo a gruelling 12-week basic training course involving a remorseless routine of physical and mental challenges – the obstacle course is reported to be among the world's toughest. The drop-out rate is high and some have died during the arduous training regimen. Those who make it through are awarded the coveted commando *balidan* (sacrifice) badge at the end. On graduation NSG commandos are assigned partners with whom they continue to train and with whom they take leave. The basic combat unit, called a *hit*, has five members – two partner pairs and a technical support member. Four *hits* form an NSG Team commanded by a captain. In order to maintain the youth profile of the NSG, all commandos are rotated back to their home units after a maximum of five years in the NSG. Throughout their duration of service, the commandos undergo constant proficiency training. For two months each year the commandos are

## Operation Black Tornado
### 2008

In 2008, the Black Cats engaged in one of their most important operations when they confronted the well-trained and equipped Pakistani terrorists who launched unprecedented multiple urban assaults against the Indian commercial capital of Mumbai on 26 November. The NSG arrived on 27 November and took on the terrorists at three different locations in the city. After 48 hours, the commandos had eliminated eight terrorists (one was captured) for the loss of two of their own.

An NSG commando abseiling from a helicopter on to the rooftop of Nariman House at Colaba Market in Mumbai.

Commandos of the National Security
Guard (NSG) stand in formation at the
inauguration in June 2009 of the Mumbai
Hub, one of the new regional centres for
the NSG to ensure their ability to act as an
effective strike force throughout India.

**'The result-oriented
action of the NSG
with successes on
more fronts than
one will reverberate
in the corridors
of time.'**

N. P. S. Aulakh, Director General of
the Indian National Security Guard, on
Operation Black Tornado, Mumbai, 2008

assigned to alert status, during which they have to maintain a target strike rate
of 85 per cent in shooting drills to remain in the force. Much of this shooting
practice consists of having to take out moving targets in minimal lighting
conditions. In order to simulate battle conditions, commandos have to stand
next to targets being shot at by their partners.

Among the NSG's famous operations are Operation Black Thunder I and II
to flush out Khalistani militants from the Sikh Golden Temple complex in
Amritsar in 1986 and 1988; Operation Ashwamedh in 1983 to rescue hostages
from a plane hijacked by Islamic terrorists; and Operation Vajra Shakti in 2002
to free hostages from the Akshardham temple in Ahmedabad, Gujarat. The unit
has also engaged in major counter-terrorism operations in Jammu and Kashmir
since 1998. Through these actions, the NSG became known to the Indian public
as the 'Black Cats' due to their black combat fatigues and helmets. In 2008 the
Black Cats emerged into the global spotlight when they confronted Pakistani
terrorists in Mumbai. The Mumbai Operation (Black Tornado) made it clear that
the single location for the NSG was too restrictive for instant deployment to
different parts of the country. In 2008 the Indian government decided to set up
regional centres in Mumbai, Bangalore, Calcutta and Hyderabad, ensuring that
the NSG remains the premier Indian anti-terrorist strike force throughout India.

# Glossary

**atlatl** Spearthrower or throwing stick – a length of wood which formed an extension of the arm and thus gave the spear or dart greater thrust, used for instance by Aztec warriors.

**arquebus** An early type of smoothbore, muzzle-loading gun (15th to 17th century), usually supported on a tripod or other rest; smaller than a musket.

**artillery** Weapons for firing projectiles long distances with some form of propulsion, such as cannon, field guns, howitzers or mortars.

**assegai** A short thrusting or stabbing spear with wooden shaft and broad metal blade used by the Zulu impis.

**aventail** Skirt or curtain of chainmail attached to the back and sides of a helmet to protect the neck and face.

**battalion** A body or unit of troops for battle, made up of several companies.

**bayonet** A pointed metal blade or spike fitted to the muzzle of a rifle or musket, for use in close hand-to-hand fighting.

**brigade** A formation within an army, comprising a group of regiments or battalions and organized into units, the precise formation varying through history and the army in question.

**busby** A military headdress or hat made of fur, originally with a cloth flap hanging down one side and often topped with a plume, associated with hussars and artillerymen.

**calibre** The diameter or bore of the interior of a gun barrel and hence of the shell or bullet fired from it.

**carbine** A firearm similar to, but with a shorter barrel than, a rifle; often used by cavalry.

**cataphract** A heavily armoured cavalrymen; the horse also armoured.

**chapka** A military cap, originally Polish, traditionally rising to a square crown.

**chasseur** A soldier, particularly in the French army, either infantry or cavalry, trained and equipped for rapid action; from the French word for hunter.

**chausses** Armour protecting the legs and feet, originally mail but later made of metal plates; part of a typical knight's armour.

**cohort** The basic Roman military unit, equivalent to one tenth of a legion.

**composite bow** A bow, shorter than the longbow, consisting of a wooden core with thin layers of horn glued to one side (the belly) and strips of animal sinew glued to the other (the back) – these made the bow very elastic and powerful. Traditionally used from horseback by the Steppe peoples of Central Asia and, for instance, the Manchu Bannermen, the Mongol *keshik* and Ottoman janissaries.

**cuirass** A protective breastplate, usually metal but also made of leather or laminated cloth, and consisting of either a single piece or made up of scales, which covered the torso, and often also with a piece for the back; sometimes shaped to the contours of the body.

**dragoon** A mounted infantry soldier trained to fight on foot but also in riding skills; later a member of certain light cavalry units. The name comes from a French musket, the *dragon*.

**en echelon** A fighting formation in which troops are arranged in parallel, overlapping lines.

**flintlock** An early gun, dating from the 17th century on, using a mechanism incorporating a flint to produce a spark to light the gunpowder and fire the ammunition.

**Frank** Name used generally for the Crusaders from western Europe, originating from the Franks of France; the Arabs used the term 'Franj'.

**fusilier** Originally the name of infantry soldiers armed with a particular type of gun, the *fusil* (a type of flintlock musket). These later became elite units, often as escorts for artillery; in battle they formed light infantry.

**ge** An ancient Chinese weapon in the form of a dagger-axe mounted on a shaft.

**grenade** Hollow spheres filled with gunpowder which could be lit by a fuse and thrown by hand. Early versions in China were made of ceramic, but later Western ones were cast iron. They were used particularly in siege and trench warfare; the name is from the French word for pomegranate because of their shape. During World War I different types were developed, and stick and ball grenades were used by German Stormtroopers.

**grenadier** Assault troops specially selected and trained to hurl grenades. As they had to be close to the enemy before throwing grenades, they had to have great courage and strength; tall soldiers were favoured also since they could throw the missiles further. They often wore tall, pointed hats, e.g. the Prussian grenadiers, as these did not impede their throwing arm. Grenadiers thus became elite soldiers and the name is still used for specialist and prestigious regiments.

**halberd** A weapon consisting of an axe-type head with a pointed spike attached to a long wooden shaft; used as a battleaxe and thrusting spear.

**hauberk** A protective chainmail shirt or coat, sometimes reaching to the knees and including sleeves.

**hoplite** Citizen-soldier of ancient Greece, armed with a spear, sword and round shield and wearing armour; typically they fought in a phalanx formation.

**hypaspist** Literally 'shield bearer' – in the army of Alexander the Great these elite soldiers were a royal bodyguard and might be used for particular tasks.

**infantry** Term used for soldiers marching and fighting on foot.

**javelin** A slender and light tapered spear.

*ji* An ancient Chinese form of halberd, combining a spearhead and dagger-axe on a single wooden shaft.

*katana* Sword used by the Japanese samurai, with a single-edged, slightly curved blade and two-handed hilt; shorter than a *tachi*.

**kepi** A military cap with a flat, sloping circular top and a horizontal peak, as worn by the French Foreign Legion in particular.

**khaki** A hard-wearing cotton or wool textile of a dull, yellowish-brown colour, used especially for military uniforms.

**laager** A defensive formation originally consisting of a circle of wagons; a South African word.

**lamellar armour** Body armour consisting of small plates, usually of metal but also leather or horn, threaded or sewn together.

**lance** A weapon consisting of a very long wooden shaft topped by a pointed steel head, used from horseback in charges.

**legion** The main organizational unit of the Roman army, numbers varying between perhaps 3,000 and 6,000 soldiers. Each legion had a strong identity, sometimes based on nationality of origin, and each had an 'eagle' (aquila) as its standard, the loss of which was regarded as a disgrace and dishonour; they each also had their own individual name and emblem, such as Caesar's 'Larks'.

**mace** A percussion weapon – a type of club, with short shaft and very heavy, often round head made usually of metal but sometimes stone. The head may also shaped with protuberances, spikes or flanges.

**machine gun** An automatic gun that can fire rounds of bullets rapidly and continuously; may be mounted or hand held.

**matchlock** A hand-held firearm that is fired by a slow-burning match held in a clamp over a hole in the breach which was lowered to ignite the gunpowder.

**miquelet-lock** A type of flintlock developed in Spain.

**musket** A muzzle-loaded firearm usually with a long, smooth-bore barrel, fired from the shoulder.

**NCO** Non-commissioned officer, appointed through promotion from the ranks.

**pelisse** A short, fur-lined or fur-trimmed cloak or jacket, especially as worn by Hussars, often loose over one shoulder.

**phalanx** A close battle formation of a body of soldiers in ancient Greece, with individuals standing in a solid line, holding their shields overlapping with spears projecting between them; especially associated with hoplites and the infantry of Alexander the Great.

**pike** A pole weapon consisting of a long wooden shaft tipped with an iron or steel point, used by footsoldiers as a thrusting spear.

**pistol** A small handgun that can be held and used in one hand.

**regiment** A large, permanent army unit typically under the command of a colonel and divided into smaller units including companies and often into two battalions; size and numbers vary. Sometimes recruited from a particular geographical region or

ethnic group, e.g. the Gurkhas, and often with their own distinct identity, history and traditions.

**rifle** Firearm with spiral grooves incised in the interior of the barrel (rifling), which makes the bullet spin as it is propelled from the gun, giving greater range and accuracy; usually fired from the shoulder.

**sabre** A curved, heavy sword with a single cutting edge, traditionally used by cavalry.

**segmental armour** Armour worn by Roman soldiers consisting of large metal plates in broad overlapping strips fastened internally with straps.

**sepoy** An Indian soldier serving in a British or other European army, trained to fight in European fashion.

*shogun* A hereditary military leader in feudal Japan and generally the real ruler of the country until the end of feudalism.

*tachi* Japanese Samurai sword with a long, single-edged, curved blade, worn slung from the belt.

**Turcopole** Locally recruited mounted archers employed as light cavalry by the Crusader Christian states of the Eastern Mediterranean.

*vélite* A swift, light-armed skirmisher on foot or horseback; in Napoleon's Imperial Guard they consisted of young volunteers from good families.

# List of Contributors

**Jeremy Black** is Professor of History at the University of Exeter. Having graduated from Cambridge University with a Starred First, he did postgraduate work at Oxford and then taught at Durham, becoming a professor, before moving to Exeter in 1996. He has lectured extensively in several countries, including the US, where he has held visiting chairs at West Point, Texas Christian University and Stillman College. A past council member of the Royal Historical Society, he is a senior fellow of the Foreign Policy Research Institute. He is, or has been, on a number of editorial boards, including the *Journal of Military History*, the journal of the Royal United Services Institute, *Media History* and *History Today*, and was editor of *Archives*. In 2008 he was awarded the Samuel Eliot Morison prize by the Society for Military History for services to military history. He is the author or editor of over a hundred books, including *The Cambridge Illustrated Atlas of Warfare: Renaissance to Revolution, 1492–1792* (1996), *World War Two: A Military History* (2003) and, for Thames & Hudson, *The Seventy Great Battles of All Time* (2005), *Great Military Leaders and Their Campaigns* (2008) and *War Since 1900* (2010). **Introduction; The Knights of Malta; The British Light Infantry**

**Gábor Ágoston** is Associate Professor at the Department of History of Georgetown University. His research focuses on Ottoman economic and military history from the 15th to 18th centuries, early modern Hungarian history, and the comparative study of the Ottoman and Habsburg empires. In addition to numerous articles, he is the author of several books, including *Guns for the Sultan: Military Power and the Weapons Industry in the Ottoman Empire* (2005) and, with Bruce Masters, *The Encyclopedia of the Ottoman Empire* (2009). **The Ottoman Janissaries**

**Simon Barton** is Professor of Spanish History at the University of Exeter. His research focuses primarily on the political and social history of the medieval Iberian Peninsula, with a particular interest in the aristocracy, chronicles and chroniclers, and Christian-Muslim relations. His most significant publications include *The Aristocracy in Twelfth-Century León-Castile* (1997), *The World of El Cid* (2000; with Richard Fletcher), *Cross, Crescent and Conversion: Studies on Medieval Spain and Christendom in Memory of Richard Fletcher* (2008; co-edited with Peter Linehan) and *A History of Spain* (2009). **The Catalan Company of the East**

**Pradeep Barua** is Professor of History at the University of Nebraska at Kearney. He is the author of *The State at War in South Asia* (2005) and *Gentlemen of the Raj: The Indian Army Officer Corps, 1817–1949* (2003). **The Sikh Khalsa; India's National Security Guard**

**Sandra Bingham** is Teaching Fellow in Classics at the University of Edinburgh. Before that she held appointments in the Department of History and Classics at the University of Alberta and in the School of Greek, Latin and Ancient History at the University of St Andrews. She is writing a book entitled *The Praetorian Guard: A Concise History of Rome's Elite Special Forces*. **Rome's Praetorian Guard**

**François Cochet** is Professor of Contemporary History at Metz University. His publications include *Les Soldats de la drôle de guerre* (2004) and *Survivre au front: Les poilus entre contrainte et consentement* (2005); he co-edited, with Colonel Rémy Porte, *Dictionnaire de la Grande Guerre* (2008) and is currently working on a dictionary on the First Indochina War. In English he has published 'World War I, 1914–1918: Daily Life in Western Societies' in *Daily Lives of Civilians in Wartime Twentieth-Century Europe* (ed. N. Atkin, 2008) and 'Democracies and the Ethics of War: The Record of the Past' in *Democracies at War against Terrorism. A Comparative Perspective* (ed. S. Cohen, 2008). **The French Chasseurs of World War I**

**James Corum** is the Dean of the Baltic Defence College in Estonia and a retired Lieutenant Colonel in the US Army Reserve. His research focuses on airpower history and counterinsurgency. In addition to dozens of articles on 20th-century military history, he is the author of seven books including *Airpower in Small Wars* (2003), *Bad Strategies: How Major Powers Fail in Counterinsurgency* (2008) and *Wolfram von Richthofen Master of the German Air War* (2008). **The Red Baron's Flying Circus; The US Navy SEALs; The Green Berets**

**Brian Davies** is Professor of History at the University of Texas San Antonio, specializing in Russian history, with other research interests in early modern European, Ottoman and Central Asian history. He has published two monographs: *State Power and Community in Early Modern Russia* (2004) and *Warfare, State and Society on the Black Sea Steppe, 1500-1700* (2007), and recently contributed two chapters to *The Cambridge History of Russia. Volume One: From Early Rus' to 1689* (2006). **Cossack Units in the Imperial Russian Army**

**David Eason** is an Assistant Professor of Japanese in the Department of East Asian Studies at the University at Albany, State University of New York. He was the recipient of a Japan Foundation Doctoral Fellowship and a Visiting Foreign Researcher at Waseda University in Tokyo. He is currently working on a study examining the interplay between legal codes, violence and emotional rhetoric in late 16th- and early 17th-century Japan. **The Japanese Samurai**

**John France** is Professor Emeritus at Swansea University. His academic interest is in crusading and warfare, and as a result he has travelled extensively in the Middle East. His books include *Victory in the East: A Military History of the First Crusade* (1994), *Western Warfare in the Age of the Crusades, 1000–1300* (1999), *The Crusades and the Expansion of Catholic Christendom, 1000–1714* (2005) and, as co-author, *How to Win on the Battlefield* (2010). **The Knights Templar and Hospitaller**

**David A. Graff** is an Associate Professor of History and Director of the East Asian Studies programme at Kansas State University. A specialist in Chinese military history, he is the author of *Medieval Chinese Warfare, 300–900* (2002) and co-editor of *A Military History of China* (2002). **Elite Contingents of the Warring States Period**

**Ross Hassig** is an anthropologist specializing in the Aztecs. His publications include *Trade, Tribute, and Transportation: The Sixteenth-century Political Economy of the Valley of Mexico* (1985), *Aztec Warfare: Imperial Expansion and Political Control* (1988), *War and Society in Ancient Mesoamerica* (1992), *Time, History and Belief in Aztec and Colonial Mexico* (2001) and *Mexico and the Spanish Conquest* (2006). **Aztec Military Orders**

**John Haywood** is an honorary research fellow at the University of Lancaster. He studied medieval history at the universities of Lancaster, Cambridge and Copenhagen. His doctoral research was on early medieval naval warfare. Now a full-time historical writer, he has more than a dozen titles to his credit, including *The Penguin Historical Atlas of the Vikings* (1995), *Encyclopaedia of the Viking Age* (2000) and *The Historical Atlas of the Celtic World* (2001). **The Viking Varangian Guard**

**Rob Johnson**, a former officer in the British Army with operational experience, is Lecturer in the History of War at Oxford University and Deputy Director of the Changing Character of War research programme. He is the author of several books, including *A Region in Turmoil: South Asian Conflicts Since 1947* (2005), *Oil, Islam and Conflict* (2007) and, as lead author, *How to Win on the Battlefield* (2010). **The Gurkhas; The Few; The Commandos of Britain's Royal Marines; The British Paratroopers; The SAS and SBS**

**Andrew Lambert** is Laughton Professor of Naval History in the Department of War Studies, King's College, London. A Fellow of the Royal Historical Society his books include *The Crimean War: British Grand Strategy against Russia 1853–1856* (1990), *The Last Sailing Battlefleet: Maintaining Naval Mastery 1815–1850* (1991), *The Foundations of Naval History: John Knox Laughton, the Royal Navy and the Historical Profession* (1998), *War at Sea in the Age of Sail 1650–1850* (2000), *Nelson: Britannia's*

*God of War* (2004), *Admirals* (2008) and *Franklin: Tragic Hero of Arctic Navigation* (2009). **The Royal Navy Bluejackets**

**John Lamphear** is Professor Emeritus of History at the University of Texas. He is a specialist on warfare in Africa, where he lived and worked for many years, mainly among pastoralist societies. His books include works on pre-colonial African conflict, resistance to colonialism, and an edited collection of African military essays. He is currently writing a military history of East Africa. **The Zulu Impis**

**Lloyd Llewellyn-Jones** is Lecturer in Ancient History at Edinburgh University, specializing in the history, culture and society of Greece and Achaemenid Iran, and of ancient perceptions of Persia. He is the author of *Aphrodite's Tortoise: The Veiled Woman of Ancient Greece* (2002) and *Ctesias' History of Persia: Tales of the Orient* (2009; with James Robson), as well as numerous articles. He has led study tours and filmed documentaries in Iran. **The Persian Immortals; The Persian Cataphracts**

**Paul Lococo Jr** is Professor of History at the University of Hawaii-Leeward. His research focuses on Chinese military history, especially the late imperial period. Among his publications are *Genghis Khan: History's Greatest Empire Builder* (2008) and *War in World History: Society, Technology, and War from Ancient Times to the Present* (2009; with Jeremy Black and Stephen Morillo). **The Manchu Bannermen**

**Philip Matyszak** has a doctorate in Roman history from St John's College, Oxford, and is the author of numerous books, including *Chronicle of the Roman Republic* (2003), *Enemies of Rome* (2004), *Ancient Rome on Five Denarii a Day* (2007), *Ancient Athens on Five Drachmas a Day* (2008), *Legionary* (2009) and *Philip Matyszak's Classical Compendium* (2009), all published by Thames & Hudson. He teaches an e-learning course on ancient Rome for the Institute of Continuing Education at Cambridge University. **The Spartan Hoplites; Caesar's 'Larks'**

**Timothy May** is Associate Professor of Central Eurasian and Middle Eastern history at North Georgia College and State University, specializing in the Mongol Empire and its impact on world history. He is the author of *The Mongol Art of War* (2007) and *Culture and Customs of Mongolia* (2008), and is the editor of the University Press of North Georgia's War and Leadership series. **The Mongol Keshik; The Mamluk Core Cavalry**

**Ciro Paoletti** is a military historian and director of the Associazione Studi Storici. He is the author of around 19 books in Italian; in English he has published many scholarly articles as well as *A Military History of Italy* (2007). **Garibaldi's Redshirts; The Italian Arditi of World War I**

**Douglas Porch** is Professor and former Chair of the Department of National Security Affairs at the Naval Postgraduate School in Monterey, California. His numerous books include *The Conquest of the Sahara* (1984), *The French Foreign Legion. A Complete History of the Legendary Fighting Force* (1991), *The French Secret Services. From the Dreyfus Affair to Desert Storm* (1995) and *Wars of Empire* (2000). His latest book, *The Path to Victory. The Mediterranean Theater in World War II* (2004) received the Award for Excellence in US Army Historical Writing from The Army Historical Foundation. He advises on security issues all over the world, and has conducted specialized seminars in Monterey, Camp Lejeune and Fort Bragg. In 2008 he was presented the Navy Superior Civilian Services Award. **The French Foreign Legion**

**Michael Prestwich** taught history at Durham University and is now Professor Emeritus. His research interests centre on 13th- and 14th-century England. His books include *War, Politics and Finance under Edward I* (1972), *The Three Edwards* (1980), *Edward I* (1988), *Armies and Warfare in the Middle Ages: The English Experience* (1996) *Plantagenet England, 1225–1360* (2005) and *Knight* (2010). **Edward III's Longbowmen**

**Ethan S. Rafuse** is an Associate Professor of Military History at the US Army Command and General Staff College. He is the author or editor of several books, including *The American Civil War* (2005) and *Robert E. Lee and the fall of the Confederacy, 1863–1865* (2008), and over 100 essays, articles and book reviews. **Rogers' Rangers; The Iron Brigade in the American Civil War; Mosby's Rangers in the American Civil War**

**Roger Reese** is Professor of History at Texas A&M University. He is the author of three books on the history of the Soviet Red Army, most notably *Stalin's Reluctant Soldiers: A Social History of the Red Army 1925–1941* (1996) and *Red Commanders: A Social History of the Soviet Army Officer Corps, 1918–1991* (2005). His future research will investigate the Soviet soldier in World War II, and other war- and society-related topics. **Soviet Shock Armies**

**Jochen G. Schenk** is Research Fellow at the German Historical Institute, London, and a Senior Member of Wolfson College Cambridge. He is the author of a number of articles on the medieval military orders and his book, *Templar Families. Landowning Families and the Order of the Temple in France, c. 1120–c. 1312*, is forthcoming. **The Teutonic Knights**

**Frederick C. Schneid** is Professor of History at High Point University in North Carolina. He is Southern Regional Director for the Society for Military History and a member of the Board of Directors of the Consortium on the Revolutionary Era, 1750–1850. He specializes in 18th- and 19th- century European military history, and the Napoleonic Wars. He is the author and editor of more than a dozen books, including *Napoleon's Italian Campaigns* (2002), *Napoleon's Conquest of Europe: The War of the Third Coalition* (2005) and, forthcoming, *War of the Risorgimento: 1859-1861*. **Napoleon's Imperial Guard**

**Dennis Showalter** is Professor of History at Colorado College and a past president of the Society for Military History. The joint editor of *War in History*, he specializes in comparative military history. His recent monographs include *The Wars of German Unification* (2004), *Patton and Rommel: Men of War in the Twentieth Century* (2005) and *Hitler's Panzers* (2009). **The German Stormtroopers of World War I; Paratroopers of the Third Reich; Panzerkorps Grossdeutschland**

**Louis Sicking** is Lecturer in the Department of History at the University of Leiden. His publications on maritime history and the history of European expansion include *Neptune and the Netherlands: State, Economy, and War at Sea in the Renaissance* (2004), *Colonial Borderlands. France and the Netherlands in the Atlantic in the Nineteenth Century* (2008) and, as co-editor, *Beyond the Catch. Fisheries of the North Atlantic, the North Sea, and the Baltic, 900–1850* (2009). He is also co-author of a new military history of the Eighty Years War (forthcoming). **The Dutch Marine Corps**

**Kenneth P. Werrell** is a Professor Emeritus who taught history at Radford University, Virginia. He has written a number of books on aviation history, the most recent of which are *Sabres over MiG Alley: The F-86 and the Battle for Air Superiority in Korea* (2005) and *Death from the Heavens: A History of Strategic Bombing* (2009). **American 'Top Gun' Pilots of the Korean War**

**Michael Whitby** is Head of the College of Arts and Law, University of Birmingham and was formerly Professor of Classics and Ancient History at the University of Warwick. His publications include *The Cambridge Ancient History XIV, Late Antiquity and its Successors, AD 425–600* (2000; co-ed.), *Sparta* (2001), and *The Cambridge History of Greek and Roman Warfare* (2007; co-ed.), which received the 2009 Distinguished Book Award from the Society for Military History, and, as co-author, *How to Win on the Battlefield* (2010). **The Theban Sacred Band; Alexander the Great's Companion Cavalry**

**Peter H. Wilson** is G.F. Grant Professor and History Research Director at the University of Hull, having worked previously at Sunderland and Newcastle universities. He has published widely on the military, political, cultural and social history of German-speaking Europe and the role of war between 1500 and 1914. His recent books include *Europe's Tragedy: A History of the Thirty Years War* (2009) and (as editor) *A Companion to Eighteenth-Century Europe* (2008). **The Swiss Pikemen; Ivan the Terrible's Streltsy; The Polish Hussars; The Prussian Grenadiers**

# Further Reading

## THE ANCIENT WORLD

### The Persian Immortals

Briant, P., *From Cyrus to Alexander. A History of the Persian Empire* (Winona Lake, 2002)

Farrokh, K., *Shadows of the Desert. Ancient Persia at War* (Oxford, 2007)

Head, D., *The Achaemenid Persian Army* (Stockport, 1992)

Hignett, C., *Xerxes' Invasion of Greece* (Oxford, 1963)

Olmstead, A. T., *History of the Persian Empire* (Chicago, 1948)

Sekunda, N., *The Persian Army 560–330 BC* (Oxford, 1992)

### The Spartan Hoplites

Anderson, J. K., *Military Theory and Practice in the Age of Xenophon* (Berkeley, 1970)

Cartledge, P., *The Spartans: The World of the Warrior-Heroes of Ancient Greece, from Utopia to Crisis and Collapse* (Woodstock, NY, 2003)

Forrest, W. G., *A History of Sparta: 950–192 BC* (London, 2nd ed., 1980)

Goldsworthy, A. K., 'The Othismos, Myths and Heresies: The Nature of Hoplite Battle', *War in History*, Vol. 4, Issue 1, 1997

Lazenby, J. F., *The Spartan Army* (Warminster, 1985)

### The Theban Sacred Band

Anderson, J. K., *Military Theory and Practice in the Age of Xenophon* (Berkeley, 1970)

Buckler, J., *The Theban Hegemony, 371–362 BC* (Cambridge, MA, 1980)

DeVoto, J. G., 'The Theban Sacred Band', *The Ancient World 23* (1992), 3–19

### Elite Contingents of the Warring States Period

Loewe, M. & Shaughnessy, E. L. (eds), *The Cambridge History of Ancient China* (Cambridge, 1999)

Portal, J. (ed.), *The First Emperor: China's Terracotta Army* (Cambridge, MA, 2007)

Sawyer, R. D. (trans.), *The Seven Military Classics of Ancient China* (Boulder, CO, 1993)

### Alexander the Great's Companion Cavalry

Bosworth, A. B., *Conquest and Empire: the Reign of Alexander the Great* (Cambridge & New York, 1988)

Brunt, P. A., *Arrian, History of Alexander* (Cambridge, MA, 1976–83)

Hammond, N. G. L. & Griffith, G. T., *A History of Macedonia II, 550–336 BC* (Oxford, 1979)

### The Persian Cataphracts

Daryaee, T., *Sasanian Persia. The Rise and Fall of an Empire* (London, 2009)

Dignas, B. & Winter, E., *Rome and Persia in Late Antiquity: Neighbours and Rivals* (Cambridge, 2007)

Herrmann, G., *The Iranian Revival* (Oxford, 1977)

### Caesar's 'Larks': Legio V Alaudae

Bishop M. C., 'Legio V Alaudae and the crested lark', *Journal of Roman Military Equipment Studies 1* (1990), 161–64

Caesar, Julius, *The Gallic War* (Loeb Classical Library, 1917)

Goldsworthy, A. K., *The Complete Roman Army* (London & New York, 2003)

Matyszak, P., *Legionary. The Roman Soldier's Unofficial Manual* (London & New York, 2009)

### Rome's Praetorian Guard

Bingham, S., *The Praetorian Guard: A Concise History of Rome's Elite Special Forces* (London, 2011)

Coulston, J., '"Armed and belted men": the soldiery in imperial Rome', in J. Coulston & H. Dodge (eds), *Ancient Rome: the Archaeology of the Eternal City* (Oxford, 2000), 76–118

Rankov, B., *The Praetorian Guard* (London, 1994)

## THE MEDIEVAL WORLD

### The Viking Varangian Guard

Blöndal, S., *The Varangians of Byzantium: An Aspect of Byzantine Military History*, trans., rev. and rewritten by B. S. Benedikz (Cambridge, 2007)

Ellis Davidson, H. R., *The Viking Road to Byzantium* (London, 1976)

Sturluson, S., *King Harald's Saga*, trans. M. Magnusson and H. Pálsson (Harmondsworth, 1966)

### The Knights Templar and Hospitaller

Barber, M., *The New Knighthood: A History of the Order of the Temple* (Cambridge & New York, 1994)

Nicholson, H., *Templars, Hospitallers and Teutonic Knights: Images of the Military Orders, 1128–1291* (Leicester, 1993)

Riley-Smith, J., *Hospitallers: The History of the Order of St John* (London, 1999)

### The Japanese Samurai

Conlan, T. D., *State of War: The Violent Order of Fourteenth-Century Japan* (Ann Arbor, 2003)

Farris, W. W., *Heavenly Warriors: The Evolution of Japan's Military, 500–1300* (Cambridge, MA, 1995)

Friday, K. F., *Samurai, Warfare, and the State in Early Medieval Japan* (London & New York, 2004)

Kobayakawa Kazutake & Noritake Yūichi, Sensō 1: Chūsei sensōron no genzai (Tokyo, 2003)

### The Mongol Keshik

Allsen, T. T., *Mongol Imperialism* (Berkeley, 1987)

May, T., *The Mongol Art of War* (Barnsley, 2007)

Morgan, D., *The Mongols* (Oxford & Malden, MA, 2nd ed., 2007)

Rachewiltz, I. de (ed. and trans.), *The Secret History of the Mongols* (Leiden, 2004)

### The Mamluk Core Cavalry

Amitai-Preiss, R., *Mongols and Mamluks: The Mamluk-Ilkhanid War, 1260–1281* (Cambridge & New York, 1995)

Crone, P., *Slaves on Horses: The Evolution of the Islamic Polity* (Cambridge & New York, 1980)

Irwin, R., *The Middle East in the Middle Ages: The Early Mamluk Sultanate* (London, 1986)

Maalouf, A., *The Crusades Through Arab Eyes* (London & New York, 1984)

Petry, C. F., *Protectors or Praetorians? The Last Mamluk Sultans and Egypt's Waning as a Great Power* (Albany, NY, 1994)

Waterson, J., *The Knights of Islam: The Wars of the Mamluks* (London, 2007)

### The Teutonic Knights

Morton, N., *The Teutonic Knights in the Holy Land, 1190–1291* (Woodbridge & Rochester, NY, 2009)

Sarnowsky, J., *Der Deutsche Orden* (Munich, 2007)

Riley-Smith, J., *The Crusades. A History* (London & New York, 2nd ed., 2005)

Urban, W., *The Teutonic Knights: A Military History* (London & St Paul, MN, 2003)

### Edward III's Longbowmen

Bartlett, C., *The English Longbowman, 1330–1515* (Oxford, 1995)

Bradbury, J., *The Medieval Archer* (Woodbridge, 1985)

Strickland, M. & Hardy, R., *The Great Warbow* (Stroud, 2005)

Sumption, J., *The Hundred Years War*, Vol. 1, *Trial by Battle* (London, 1990); Vol. 2, *Trial by Fire* (London, 1999)

### The Catalan Company of the East

Chaytor, H. J., *A History of Aragon and Catalonia* (London, 1933), Chapter 10

Hughes, R. D. (trans.), *The Catalan Expedition to the East: from the Chronicle of Ramon Muntaner*, intro. by J. N. Hillgarth (Barcelona & Woodbridge, 2006)

Setton, K. M., *The Catalan Domination of Athens 1311–1380* (London, rev. ed., 1975)

### The Swiss Pikemen

McCormack, J., *One Million Mercenaries. Swiss Soldiers in the Armies of the World* (London, 1993)

Schaufelberger, W., *Der alte Schweizer und sein Krieg* (Frauenfeld, 3rd ed., 1987)

Taylor, F. L., *The Art of War in Italy 1494–1521* (reprint, Westport, CT, 1973)

### Aztec Military Orders

Hassig, R., *Aztec Warfare: Imperial Expansion and Political Control* (Norman, 1988)

Hassig, R., *War and Society in Ancient Mesoamerica* (Berkeley & Los Angeles, 1992)

Pohl, J. & Hook, A., *Aztec Warrior: AD 1325–1521* (Oxford, 2001)

Pohl, John & McBride, A., *Aztec, Mixtec and Zapotec Armies* (Oxford, 1991)

## THE EARLY MODERN WORLD

### The Ottoman Janissaries

Goodwin, G., *The Janissaries* (London, 1997)

Mihailović, K., *Memoirs of a Janissary*, trans. Benjamin Stoltz (Ann Arbor, 1975)

Murphey, R., *Ottoman Warfare, 1500–1700* (New Brunswick, 1999)

### Ivan the Terrible's Streltsy

Hellie, R. F., *Enserfment and Military Change in Muscovy* (Chicago, 1971)

Keep, J. L. H., *Soldiers of the Tsar. Army and Society in Russia 1462–1874* (Oxford, 1985)

Massie, R. K., *Peter the Great* (London, 1981)

### The Knights of Malta

Bradford, E. D. S., *The Great Siege* (London, 1961)

Guilmartin, J. F., *Gunpowder and Galleys: Changing Technology and Mediterranean Warfare at Sea in the Sixteenth Century* (London, rev. ed., 1974)

Pryor, J. H., *Geography, Technology and War: Studies in the Maritime History of the Mediterranean, 649–1571* (Cambridge, 1988)

### The Dutch Marine Corps

Bosscher, Ph. M., *De Nederlandsche mariniers* (Bussum, 1966)

Bruijn, J. R., *Varend verleden. De Nederlandse oorlogsvloot in de zeventiende en achttiende eeuw* (Amsterdam, 1998)

Dorren, C. J. O., *De geschiedenis van het Nederlandsche Korps Mariniers van 1665–1945* (The Hague, 1948)

Sicking, L., *Neptune and the Netherlands: State, Economy, and War at Sea in the Renaissance* (Leiden & Boston, 2004)

### The Manchu Bannermen

Crossley, P. K., *The Manchus* (Cambridge, MA & Oxford, 1997)

Elliot, M. C., *The Manchu Way: The Eight Banners and Ethnic Identity in Late Imperial China* (Stanford, 2001)

Wakeman Jr, F., *The Great Enterprise: The Manchu Reconstruction of Imperial Order in Seventeenth-Century China* (Berkeley, 1986)

### The Polish Hussars

Barker, T. M., *Double Eagle and Crescent. Vienna's Second Turkish Siege and its Historical Setting* (Albany, 1967)

Brzezinski, R. & McBride, A., *Polish Armies 1569–1696*, 2 vols (Oxford, 1987–88)

Wasilkowska, A., *Husaria. The Winged Horsemen* (Warsaw, 1998)

### The Prussian Grenadiers

Bleckwenn, H., *Die friderizianischen Uniformen 1753–1786*, 4 vols (Osnabrück, 1987)

Duffy, C., *The Army of Frederick the Great* (Chicago, 2nd ed., 1996)

Nosworthy, B., *The Anatomy of Victory. Battle Tactics 1689–1763* (New York, 1990)

Showalter, D. E., *The Wars of Frederick the Great* (London & New York, 1996)

### Rogers' Rangers

Grenier, J., *The First Way of War: American War Making on the Frontier* (New York, 2005)

Loescher, B. G., *The History of Rogers Rangers*, 4 vols (Bowie, MD, 2001)

Rogers, R., *Journals of Major Robert Rogers* (Albany, NY, 1883 [1765])

Ross, J. F., *War on the Run: The Epic Story of Robert Rogers and the Conquest of America's First Frontier* (New York, 2009)

### Napoleon's Imperial Guard

Chandler, D. G., *The Campaigns of Napoleon* (New York, 1966)

Elting, J. R., *Swords Around a Throne: Napoleon's Grande Armée* (New York, 1988)

Lachouque, H. & Brown, A., *The Anatomy of Glory, Napoleon and his Guard: A Study in Leadership* (Providence, RI, 1962)

Rothenberg, G. E., *The Art of Warfare in the Age of Napoleon* (Bloomington, 1976)

### The British Light Infantry

Caldwell, G. & Cooper, R., *Rifles at Waterloo* (Leicester, 1995)

Haythornthwaite, P., *Napoleon's Light Infantry* (London, 1983)

Kincaid, Capt. J., *Adventures in the Rifle Brigade, in the Peninsula, France and the Netherlands* (London, 1830)

Oman, C. W. C., *Wellington's Army* (London, 1912)

### The Royal Navy Bluejackets

Brooks, R., *The Long Arm of Empire: Naval Brigades from the Crimea to the Boxer Rebellion* (London, 1999)

Lambert, A., *War at Sea in the Age of Sail 1650–1850* (London, 2000)

### Cossack Units in the Imperial Russian Army

McNeal, R. H., *Tsar and Cossack, 1855–1914* (Oxford & New York, 1987)

O'Rourke, S., *Warriors and Peasants: The Don Cossacks in Late Imperial Russia* (New York & Oxford, 2000)

Zolotarev, I., *Donskie kazaki i gosudarstvennaia sluzhba* (Rostov-na-Donu, 2001)

### The Zulu Impis

Knight, I., *Zulu 1816–1906* (London, 1995)

Knight, I., *Anatomy of the Zulu Army: From Shaka to Cetshwayo, 1818–1879* (London & Mechanicsburg, PA, 1999)

Krige, E. J., 'The Military Organization of the Zulus', in Elliot P. Skinner (ed.), *Peoples and Cultures of Africa* (New York, 1973)

Morris, D. R., 'The Zulu Army', *Tradition*, IV, 23 (1967)

### The Sikh Khalsa

Bajwa, Fauja Singh, *Military System of the Sikhs 1799–1849* (Delhi, 1964)

Cook, H., *The Sikh Wars* (London, 1975)

Stronge, S., *The Arts of the Sikh Kingdoms* (London, 1999)

### Garibaldi's Redshirts

Abba, G. C., *Da Quarto al Volturno* (Florence, 1966)

Bandi, G., *I Mille: da Genova a Capua* (Milan, 1977)

Garibaldi, G., *Memorie* (Turin, 1975)

Paoletti, C., 'Latin American Warfare and Garibaldi's Tactics', in *Acta of the XXIV ICMH Annual Conference* (1998)

Ridley, J., *Garibaldi* (London, 2001)

Sacerdote, G., *La vita di Giuseppe Garibaldi* (Milan, 1933)

### The Iron Brigade in the American Civil War

Dawes, R. R., *A Full Blown Yankee of the Iron Brigade: Service with the Sixth Wisconsin Volunteers* (Lincoln, NE, 1999 [1890])

Herdegen, L. J., *Those Damned Black Hats! The Iron Brigade in the Gettysburg Campaign* (El Dorado Hills, CA, 2008)

Nolan, A. T., *The Iron Brigade: A Military History* (New York, 1961)

Nolan, A. T. & Vipond, S. E. (eds.), *Giants in Their Tall Black Hats: Essays on the Iron Brigade* (Bloomington, IN, 1998)

Wert, J. D., *A Brotherhood of Valor: The Common Soldiers of the Stonewall Brigade, C.S.A., and the Iron Brigade, U.S.A.* (New York, 1997)

### Mosby's Rangers in the American Civil War

Keen, H. C. & Mewborn, H., *43rd Battalion Virginia Cavalry Mosby's Command* (Lynchburg, VA, 1993)

Ramage, J. A., *Gray Ghost: The Life of Colonel John Singleton Mosby* (Lexington, KY, 1999)

Wert, J. D., *Mosby's Rangers* (New York, 1991)

### The French Foreign Legion

Clayton, A., *France, Soldiers and Africa* (London & Washington, 1988)

Cooper, A. R., *Born to Fight* (Edinburgh & London, 1969)

Murray, S., *Legionnaire. Five Years in the French Foreign Legion* (San Francisco, 2006)

Porch, D., *The French Foreign Legion. A Complete History of the Legendary Fighting Force* (New York, 1991)

Windrow, M., *The Last Valley. Dien Bien Phu and the French Defeat in Vietnam* (London & Cambridge, MA, 2005)

## THE MODERN WORLD

### The Red Baron's Flying Circus

Hallion, R., *Rise of the Fighter Aircraft 1914–1919* (Annapolis, MD, 1984)

Kilduff, P., *Richthofen: Beyond the Legend of the Red Baron* (London & New York, 1993)

Morrow, J., *The Great War in the Air* (Washington, 1993)

Treadwell, T. & Wood, A., *German Fighter Aces of World War I* (Stroud, 2003)

### The German Stormtroopers of World War I

Gudmundsson, B. I., *Stormtroop Tactics. Innovation in the German Army, 1914–1918* (New York, 1985)

Naud, P., 'Les Sturmtruppen de l' armée allemande', *Batailles. L'histoire militaire du XX siècle*, Hors-Serie No. 9 (Paris, 2006)

### The Italian Arditi of World War I

Businelli, A., *Gli Arditi del IX* (Rome, 1935)

Di Martino, B. & Cappellano, F., *I Reparti d'Assalto nella Grande Guerra (1915–1918)* (Rome, 2006)

Fulmine, A., *Dal Piave a Via Cerva* (Milan, 1938)

Longo, L. E., *Giovanni Messe, l'ultimo Maresciallo d'Italia* (Rome, 2006)

### The French Chasseurs of World War I

Martin, W., *Verdun, 1916: They Shall* (Westport, CT, & London 2004)

Sanchez, J.-C. & Herniou, Y., *Bataillons de chasseurs, les diables bleus: une troupe d'élite* (Boulogne-Billancourt, 2009)

### The Gurkhas

Cross, J. P. & Buddhiman Gurung, *Gurkhas at War: Eyewitness Accounts from World War II to Iraq* (London, 2007)

Gould, T., *Imperial Warriors: Britain and the Gurkhas* (London, 1999)

Parker, J., *The Gurkhas: The Inside Story of the World's Most Feared Soldiers* (London, 2005)

### The Few

Deighton, L., *Fighter: The True Story of the Battle of Britain* (London & New York, 1977)

Halpenny, B., *Fight for the Sky: Stories of Wartime Fighter Pilots* (Wellingborough, 1986)

Hough, R. & Richards, D., *The Battle of Britain: The Greatest Air Battle of World War II* (New York & London, 1989)

Overy, R., *The Battle of Britain: The Myth and the Reality* (New York & London, 2001)

Wood, D. & Dempster, D., *The Narrow Margin: The Battle of Britain and the Rise of Air Power 1930–1940* (Shrewsbury & Washington, rev. ed., 1990)

### The Commandos of Britain's Royal Marines

Neillands, R., *The Raiders: Army Commandos 1940–1946* (London, 1989)

Parker, J., *The Royal Marine Commandos: The Inside Story of a Force for the Future* (London, 2007)

Terrill, C., *Commando* (London, 2008)

Thompson, General J., *The Royal Marines: From Sea Soldiers to a Special Force* (London, 2001)

### Paratroopers of the Third Reich

Lucas, J., *Storming Eagles: German Airborne Forces in World War II* (London, 1988)

Quarrie, B., *German Airborne Divisions: Blitzkrieg 1940–41* (Oxford, 2004)

Quarrie, B., *German Airborne Divisions: Mediterranean Theatre 1942–45* (Oxford, 2005)

### The British Paratroopers

Bishop, P., *3 Para* (London, 2008)

Buckingham, W. F., *The Paras: The Untold Story of the Birth of the British Airborne Forces* (London, 2008)

Clark, L., *Arnhem. Jumping the Rhine, 1944 and 1945: The Greatest Airborne Battle in History* (London, 2008)

Cooksey, J., *3 Para: Mount Longdon, the Bloodiest Battle* (Barrnsley, 2004)

Parker, J., *The Paras: The Inside Story of Britain's Toughest Regiment* (London, 2000)

### Panzerkorps Grossdeutschland

Sajer, G., *The Forgotten Soldier*, trans. L. Emmett (London & New York, 1971)

Sharpe, M. & Davis, B. L., *Grossdeutschland. Guderian's Eastern Front Elite* (Horsham, 2001)

Spaeter, H., *History of the Panzerkorps Grossdeutschland*, 2 vols., trans. David Johnson (Winnipeg, 1990–95)

### Soviet Shock Armies

Glantz, D. M. & House, J., *When Titans Clashed: How the Red Army Stopped Hitler* (Lawrence, KS, 1995)

Glantz, D. M., *The Battle for Leningrad, 1941–1944* (Lawrence, KA, 2002)

Zhukov, G. K., *Marshal Zhukov's Greatest Battles*, trans. T. Shabad (New York, 1969)

### American 'Top Gun' Pilots of the Korean War

Dorr, R., Lake, J. & Thompson, W., *Korean War Aces* (London, 1995)

David, L., *MiG Alley: Air to Air Combat over Korea* (Carrollton, TX, 1978)

Germon, A. A., *Red Devils on the 38th Parallel* (Kiev, 1998)

Thompson, W. & McLaren, D., *MiG Alley: Sabres vs. MiGs Over Korea* (North Branch, MN, 2002)

Werrell, K. P., *Sabres over MiG Alley: The F-86 and the Battle for Air Superiority in Korea* (Annapolis, MD, 2005)

Zhang, X., *Red Wings over the Yalu: China, the Soviet Union, and the Air War in Korea* (College Station, TX, 2002)

### The SAS and SBS

Fremont-Barnes, G. & Winner, P., *Who Dares Wins: The SAS and the Iranian Embassy Siege, 1980* (Oxford, 2009)

Davies, B., *Heroes of the SAS: True Stories of the British Army's Elite Special Forces Regiment* (London, 2000)

Warner, P., *The SAS. The Official History* (London, 1981)

### The US Navy SEALs

Adams, T., *US Special Operations Forces in Action* (London & Portland, OR, 1998)

Bahmanyar, M., *US Navy Seals* (Oxford, 2005)

Coach, D., *The Sheriff of Ramadi: Navy Seals and the Winning of al-Anbar* (Annapolis, MD, 2008)

### The Green Berets

Adams, T., *US Special Operations Forces in Action* (London & Portland, OR, 1998)

Simpson III, C. M., *Inside the Green Berets: The First Thirty Years* (Novato, CA & London, 1983)

Stanton, S. L., *Green Berets at War: US Special Forces in Southeast Asia 1956–1975* (Novato, CA & London, 1985)

Tucker, D. & Lamb, C., *United States Special Operations Forces* (New York, 2007)

### India's National Security Guard

Conboy, K. & Hannon, P., *Elite Forces of India and Pakistan* (London, 1992)

# Sources of Illustrations

a = above, b= below, c = centre, l = left, r = right

1 akg-images; 2–3 Leif Skoogfors/Corbis; 4 Furusiyya Art Foundation, Liechtenstein; 6 Bibliothèque National de France, Paris; 7 Alain Keler/Sygma/Corbis; 8–9 Danny Lehman/Corbis; 10 Musée du Louvre, Paris; 11a British Museum, London; 11b akg-images/Erich Lessing; 12 akg-images/John Hios; 13a Archaeological Museum, Olympia; 13b Kobal Collection; 14a Museum of Classical Antiquity, Sparta; 14b Antikensammlung, Staatliche Museen zu Berlin; 15 The Art Archive/Archaeological Museum, Châtillon-sur-Seine/Gianni Dagli Orti; 16 bpk/Antikensammlung, Staatliche Museen zu Berlin. Photo Johannes Laurentius; 17a Musée du Louvre, Paris; 17b Kunsthistorisches Museum, Vienna; 18 Qin Terra-cotta Museum, Lintong, Shaanxi Province; 19al, 19ar, 19c Xia Juxian, Guo Yan; 19b Qin Terra-cotta Museum, Lintong, Shaanxi Province; 20a Keren Su/Corbis; 20b, 21 Qin Terra-cotta Museum, Lintong, Shaanxi Province; 22 Museo Archeologico, Florence; 23 akg-images/Erich Lessing; 25 Museo Archeologico Nazionale, Naples; 26 Dura Europos Project, Yale University, New Haven CT; 27 Roger Wood/Corbis; 28 British Museum, London; 29 akg-images/Peter Connolly; 30 British Museum, London; 31 Musée du Louvre, Paris; 32 Photo Scala, Florence; 33 akg-images; 34–35 Bibliothèque Nationale de France, Paris; 36 Biblioteca Nacional d'España, Madrid; 37a Ted Speigel/Corbis; 37b Werner Forman Archive; 38a British Library, London; 38b British Museum, London; 39 Koninklijke Bibliotheek, The Hague; 40a akg-images/Erich Lessing; 40b Corpus Christi College, Cambridge; 41l Museum of London; 41r Wallace Collection, London; 42l akg-images; 42r Bodleian Library, Oxford; 43 British Library, London; 44–45 Museum of Fine Arts, Boston; 46, 47 Private Collection; 48 Werner Forman Archive; 49 Uesugi Shrine, Yonezawa, Yamagata Prefecture; 50a, 50b Private Collection; 51 Pauline Taylor/Alamy; 52 Private Collection; 53a British Library, London; 53b, 54 Furusiyya Art Foundation, Liechtenstein; 55 British Library, London; 56a Museum of the Polish Army, Warsaw; 56b akg-images; 57 Woody Stock/Alamy; 58, 59 British Library, London; 60–61 akg-images/Erich Lessing; 62, 63 akg-images/Oronoz; 64 Wallace Collection, London; 65a Galleria Nazional di Capodimonte, Naples; 65b akg-images; 66, 67 Zentralbibliothek, Zurich; 68 National Museum of Anthropology, Mexico City; 69a, 69b Bodleian Library, Oxford; 70–71 Archiwum Zamku Królewskiego, Warsaw; 72a Tareq Rajab Museum, Kuwait; 72b British Museum, London; 73 Topkapi Sarayi Museum, Istanbul; 74 British Museum, London; 75 Tareq Rajab Museum, Kuwait; 76 Topkapi Sarayi Museum, Istanbul; 77 Private Collection; 78, 79 akg-images; 80a akg-images/Erich Lessing; 80b, 81 akg-images/Rainer Hackenberg; 82 National Maritime Museum, Greenwich, London; 83 akg-images/Erich Lessing; 84l Rijksmuseum, Amsterdam; 84r, 85a, 85b National Maritime Museum, Greenwich, London; 86l Private Collection; 86c, 87a, 87b, 88 Palace Museum, Beijing; 89 Sotheby's Picture Library; 90a, 90b, 91a Muzeum Narodowe, Krakow; 91b Zbiory Biblioteki w Kórniku, Poland; 92a, 92b, 93, 94, 95 Private Collection; 96 akg-images; 97a Private Collection; 97b Corbis; 99 New York Public Library; 100, 101, 102a, 102b Private Collection; 103 Musée de l'Armée, Brussels, Belgium/Patrick Lorette Giraudon/Bridgeman Art Library; 104–05 akg-images; 106c National Army Museum, London/Bridgeman Art Library; 106b The Art Archive; 107c The Art Archive/Gunshots; 107b Apsley House, The Wellington Museum, London/English Heritage Photo Library/Bridgeman Art Library; 108 akg-images; 109 Imperial War Museum, London; 110a, 110b, 111 National Maritime Museum, Greenwich, London; 112 akg-images; 113a Mary Evans Picture Library; 113b Royal Naval Museum, Portsmouth/Bridgeman Art Library; 114 Mary Evans Picture Library; 115a Bibliothèque Nationale de France/Giraudon/Bridgeman Art Library; 115b Private Collection/Bridgeman Art Library; 116a The Art Archive/Gunshots; 116b akg-images; 117 Private Collection; 118l Private Collection; 118r The Art Archive; 119a National Army Museum, London/Bridgeman Art Library; 119b Private Collection; 120 British Library, London; 121a Kapany Collection; 121b Musée national des Arts asiatiques-Guimet, Paris; 122 Getty Images; 123 Private Collection; 124 Gettysburg National Military Park, PA; 125 Corbis; 126, 127 Library of Congress, Washington, D.C.; 128c Gettysburg National Park, PA; 128b James J. Williamson, Mosby's Rangers, New York, 1896; 129a The Museum of the Confederacy, Richmond, Virginia, photograph by Katherine Wetzel; 129b Library of Congress, Washington, D.C.; 130 Private Collection; 131 Leonard de Selva/Corbis; 132 Hulton-Deutsch Collection/Corbis; 133 Alain Nogues/Corbis; 134–35 Leading Airman Gaz Faulkner/epa/Corbis; 136a Private Collection; 136b akg-images; 137a James Corum; 137b Private Collection; 138 akg-images; 139a akg-images/Erich Lessing; 139b James Corum; 140a Private Collection; 140b, 141a Imperial War Museum, London; 141r Private Collection; 142, 143 Private Collection; 144, 145 Musée de l'Armée, Paris/RMN; 146a Wallace Collection, London; 146b Imperial War Museum, London; 147 Patrick Chauvel/Corbis; 148 Imperial War Museum, London; 149 Ministry of Defence, London; 150a H. F. Whittick; 150b Imperial War Museum, London; 151a Getty Images; 151b, 152a H. F. Whittick; 152b Private Collection; 153 Imperial War Museum, London; 154a H. F. Whittick; 154b, 155, 156, 157 Imperial War Museum, London; 158ar Hulton-Deutsch Collection/Corbis; 158al Popperfoto/Getty Images; 159 Imperial War Museum, London; 160a akg-images; 160b Imperial War Museum, London; 161 akg-images/ullstein bild; 162 akg-images; 163 Imperial War Museum, London; 164r H. F. Whittick; 164l Hulton-Deutsch Collection/Corbis; 165a Francois Marit/AFP/Getty Images; 165b Ghaith Abduli-Ahad/epa/Corbis; 166 Private Collection; 167a Imperial War Museum, London; 167b, H. F. Whittick; 168 akg-images/ullstein bild; 169 Private Collection; 170 Private Collection; 171 akg-images; 172 Private Collection; 173 Imperial War Museum, London; 174l Peter Newark's Military Pictures; 174r Deutsche Fototek, Dresden; 175a Private Collection; 175b akg-images; 176a USAF, Historical Research Agency, Maxwell AFB, AL; 176b George Hall/Corbis; 177 USAF, Historical Research Agency, Maxwell AFB, AL; 178, 179 USAF Museum, Wright-Patterson AFB OH; 180a H. F. Whittick; 180b John Rogers/Getty Images; 181a Popperfoto/Getty Images; 181b Imperial War Museum, London; 182a Charles Hewitt/Getty Images; 182b H. F. Whittick; 183a Hulton-Deutsch Collection/Corbis; 183b John Rogers/Getty Images; 184a Jim Sugar/Corbis; 184b Private Collection; 185 U.S. Navy; 186 Corbis; 187a Revolution Studios/Album/akg-images; 187b John Moore/Getty Images; 188–89 Getty Images; 190, 191 JP Laffont/Sygma/Corbis; 192 U.S. Army; 193 JP Laffont/Sygma/Corbis; 193 Pedro Ugarte/AFP/Getty Images; 194 Indranil Mukherjee/AFP/Getty Images.

# Sources of Quotations

11 Herodotus, The Histories, 7.211; 13 Herodotus, The Histories, 7.226; 16 Plutarch, Life of Pelopidas, 18.3; 20 The Seven Military Classics of Ancient China, trans. Ralph D. Sawyer (Boulder, CO, 1993), 211; 24 Arrian, Campaigns of Alexander, 3.13.2; 27 Ammianus Marcellinus, Roman Antiquities, 25.477; 29 Julius Caesar, The African Wars, 60; 33 Tacitus, Annals, 4.2; 36 Michael Psellus, Chronographia, Book II; 41 St Bernard of Clairvaux, In Praise of the New Knighthood, trans J. Riley-Smith, The Atlas of the Crusades (London, 1991), 52; 50 The Secret History of the Mongols, ed. and trans. Igor de Rachelwiltz (Leiden, 2004); 54 A. Maalouf, The Crusades Through Arab Eyes (London, 1984); 56 Oliver of Paderborn, The Capture of Damietta, trans. J. J. Gavigan (Philadelphia, 1948); 58 Sir John Froissart's Chronicles of England, ed. T. Johnes (London, 1839), 166; 62 The Catalan Expedition to the East: from the Chronicle of Ramon Muntaner, trans. R. D. Hughes (Barcelona/Woodbridge, 1933), 148–49; 68 Diego Durán, Historia de las Indias de Nueva España, ed. A. M. Garibay (Mexico City, 1967), vol. 2, 167; 75 Konstantin Mihailovic, Memoirs of a Janissary, trans. B. Stoltz (Ann Arbor, 1975), 169; 113 Quoted in W. L. Clowes, The Royal Navy: A History from the Earliest Times to the Death of Queen Victoria (London, 1903); 116 Armand de Caulaincourt, Memoirs... (London, 1935); 118 Quoted in D. Leslie, Among the Zulus and Amatongas (Edinburgh, 1875), 39; 138 H. A. Jones, The War in the Air, vol. IV (Oxford, 1934), 396–97; 140 Ernst Jünger, Storm of Steel, trans B. R. Creighton (London, 1975), 254–55; 170 Alfred Novotny, The Good Soldier. From Austrian Social Democracy to Communist Captivity with a Soldier of Panzer Grenadier Division Grossdeutschland (Bedford, PA, 2002), 76; 175 Quoted in David M. Glantz, 'Forgotten Battles of the German-Soviet War (1941–45)', part 5, Journal of Slavic Military Studies, 13:4 (2000), 181.

# Index